# ANNE FRANK REMEMBERED

## The Story of the Woman
## Who Helped to Hide
## the Frank Family

Miep Gies

and

Alison Leslie Gold

SIMON & SCHUSTER PAPERBACKS

New York   London   Toronto   Sydney

Simon & Schuster Paperbacks
A Division of Simon & Schuster, Inc.
1230 Avenue of the Americas
New York, NY 10020

This Simon & Schuster trade paperback edition February 2009

SIMON & SCHUSTER PAPERBACKS and colophon are registered
trademarks of Simon & Schuster, Inc.

For information about special discounts for bulk purchases,
please contact Simon & Schuster Special Sales at
1-800-456-6798 or business@simonandschuster.com.

Designed by Edith Fowler

Manufactured in the United States of America

20  19

The Library of Congress has cataloged the hardcover edition as follows:
Gies, Miep, 1909–.
Anne Frank remembered
   1. Gies, Miep, 1909–. 2. Righteous Gentiles in the Holocaust—
Netherlands—Amsterdam—Biography. 3. Frank, Anne, 1929-1945.
4. Holocaust, Jewish (1939-1945)—Netherlands—Amsterdam.
5. Amsterdam (Netherlands)—Ethnic relations. I. Gold, Alison Leslie.
II. Title.
DS135.N5A536 1987
940.53'15'03924
86–25991

ISBN-13: 978-0-671-54771-4
ISBN-10:      0-671-54771-2
ISBN-13: 978-1-4165-9885-5 (pbk)
ISBN-10:      1-4165-9885-5 (pbk)

# CONTENTS

# ACKNOWLEDGMENTS

Thanks to:

Jan Gies, our backbone then and always, Paul Gies for his help, Jacob Presser for excellent reference material, Jan Wiegel for use of photos, Anne Frank Stichting, Amsterdam and Anne Frank-Fonds/Cosmopress, Genève for photos, repoductions, permissions. Doubleday & Co., Inc. for permission to reprint excerpt from *Anne Frank: The Diary of a Young Girl* by Anne Frank, copyright 1952 by Otto H. Frank; Meredith Bernstein for enthusiastic agenting; Bob Bender for skillful editing; Sharon H. Smith for special help freely given; and Lily Mack for inspiration—athough her youth was destroyed by the Nazis, her capacity for seeing beauty everywhere has not been diminished.

"*Monday, 8 May 1944*

*It seems as if we are never
far from Miep's thoughts. . . ."*

ANNE FRANK

# PROLOGUE

I am not a hero. I stand at the end of the long, long line of good Dutch people who did what I did or more—much more—during those dark and terrible times years ago, but always like yesterday in the hearts of those of us who bear witness. Never a day goes by that I do not think of what happened then.

More than twenty thousand Dutch people helped to hide Jews and others in need of hiding during those years. I willingly did what I could to help. My husband did as well. It was not enough.

There is nothing special about me. I have never wanted special attention. I was only willing to do what was asked of me and what seemed necessary at the time. When I was persuaded to tell my story, I had to think of the place that Anne Frank holds in history and what her story has come to mean for the many millions of people who have been touched by it. I'm told that every night when the sun goes down, somewhere in the world the curtain is going up on the stage play made from Anne's diary. Taking into consideration the many printings of *Het Achterhuis* ("The Annex")—published in English as *Anne Frank: The Diary of a Young Girl*—and the many translations that have been made of Anne's story, her voice has reached the far edges of the earth.

My collaborator, Alison Leslie Gold, said that people would respond to my remembrances of how these sad events all happened. Since everyone else is now dead, there remain only my husband and me. I am writing of these events as I remember them.

In keeping with the spirit of the original version of Anne's diary, I have chosen to continue using some of the names that Anne invented for many of the persons involved. Anne made up a list of pseudonyms which was found among her papers. Apparently she intended to disguise the identities of people in case anything of her hiding experiences was published after the war. For example, my nickname is Miep, a very common Dutch nickname that Anne didn't bother to change. My husband's name, Jan, Anne changed to "Henk." And our last name, Gies, became "Van Santen."

When the diary was first published, Mr. Frank decided to use Anne's names for everyone other than his own family, out of respect for people's privacy. For reasons of consistency with Anne's diary, as well as privacy, I have done the same, using either variations of Anne's made-up names or names I've made up for some people not mentioned in Anne's diary. The notable exception is that this time I have used my real last name, Gies. The true identities of all these people are carefully documented in the official archives of the Netherlands.

In some instances, more than fifty years have passed, and many details of events recorded in this book are half-forgotten. I have reconstituted conversations and events as closely as possible to the way I remember them. It is not easy to recall these memories in such detail. Even with the passing of time, it does not get easier.

My story is a story of very ordinary people during extraordinarily terrible times. Times the like of which I hope with all my heart will never, never come again. It is for all of us ordinary people all over the world to see to it that they do not.

MIEP GIES

*Part One*

REFUGEES

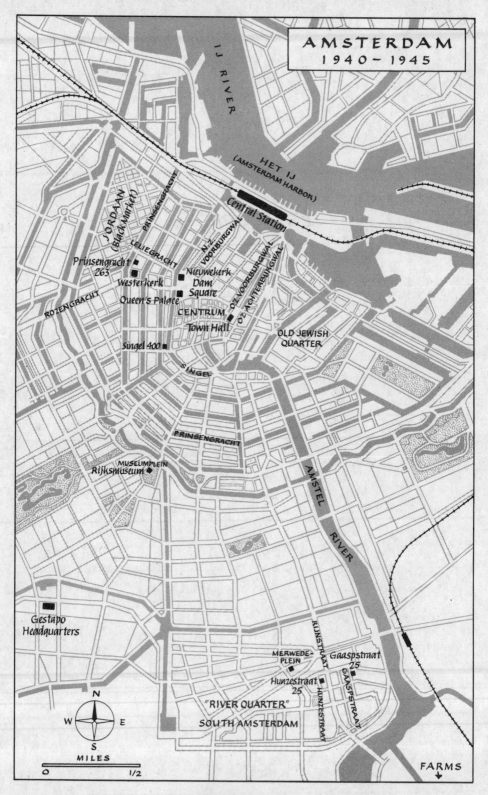

AMSTERDAM 1940 - 1945

IJ RIVER

HET IJ
(AMSTERDAM HARBOR)

Central Station

JORDAAN
(Black Market)

PRINSENGRACHT

LELIEGRACHT

N.Z. VOORBURGWAL

O.Z. VOORBURGWAL

O.Z. ACHTERBURGWAL

Prinsengracht
263

Westerkerk

Queen's Palace

Nieuwekerk
Dam
Square

ROZENGRACHT

CENTRUM

Town Hall

OLD JEWISH
QUARTER

Singel 400

SINGEL

PRINSENGRACHT

AMSTEL RIVER

MUSEUMPLEIN

Rijksmuseum

Gestapo
Headquarters

MERWEDE-
PLEIN

RIJNSTRAAT

Gaaspstraat
25

GAASPSTRAAT

Hunzestraat
25

HUNZESTRAAT

"RIVER QUARTER"

SOUTH AMSTERDAM

N
W        E
S

MILES
0        1/2

FARMS

AMSTERDAM

# CHAPTER ONE

In 1933, I LIVED with my adoptive parents, the Nieuwenhuises, at Gaaspstraat 25, sharing a small, cozy attic room with my adoptive sister, Catherina. Our quarter was a quiet area of South Amsterdam known as the River Quarter because the streets were named after Dutch and other European rivers whose lower courses flowed through the Netherlands to the sea, like the Rhine, the Maas, the Jeker. In fact, the Amstel flowed practically into our own backyards.

This section had been built up during the 1920s and early '30s when large, progressive corporations had built great blocks of apartments for their members with the help of government loans. We were all quite proud of this forward-looking treatment of ordinary working people: comfortable housing, indoor plumbing, tree-filled gardens in the rear of each block. Other big blocks were built entirely by private firms.

Actually, our quarter wasn't altogether quiet. Almost always, lively children filled the air with shouts and laughter; if they weren't playing games, they were whistling upward to call their friends out to play. A friendship included a one-of-a-kind tune whistled loudly to call the friend and identify who was downstairs. Children were always in each other's company, charging off in little packs to the Amstelpark swimming pool, or perhaps speaking in singsong as they walked to and from school in bunches. Dutch children, like their parents, learned faithfulness in friendship very young, and would just as quickly turn implacable if any wrong was done to a friend.

Gaaspstraat was much like all the other streets, filled with a great five-story block of apartments. There were doorways up and down the street leading to steep stairways. The buildings were constructed of dark brown brick with sloping orange roofs. There were windows both front and back, all wood-trimmed and painted white, each window with a different white lace curtain, and never without flowers or plants.

Our backyard was filled with elm trees. Across the way was a little grassy playground, and on the other side of the playground was a Roman Catholic church whose ringing bells punctuated the day and sent birds flying against the sky: sparrows; pigeons, which were kept on the roofs; gulls. Always gulls.

Our quarter was bordered on the east by the Amstel, with boats going back and forth, and on the north by the stately Zuideramstellaan Boulevard, where streetcar number 8 ran, and poplars grew on either side, in straight rows. Zuideramstellaan met Scheldestraat, one of the neighborhood shopping streets filled with shops, cafés, and open flower stalls with cans of bright, fresh flowers.

BUT AMSTERDAM was not my native city. I had been born in Vienna, Austria, in 1909. When I was five years old, the First World War began. We children had no way of knowing that the war had begun, except that one day we heard soldiers marching in the streets. I remember feeling great excitement, and I ran out alone to take a look. I was aware of uniforms, equipment, and many emotional displays between people. To get a better look, I ran between the marching men and horses. A man from the fire brigade grabbed me, hoisted me into his arms, and carried me home, as I craned my neck to see more.

In Vienna, there were old buildings, not in good condition, built around central courtyards and broken up into many apartments filled with working people. We lived in one of these dark apartments. The man from the fire brigade returned me to my anxious mother and left. My mother told me gravely, "There are soldiers in the streets. It's not safe. Don't go out there."

I didn't understand, but I did as I was told. Everyone was acting so strangely. As I was so young, I remember very little about those days, except that two uncles who lived with us had to go to war, and much was made of this.

Both uncles returned safely, and by that time one had married. Neither one came back to live with us, so by the time the war ended I lived with just Mother, Father, and Grandmother.

I was not the strongest child, and because of the serious food shortages during the war, I had become undernourished and sick. I was a small child to begin with, and seemed to be wasting away, rather than growing normally. My legs were sticks dominated by bony kneecaps. My teeth were soft. When I was ten years old, my parents had another child; another daughter. Now there was even less food for us all. My condition was worsening, and my parents were told that something had to be done or I would die.

Because of a program that had been set up by foreign working people for hungry Austrian children, a plan was devised that might rescue me from my fate. I was to be sent with other Austrian workers' children to the faraway country called the Netherlands to be fed and revitalized.

It was winter—always bitter in Vienna—December of 1920, and I was bundled up in whatever my parents could find and taken to the cavernous Vienna railway station. There we waited long, tiring hours, during which we were joined by many other sickly children. Doctors looked me over, probing and examining my thin, weak body. Although I was eleven, I looked much younger. My long, fine dark blond hair was held back with a large piece of cotton cloth tied into a big puffed bow. A card was hung around my neck. On it was printed a strange name, the name of people I had never met.

The train was filled with many children like me, all with cards around their necks. Suddenly, the faces of my parents were no longer in sight anywhere and the train had begun to move. All the children were scared and apprehensive about what was to become of us. Some were crying. Most of us had never even been outside our streets, certainly never outside Vienna. I felt too weak to observe much, but found the chugging motion of the train made me sleepy. I slept and woke. The trip went on and on and on.

It was pitch-black, the middle of the night, when the train stopped and we were shaken awake and led off the train. The sign beside the still-steaming train said LEIDEN.

Speaking to us in a totally foreign language, people took us into a large, high-ceilinged room and sat us on hard-backed wooden chairs. All the children were in long rows, side by side. My feet didn't reach the floor. I felt very, very sleepy.

Opposite the exhausted, sick children crowded a group of adults. Suddenly, these adults came at us in a swarm and began to fumble with our cards, reading off the names. We were helpless to resist the looming forms and fumbling hands.

A man, not very big but very strong-looking, read my tag. "*Ja*," he said firmly, and took my hand in his, helping me down from the chair. He led me away. I was not afraid and went with him willingly.

We walked through a town, past buildings that had very different shapes from those of Viennese buildings I had seen. The moon was shining down, creamy, luminous. It was clear weather.

The shining moonlight made it possible to see. I was intently look-ing for where we were going.

I saw that we were walking away from the town. There were no more houses; there were trees. The man had begun to whistle. I became angry. He must be a farmer, I thought. He must be whis-tling for his dog to come. I was desperately frightened of big dogs. My heart sank.

However, we kept on walking and no dog came, and suddenly more houses appeared. We came to a door. It opened and we went upstairs. A woman with an angular face and soft eyes stood there. I looked into the house, past a stairway landing, and saw heads of many children staring down at me. The woman took me by the hand into another room and gave me a glass of frothy milk. Then she guided me up the stairs.

All the children were gone. The woman took me into a small room. It contained two beds. In one bed was a girl my age. The woman took off all my layers of clothes, removed the bow from my hair, and put me between the covers in the center of the other bed. Warmth enfolded me. My eyelids dropped shut. Immediately, I was asleep.

I will never forget that journey.

The next morning the same woman came to the room, dressed me in clean clothes, and took me downstairs. There at the big table sat the strong man, the girl my age from the bedroom, and four boys of all different ages; all the faces that had stared at me the night before now looked curiously at me from around the table. I understood nothing of what they said and they understood nothing of what I said, until the oldest boy, who was studying to be a teacher, began to use the bits of German he had learned in school to trans-late simple things for me. He became my interpreter.

Despite the language problem, all the children were kind to me. Kindness, in my depleted condition, was very important to me. It was medicine as much as the bread, the marmalade, the good

Dutch milk and butter and cheese, the toasty temperature of the warm rooms. And, ahhh, the little chocolate flakes known as "hailstones" and other chocolate bits called "little mice" they taught me to put on thickly buttered bread—treats I'd never imagined before.

After several weeks, some of my strength began to return. All the children were in school, including the eldest, my interpreter. Everyone believed that the quickest way for a child to learn the Dutch language was to go to a Dutch school. So the man took me again by the hand to the local school and had a long talk with the school's director. The director said, "Have her come to our school."

In Vienna, I had been in the Fifth Class, but here in Leiden I was put back into the Third Class. When the director brought me into the strange class, explaining in Dutch to the children who I was, they all wanted to help me; so many hands reached out to guide me that I didn't know which one to grab first. The children all adopted me. There is a children's story in which a little child in a wooden cradle is washed away by a flood and is floating on the raging waters, in danger of sinking, when a cat leaps onto the cradle and jumps from side to side of it, keeping the cradle afloat until it touches solid ground again and the child is safe. I was the child, and all these Dutch people in my life were the cats.

By the end of January, I could understand and speak a few words of Dutch.

By spring I was the best in the class.

My stay in Holland was to have been for three months, but I was still weak by that time and the doctors extended it another three months, and then another. Quickly, this family began to absorb me. They started to consider me one of them. The boys would say, "We have two sisters."

The man I was beginning to think of as my adoptive father was a supervisor of workers in a coal company in Leiden. Despite five children of his own, this man and his wife, although not well off by any means, took the attitude that where seven could eat, so could eight, and so they slowly revitalized their little hungry child from Vienna. At first, they called me by my proper name, Hermine, but as the ice between us melted, they found the name too formal and began calling me by an affectionate Dutch nickname, Miep.

I took to Dutch life quite naturally. *Gezellig,* or coziness, is the Dutch theme. I learned to ride a bicycle, to butter my bread sandwiches on *two* sides. I was taught a love of classical music by these people, and that it was my duty to be politically aware and read the newspaper each evening, later discussing what I'd read.

I failed miserably in one area of Dutch life. When the winter became cold enough for the water of the canals to freeze, the Nieuwenhuises bundled me up with the other children and took us to the frozen canal. It was a festive atmosphere: stalls selling hot chocolate and hot anise milk; whole families skating together, one behind the next, their arms hooked to a long pole to swing themselves around; the horizon always flat and luminous, the winter sun reddish.

They strapped a pair of wooden skates with curling blades to my shoes with leather thongs, and pushed me out onto the frozen surface. Seeing my panic, they pushed a wooden chair out onto the ice and instructed me to push the chair ahead of me. My misery must have shown, because shortly I was helped to the side of the canal. Frozen and miserable, I fought to untie the knotted, wet thongs without my gloves. The knots wouldn't budge as my fingers grew more and more frozen. My rage and misery mounted, and I vowed to myself never again to go anywhere near the ice. I've kept that vow.

WHEN I WAS thirteen, the whole family moved to South Amsterdam, to the quarter where all the streets are named for rivers. Even though this quarter was at the very edge of the City of Amsterdam and bordered on the Amstel River, with green pastureland and black-and-white cows grazing, we were living in the city. I loved city life. I particularly delighted in Amsterdam's electric streetcars and canals and bridges and sluices, birds, cats, speeding bicycles, bright flower stalls and herring stands, antiquities, gabled canal houses, concert halls, movie theaters, and political clubs.

In 1925, when I was sixteen, the Nieuwenhuises took me back to Vienna to see my blood relatives. I was surprised at the beauty of Vienna, and felt strange with these now-unfamiliar people. As the visit drew to a close, my anxiety mounted about my departure. But my natural mother spoke frankly to my adoptive parents. "It's better if Hermine goes back to Amsterdam with you. She has become Dutch. I think that she would not be happy if she stayed now in Vienna." My knots untied and I felt great relief.

I did not want to hurt my natural family's feelings, and I was still young and needed their consent. But I wanted desperately to return to the Netherlands. My sensibilities were Dutch, the quality of my feelings also Dutch.

During my late teens, some of my heartiness turned inward. I became staunchly independent and began to read and think about philosophy. I read Spinoza and Henri Bergson. I began to fill notebooks with my most private thoughts, jotting endlessly. I did all this in secret, for myself only, not for discussion. I had a deep longing for an understanding of life.

Then, as forcefully as it had assaulted me, the passion for notebook-keeping lifted. I felt suddenly embarrassed, self-conscious, fearful that someone would chance upon these very private thoughts. In one purge I tore all my writings in two and threw them away, never again to write in this way. At eighteen, I left school and went to work in an office. Although I continued to be a staunchly private and independent woman, my zest for life turned outward again.

In 1931, at twenty-two, I returned again to Vienna to see my parents. This time I was a grown woman and traveled alone. Having been employed for some time, I had corresponded regularly with them and had sent money whenever I could. It was a good visit, but this time no mention was made of the possibility of my returning to Austria. I was now Dutch through and through. The hungry little eleven-year-old Viennese girl with the tag tied around her neck and a bow in her hair had faded away entirely. I was now a robust young Dutch woman.

Because during my visits to Vienna none of us had thought to have any change made in my passport, on paper I was still an Austrian citizen. But when I bade farewell to my mother, father, and sister in Austria, I did so with a clarity about my identity. I knew I would continue to write and send money regularly, that I would periodically visit them and bring my children to see them when that time came, but that Holland would be my home forever.

# CHAPTER TWO

I WAS TWENTY-FOUR in 1933. It was a difficult year for me. I had been without a job for several months, fired, along with another employee, from the textile company where I'd had my first and only job as an office worker. Times were bad and unemployment was high, especially for the young. Jobs were hard to come by, but being a young woman with an independent spirit, I was longing to be working again.

My adoptive family and I lived several floors above an older woman, Mrs. Blik, who occasionally had coffee with my adoptive mother. Mrs. Blik had a rather unusual job for a woman, even though it was not unusual for Dutch women to work outside the home. She was a traveling saleswoman and often would be away from home all week—until Saturday, that is—demonstrating and selling household products to farmers' wives and to clubs made up of housewives.

Every Saturday she would return with her empty sample case and report to the firms that employed her in order to refill her demonstration kit and submit her orders. One Saturday, at one of her steady places of employment, she heard that one of the office girls was sick and the firm was looking for a temporary replacement.

That very afternoon, straight from the streetcar, she trudged up the extra steps to our apartment and knocked on the door. My adoptive mother called me in from the kitchen and enthusiastically told me about the job. Mrs. Blik handed me a sheet of paper, saying, "First thing Monday morning . . ."

I thanked her, becoming excited about the prospect of asserting my independence by working again . . . that is, if I could get there early enough and get hired. Where was the office? I glanced at the paper. Easy, I thought, not twenty minutes by bicycle. Fifteen, perhaps, the way I usually rode—fast. The paper read:

MR. OTTO FRANK
N.Z. Voorburgwal 120–126

BRIGHT AND EARLY on Monday morning, I lifted my sturdy second-hand black bicycle down the steep front steps, careful not to muss my freshly washed and ironed skirt and blouse. I prided myself on well-styled clothes, most made by hand to save money but not very different from clothes displayed in fashionable shops. I wore my hair in the most fashionable way as well, a loose chignon, and it was said laughingly by some of my friends that I resembled the American movie star Norma Shearer. I was short, just over five feet, blue-eyed, with thick dark blond hair. I tried to make up for my size with my shoes, adding as much height as possible.

I nosed my bicycle north and quickly left our quiet neighborhood. Pedaling at my usual breakneck speed, my skirt blowing out around me, I wove effortlessly in and out through the flowing stream of workers on bicycles whooshing toward their jobs in the Centrum, the business center of Amsterdam.

Glancing in passing into the shiny windows of the giant

department store De Bijenkorf to ogle the newest outfits, I crossed
the large, busy, pigeon-filled Dam Square, where many streetcar
lines passed on their way to the Centraal Station. Then I whisked
around the Royal Palace and the ancient Nieuwe Kerk—the "New
Church"—where Wilhelmina was inaugurated Queen in 1898, when
she turned 18. (She had succeeded Wilhelm III in 1890 under the
regency of Queen mother Emma.) I turned into the busy N.Z. Voorburgwal.

The N.Z. Voorburgwal, another winding street full of streetcars and workers, was lined with mostly seventeenth- and eigh-
teenth-century gabled buildings. Finding the block, I walked my
bike the last few steps.

The building before me was the most modern on the street,
practically a skyscraper. Above the beige-stone entrance was a cir-
cular awning. Nine totally glass-enclosed stories, separated by taupe-
colored stone, soared toward the cloud-filled sky. This unusual
building was named, in black lettering on the street level, GEBOUW
CANDIDA (Candida Building). I wiggled my bicycle into the bicycle
rack and smoothed my hair back into place.

The firm of Travies and Company was contained in a small
two-room office. I was admitted by a sweet-faced, brown-haired boy
of about sixteen. He was dressed in working clothes and had been
unpacking and sorting merchandise in what looked like a shipping
area of the room. The room was not bright, and besides the shipping area, it contained a wooden desk with a black typewriter and
a black telephone on top. The boy told me that his name was
Willem, that he was the shipping clerk and ran errands for the
company. I saw right away that he was a friendly and likable Dutch
boy, but before I could observe him further, a soft, heavily accented
voice called out to me from the second office.

In a shy but gentlemanly way, this tall, slim, smiling man
introduced himself, as did I, and began the usual preliminaries of

a job interview. His dark eyes held mine, and I felt immediately his kind and gentle nature, stiffened somewhat by shyness and a slightly nervous demeanor. He had come from behind an orderly desk. There were two desks in his office. He apologized for his poor Dutch, explaining that he had very recently come from Frankfurt, Germany—so recently, in fact, that his wife and children had not yet joined him.

I gladly spoke German to make things easier for him. A ripple of gratitude shone in his eyes as he switched back into the comfort of his native language. His name was Otto Frank. I judged him to be in his forties. He wore a mustache, and his smile, which came often, revealed uneven teeth.

He must have responded favorably to me, because he said to me, "Before you can start, you must come with me to the kitchen." My cheeks felt hot. Did I have the job? I couldn't imagine what he could want in the kitchen: perhaps a cup of coffee? But naturally, I followed him into the kitchen. I was introduced in passing to another person, Mr. Kraler, with whom Mr. Frank shared his office. Afterward, I learned that Victor Kraler, like me, had been born in Austria.

In the kitchen, Mr. Frank began assembling sacks of fruit, sugar wrapped in paper, and packets of other ingredients, all the while speaking in his cultured, quiet way. It seemed that the headquarters of Travies and Company was in Cologne, Germany. The firm specialized in products for the homemaker, and among them was one called pectin, which Mr. Frank was presently marketing to Dutch housewives. It was made from apples—"apple pits," Mr. Frank joked—and Mr. Frank imported it from Germany. The housewife combined it with sugar, fresh fruit, and various other ingredients to make her own jam in about ten minutes.

He handed me a sheet of paper. "Here's the recipe. Now make jam!" He turned and left, leaving me standing alone in the kitchen.

I was suddenly on unsteady ground. How could Mr. Frank know that I still lived in my adoptive parents' home and had very little to do with the kitchen and cooking? I could make the best coffee in the family, yes, but jam? I quieted the voices in my head and read through the recipe. It was an unfamiliar procedure. I reminded myself that I could do anything I set my mind to do. So I set my mind and simply followed the instructions.

I made jam.

For the next two weeks, I stayed in the small kitchen making pot after pot of jam. Each day Mr. Frank brought a sackful of different fruit. He'd lay it on the counter. Each fruit had a different formula. Very quickly, I got the hang of it, and by the third or fourth day had become something of an expert. My jams were always perfect: good, bright color, stiff consistency, juicy flavor. Jars of delicious jam piled up.

Mr. Frank suggested that Willem and I take jam home to our families. We did. He took none for himself, as he was living alone at a small hotel in the Centrum, and would remain there until his family could be brought to Amsterdam to join him. Mr. Frank said little about his family, just that they were staying with his wife's mother in Aachen, a German city very near the southeast corner of Holland. He had a wife named Edith and two very young daughters, Margot Betti, the elder, and Anneliese Marie, the baby, whom for short he called Anne. He also had an old mother and other family in Basel, Switzerland.

I sensed that he was lonesome, that he was a family man without his family. Naturally, I said nothing about it. It would be too personal a subject.

I called him Mr. Frank and he called me Miss Santrouschitz, as Northern Europeans of our generation did not use first names with each other. Feeling at ease with him quite quickly, I threw formality aside and pleaded, "Please call me Miep." Mr. Frank did as asked.

Mr. Frank and I quickly established a rapport as well, discovering our common passion for politics. We found ourselves on the same side of things. Although I had been brought up not to hate, I disapproved of the fanatic Adolf Hitler, who had recently seized power in Germany. Mr. Frank felt the same way, although much more personally, as he was Jewish. Mr. Frank had left Germany because of Hitler's anti-Jewish policies.

Although the campaign against Jews in Germany seemed to have ended, it left me galled. I had never felt strongly one way or another about Jewish people. In Amsterdam, they were so much a part of the fabric of city life there was nothing unusual about them. It was simply unjust for Hitler to make special laws about them. Fortunately, Mr. Frank had come to Holland, and soon his family would be safely living here as well. Holding our little discussions in German, we agreed that it was just as well to turn one's back on Hitler's Germany and be secure and protected by our adopted homeland, Holland.

Days passed and there seemed to be no sign of the sick girl whom I had replaced returning. One morning, toward the end of my second week in the kitchen, Mr. Frank's arms were empty of fruit when he arrived at work. He came to the door of the kitchen and motioned for me to remove the apron I'd been wearing to protect my clothes from jam.

"Come, Miep!" he requested, and led the way into the front office.

He pointed me toward the desk beside the window and explained, "You'll now sit at this desk. I call it the Complaint and Information Desk. You'll know why shortly."

I settled myself into the corner of the room, with half an eye on the lively view of streetcars and hustle and bustle below in the street. Quickly, I understood the title that went with the desk. My job, now that I was an expert at our jam-making process, was to deal directly with our homemaker customer.

What we sold for jam-making was an envelope with four packets of pectin. Sample recipes for different jams were written on the back of the packets. Inside were also orange-and-blue stickers for labeling the jars and cellophane squares which were to be wetted, pressed over the top of the jar, and secured with a rubber band. Our representative, Mrs. Blik, sold our product all across Holland, and we sold our little kits directly in shops and drugstores.

Many housewives were beginning to use our process, but often they wouldn't follow the recipe exactly. Women were used to adding a little extra imagination to everything they did in their kitchens and would often innovate on our instructions, a little more here, a little less there. Suddenly their jams would turn into either congealed sludge or watery disasters.

Dutch homemakers are always prudent with money, both by necessity and on principle. To be Dutch is to be truly tight with money and to frown on waste. So these women, having wasted their investment in our product, would become irate. They would phone us to tell us that our product was no good. It was my job to listen politely and figure out what they'd done wrong, how they had innovated their way into a mess of ruined jam. I would calm them down and get them to describe their results, and by the nature of the disaster, I could tell what they'd done wrong. Then I would tell them how to set it right. Travies and Company would now have a satisfied and loyal customer.

Mr. Kraler, who shared the office, was a husky, good-looking man, dark-haired and precise. He was always serious, never joked. He was about thirty-three years old. Mr. Kraler came and went about his business, always quite formal and polite, sending young Willem on errands and supervising his work. So far, he had almost nothing to do with me. I seemed to be in Mr. Frank's hands, and, because of my easy feeling with Mr. Frank, I was glad to be under his jurisdiction.

Mr. Frank must have been satisfied with me, because he also

began to give me other work to do, like bookkeeping and typing. Business was slow, but it was picking up because of Mr. Frank's innovations and Mrs. Blik's skill in selling.

One day Mr. Frank told me, with a pleased look on his face, that he had rented an apartment in my quarter, South Amsterdam, where many German refugees had recently begun to live. At last, his family had come from Germany. I could see that he was happy.

Not long after this, Mr. Frank announced that the sick office worker, Miss Heel, would be returning to work, her health restored. Trying not to show my immediate desolation, I nodded, thinking, Yes, it was bound to come.

"But," he added, "we would like it very much if you would stay on as a regular office worker also. Would you stay on here, Miep?"

My heart leaped. "Yes, of course I will, Mr. Frank!"

"Business is improving," he explained. "There'll be enough work for both you *and* Miss Heel. We'll get another desk and all the trappings for you. Right away."

One morning, Mr. Frank inquired if we had extra coffee and milk in the kitchen. I assumed that we were to receive a caller. But I was lost in my work when I heard the front door. Mr. Frank's visitors, I thought, and looked at the door. In walked a round-faced, conservatively well-dressed woman, her dark hair tied in a bun. She was in her thirties. Beside her walked a tiny dark-haired little girl wearing a snow-white fur coat.

Mr. Frank must also have heard the door, and strode out to greet the visitors. As I was nearest, he brought them to me first. "Miep," he said in German, "I'd like you to meet my wife, Edith Frank-Holländer. Edith, this is Miss Santrouschitz." Mrs. Frank presented herself as one would who came from a cultured, wealthy background—aloof, but sincere. And then, in a smiling voice, Mr. Frank added, "And this is my younger daughter, Anne."

The little girl in the fluffy white fur looked up at me and then curtsied. "You'll have to speak German," Mr. Frank explained. "I'm afraid she doesn't speak Dutch yet. She's only four."

I could see that little Anne was shy, and hanging against her mother at first. But her dark, shining, alert large eyes, which dominated her delicate face, were drinking in everything around her. "I'm Miep," I told them both. "I'll bring coffee." I hurried into the kitchen to prepare a tray of refreshments.

By the time I brought the tray back into the office, Frank had taken his wife and daughter around to meet Mr. Kraler and Willem. Anne was all eyes for Willem, and for all the objects about the office. Although still feeling shy, she seemed to be warming up to me, showing curiosity at things that for us adults were dull and commonplace: shipping boxes, wrapping paper, string, invoice holders.

Anne drank a glass of milk while Mr. and Mrs. Frank took their coffee into Mr. Frank's private office. Anne and I walked toward my desk. She looked with fascination at my shiny black typewriter. I held her little fingers to the keys and pressed. Her eyes flashed when the keys jumped up and printed black letters onto the invoice rolled into the machine. Then I directed her attention to the window—just the kind of lively scene I thought any child would like. I was right. The view caught her interest: the streetcars, the bicycles, the passersby.

Watching Anne, I thought, Now, here's the kind of child I'd like to have someday. Quiet, obedient, curious about everything. She finished the glass of milk and turned her eyes up toward me. She didn't have to speak; her eyes told me what she wanted. I took away the empty glass and refilled it.

THE COMPLAINT and Information part of my job with Otto Frank became less and less important as our customers became more adept at following the recipes and making jam. My bookkeeping, typing, and invoicing duties increased as business improved. Willem was a friendly companion in the office, like a good-natured younger brother. We got along very well.

Each morning I'd pack my lunch and bicycle to the office. I'd pass the Montessori school where Mr. Frank had enrolled little Anne and his other daughter, Margot, two years older than Anne. It was a modern brick building whose sidewalks were always full of laughing and running children. The Franks had moved to an address on the Merwedeplein, a street just like my own, a large block of brown brick apartments, perhaps three or four streets northeast of me, also in the River Quarter.

Each day, more and more refugees from Germany were moving into our neighborhood, mostly Jews, and the joke became that on the number 8 streetcar "the ticket taker also speaks Dutch." Many of these refugees were more affluent than the Dutch workers in the neighborhood, and they created a stir when seen in furs or with other fancy possessions.

I've never walked when I could run, so I'd always fly to work on my secondhand bicycle and be there promptly at eight-thirty, before Mr. Frank or Mr. Kraler or even Willem had arrived. The first order of business at work was to make coffee for all of us. This was *my* job each morning. It gave me pleasure to make good, strong coffee and see that all the others had their fill. After coffee, we were all ready for work.

One day a new desk was delivered to the office and placed across the way from my desk. Soon afterward, a girl about my age, plain-looking, blond, somewhat chubby, appeared and reclaimed her desk. I moved to the other desk. She was Miss Heel, the girl whose illness had become so extended. Willem, Miss Heel, and I now shared the front office.

Miss Heel and I did not get along particularly well. We chatted about this and that, and Miss Heel presented herself as an authority on everything. Music, bookkeeping, any subject, she always tried to have the last word. She was a Little Miss Know-It-All if ever there was one.

Miss Heel began to hold forth about the new political group she had joined, the NSB, which was the Dutch version of Hitler's National Socialists. Now suddenly a Nazi party had sprung up in Holland too. The more she propounded her new dogma to Willem and me, which included racist opinions on Jews, the more irritated I became.

Finally, I could hold my tongue no longer. "Listen," I told her, locking eyes with her, "do you know that our boss, Mr. Frank, is also a Jew?"

She bent her head in her haughty way and replied, "Oh, yes, I know that. But Mr. Frank is a gentleman."

Sharply, I snapped, "So are *all* the Christian people gentlemen?"

She was silenced by this sarcasm and gave me the cold shoulder. We talked no more, and the formerly cozy atmosphere of the office grew tense and cool. None of us cared to talk politics in front of her. I wondered what Mr. Frank thought about her outspoken Nazi connections, and if he would fire her. A sense of suspense hung over the office, as though we were all waiting for another shoe to drop.

But the office was not the only thing in my life. My social life at this time was very lively. I loved to dance and belonged, like many young Dutch girls, to a dance club. I was one of the first girls in Amsterdam to learn the Charleston, the two-step, the tango, and the slow fox. My club was on Stadhouderskade. I would go with my girlfriends once a week for lessons, and we'd try out the dances with a teacher and a pianist and with each other.

On Saturday and Sunday evenings, the club gave free dances. At this time we danced with young men to records like "When You

Wore a Tulip," "My Blue Heaven," and "I Can't Give You Anything But Love, Baby." I was such a peppy dancer and loved dancing so much that I was never left sitting. Young men always seemed
to be holding their large hands out to me, to dance with me and to
escort me home afterward.

I kept company with various attractive young men, including a
very tall, well-dressed, highly appealing Dutchman a few years older
than I. His name was Henk Gies. I had met him when we worked
together at the textile office years before. I'd been an office worker
and he a bookkeeper. We'd become friendly then, and even though
we'd gone our separate ways—I to Travies and Company, Henk to
the City of Amsterdam Bureau of Social Work as a social worker—
we kept in touch. I found Henk most attractive. His thick fair hair
gleamed. His eyes were warm and full of life.

Henk too lived in the River Quarter. In fact, he'd grown up in
old South Amsterdam, near the Amstel River, when there were
farms, and cows and sheep grazing on the grasslands. Now he had a
room in the house of a family on Rijnstraat. It was a commercial
street with many shops and dark, bushy elm trees.

MR. FRANK's innovations were bringing added prosperity to Travies
and Company. Mr. Frank's Dutch had improved vastly, and he and
I spent long hours with our heads together composing advertise-
ments for our product, which I would then place in the magazines
that housewives and homemakers read.

Mr. Kraler did not always find me as much to his satisfaction
as Mr. Frank did. Victor Kraler, always serious, precise, his dark hair
combed in the same flat way, liked things done his way and his way
alone. Once Mr. Frank had given me a letter and said, "Please answer this letter, Miep."

I'd done so and had brought my reply into the office Frank
and Kraler shared and had shown it to Mr. Frank. He read it over

very quietly and said, "Fine." Kraler too took a look, but he dis-agreed with Frank, stating, "No, we do it another way."

I held my tongue. At this point I certainly knew how to write a letter. What Mr. Kraler didn't acknowledge was that because I was a woman, I knew that there was one way to write to a business-man and another way to write to a housewife. Although Kraler was married, he had no children, and he saw business etiquette in a very old-fashioned way. Frank's business sense was more modern and innovative. But aside from his conservatism, Mr. Kraler was not an unlikable person. He was fair to the employees, and he kept largely to himself.

Miss Heel failed to show up for work for several days. She sent a message to Mr. Kraler, soon followed by a letter from her doctor. The letter said, "As a result of mental illness, Miss Heel is not able to do the work required of her at Travies and Company." We con-tinued to hold our breath, and when nothing else happened, we as-sumed that we were rid of her. Jokingly, Mr. Frank announced: ". . . an easy way to lose a Nazi."

We agreed, none of us making inquiries as to whether or not her health was improving. We hoped we were rid of her for good.

IN 1937, Travies and Company moved to Singel 400, occupying several floors in a gabled old canal house, with a workroom below. Our new location was two steps from the beautiful floating flower market overlooking the curving Singel canal, one of the most charm-ing waterways in Central Amsterdam. Nearby, to my delight, were Leidsestraat, a chic shopping street, and the Spui, filled with stu-dents browsing in the many bookshops; also Kalverstraat, another shopping street. Although I was careful with my small salary, it cost me nothing to browse and admire the fashionable shops. There was nothing I enjoyed more than a stroll after lunch on a sunny day and a look at the newest dresses in the windows.

Sometimes Henk Gies and I would take a short stroll at lunchtime together. Mr. Frank had met Henk several times this way, and took note that he was becoming a steady companion. The two men were of similar build—tall, thin—but Henk was somewhat taller, his fair hair billowing up from his brow in thick waves, while Frank's dark hair was fine and receding. They were similar in character as well: men of few words, with high principles and ironic senses of humor.

One day Mr. Frank invited me to come to his home for dinner. "And bring Mr. Gies," he added. I accepted, honored to be invited home by my boss to share a meal with his family.

The correct thing to do would be to arrive promptly at six, eat, and leave relatively quickly after the meal, keeping the visit as short as possible. It would not be in keeping with the formality of the relationship to linger too long after dinner. Henk and I arrived at the Franks' on the dot of six.

Still wearing a tie and jacket, Mr. Frank was more relaxed in the comfort of his home. Mrs. Frank greeted us in her reserved way. Her dark, shining hair was parted in the center and brought back into a soft knot at the back of her head. She had dark eyes, a wide face, and a broad forehead. Her cheeks were fleshy; she carried a few extra pounds, which gave her body a sturdy, motherly look. Although Mrs. Frank was progressing with her Dutch, she still spoke with a strong accent, much stronger than Mr. Frank's. Henk was fluent in German also, so we all spoke German in our conversation. I remembered how rough Dutch had seemed to me at first all those years ago. It must be even more so for the Franks at their stage in life.

Mrs. Frank missed Germany a great deal, much more than Mr. Frank. In conversation she would very often refer with melancholy to their life in Frankfurt, to the superiority of some kinds of German sweets and the quality of German clothing. Her old mother,

Mrs. Holländer, had moved in with them, but her health was not good and she spent much of the time in bed.

The apartment's furnishings had been brought from Frankfurt, and there were many antiques, mostly in polished, dark woods; several were imposing pieces, dark and large. I especially admired a delicate, tall secretary in a nineteenth-century French style standing between two windows. Mrs. Frank mentioned that it had been part of her dowry. A stately old grandfather clock ticked softly in the background. The clock was an Ackermann, made in Frankfurt. When we admired the clock, Frank told us that when it was wound every three to four weeks, it kept precise time.

My eye caught a dreamy charcoal sketch hanging in a fine frame on the wall. It was of a large cat with two little kittens beside her. The mother cat was serene, and the two babies were snuggled against her fur, nursing. The Franks were cat lovers. And indeed, a friendly cat marched possessively across the room as though she owned the place. Frank commented that the cat belonged to his daughters. Everywhere were signs that children dominated this house: drawings, playthings.

The bloody Civil War in Spain had been much on all our minds of late. Spain's General Franco, a Fascist, had almost entirely broken the forces that had been made up of volunteers from many parts of Europe and places as far away as America and Australia. Hitler and Italy's Fascist leader, Mussolini, had been making no secret of their support and assistance to Franco. As we all shared anti-Fascist views, we discussed the latest news from Spain and shook our heads in frustration, as it seemed as though the brave resistance had just about been smashed.

We were seated at the table, and Margot and Anne were called. Anne ran in. She was now eight years old, still somewhat thin and delicate, but with electric gray-green eyes with green flecks. Her eyes were very deeply set, so that when they were half-closed, they appeared to be shrouded in dark shade. Anne had her mother's nose and her father's mouth, but with a slight overbite and cleft chin.

We were meeting Margot for the first time. She came in and sat down. Margot was ten years old, very pretty, also with shiny dark hair. Both girls had their hair cut just below their ears, parted on the side, held back by a barrette. Margot's eyes were dark. She was shy and quiet with us, and very, very well mannered, as was little Anne. Margot's smile made her face even prettier. Both girls spoke perfect Dutch.

Margot seemed to be Mommy's little girl, and Anne was very much Daddy's.

Both Frank girls had been having problems with their health during this last year. Because of repeated childhood illnesses, like measles, they had been forced to miss many days of school. I was happy to see, as dinner progressed, that despite their delicate conditions they both had hearty appetites.

After dinner, the children excused themselves, first saying good night. They went back to their rooms to do their homework. As she left, I noticed Anne's thin little legs encased in white ankle socks and little pumps. The socks drooped slightly around her thin ankles in a touching, comical way. A wave of tenderness rose in my chest. I suppressed a smile and the desire to reach down and pull her socks back up around her ankles.

Henk, the Franks, and I continued our conversation, and as soon as our coffee cups were empty for the second time we said thank you and quickly left.

This was the first of occasional dinner invitations to the Frank home. Despite our formality, I was learning more about them, mainly because Mrs. Frank liked to reminisce about the past, about her happy childhood in the small city of Aachen, her marriage to Mr. Frank in 1925, and their life in Frankfurt. Mr. Frank had grown up there. His family had been part of the highly cultured business and banking Jewish community as far back as the seventeenth century. He had been well educated, and had been a brave soldier decorated in World War I, where he had seen much action and risen to the rank of lieutenant.

In Frankfurt, after the war, Frank had become a businessman. Mr. Frank's sister lived in Basel, Switzerland. She was married to a man who worked for a firm that had its home office in Cologne and a subsidiary in Amsterdam. This was Travies and Company, specializing in food products. When Mr. Frank wanted to leave Germany, his brother-in-law suggested that the Dutch branch take in Mr. Frank and let him revitalize its business. And so Travies and Company had—a move that was turning out to be quite profitable for Travies and Company and for Mr. Frank as well.

# CHAPTER THREE

HENK GIES and I began to spend more and more time together. We slowly were discovering how much we had in common, like Mozart, whom we both loved. How pleased we were when we discovered that we both loved a particular concerto for flute and harp.

When Henk and I were together, I would sometimes catch a look of approval in someone's eye at the picture we cut together. We both prided ourselves on being well dressed. In fact, Henk always looked very elegant. I never saw him without a tie. His blue eyes sparkled with vitality. Our mutual attraction was magnetic. People who observed us could not help feeling it too.

We often went to movies. Quickly our Saturday-night visits to the Tip Top Theater in the old Jewish Quarter became a habit. This theater showed American, British, and German films, as well as newsreels and a serial which was often so intriguing that we couldn't wait to return the following Saturday to see the next episode.

Like every other young Dutch couple, we made excursions by bicycle. One bicycle, that is. Henk would pedal, and I'd sit sideways behind him, my legs raised above the ground, my skirt flapping away in the wind, my back pressed outward, balancing me, my arms loosely holding Henk by his waist.

All of Amsterdam would mount its trusty black bicycle on any warm, sunny day, just like us. Whole families could fit on a bicycle or two. With a little seat placed on a luggage carrier, one little Dutch child could ride behind, and a second could sit on a little seat in front of the driver. Two parents could transport a family of four children, children too young to pedal a bicycle of their own. However, as soon as the children were old enough, they'd get their very own secondhand bike, and would follow their mothers or fathers like little ducklings all in a row, through the cobbled streets, across the bridges, and over the flowing canals.

Henk Gies and I were both crazy about the Sunday market in the old Jewish Quarter very close to the stately Portuguese synagogue just across the Amstel River. People all over Amsterdam loved to go to this remarkable quarter, filled with seventeenth-, eighteenth-, and nineteenth-century buildings, and to stroll through the huge outdoor market, lined with pushcarts and full of activity and color, very noisy, everywhere full of exotic goodies and bargains. I had often gone with my adoptive family on Sunday mornings, as had Henk as a young man, so together we felt right at home.

In this quarter lived the poorer Jewish people of Amsterdam. Long ago Jews from countries to the east had found their way into Holland; recently German-Jewish refugees had come. Sometimes Yiddish or German could be heard. Now, however, the Dutch immigration laws were being tightened. It was becoming quite difficult for Jews and other refugees to enter Holland, and many other Western European countries as well.

The flood of refugees had narrowed to a trickle. We wondered where the unwanted refugees would go. And especially, we pondered with concern, where would the German Jews go, as Hitler was making them more and more unwelcome in Germany? Who would take them in?

ONE DAY Willem, our helper at the office, was driving the firm's three-wheel delivery cart too quickly along the Singel. It was a beautiful day. Gulls circled above the canal; tingly music trickled out of a barrel organ down the street. Young Willem pedaled the cycle bumpty-bump along the cobbled street, missed the curve, and shot right into the murky water of the Singel Canal in front of the office.

Mr. Frank and I rushed out into the street and, unable to subdue our laughter, fished Willem and the delivery cycle out of the canal. Mr. Frank sent Willem home in a taxi, and we returned to the office, laughing on and off for days over the incident.

Any lightheartedness we felt dried up on the day in March, 1938, when the whole office stood together listening to Mr. Frank's radio as the dramatic voice announced Hitler's triumphal entry into the city of his youth, Vienna. The radio announcer described the atmosphere of flowers and flags and cheering, euphoric crowds.

In Vienna, Hitler had lived the life of an outcast. There I had lived as well. I ached inside. I imagined the hysterical joy of the Austrian rabble that cheered him on. I was reminded of my Austrian passport and deeply regretted that I hadn't taken the time to rid myself of it.

All of us were soon stunned when the news came that Viennese Jews had been made to clean out public toilets and to scrub the streets in an orgy of Nazi depravity, and that these people's possessions had been seized by the Nazis.

Shortly afterward, I made my annual visit to the Aliens Department of the police at O.Z. Achterburgwal 181. Year after year I had come here to have my passport stamped and my visa extended. That year, 1938, to my shock and dismay, I was sent to the German consulate, where my Austrian passport was taken away, and in return I was given a German passport with a black swastika stamped next to my photo. On paper now my nationality was German. But this was nonsense, because in my heart I was Dutch, through and through.

One evening several weeks after my visit to the alien registration office and the German consulate, I was at home with my adoptive family on Gaaspstraat. We'd just finished dinner, and I was relaxing with the newspaper and a second cup of coffee. There was a knock at the door and I was called to come.

There stood a very blond young woman about my age wearing a sugary smile. Could she please speak with me? she asked.

I invited her into the apartment and asked the nature of her visit. In a gush, this girl explained that she had been given my name at the German consulate. That she was, just like me, a German national. The purpose of her visit was to invite me to join a Nazi Girls' Club. The ideals of the club were those of "our" Führer, Adolf Hitler, and clubs just like "ours" were springing up all over Europe.

She continued to explain that when I joined—not "if" I joined— I would receive a membership pin and could begin to attend meetings. Soon, she bragged, "our" group would be given a trip to the Fatherland, Germany, in order to participate in activities with our Aryan sisters. She continued in this vein as though I were a fellow member already.

The sugar coating melted from her face when I declined her invitation. "But why?" she demanded, in dismay.

"How can I join such a club?" I icily asked. "Look at what the Germans are doing to the Jews in Germany."

Her eyes narrowed and drank in my face with a fixed stare, as though to memorize my every feature. I was glad to present my contemptuous face to her little Nazi eyes. Let her take a good look at me and see with her own eyes that some "Aryan" women were not to be swept in by the Nazis.

I bade her good night and closed the front door behind her.

THE WEATHER in Holland hadn't turned cold yet—just drizzle and rain, clouds and overcast. That November, one of our evenings with the Frank family was particularly fraught with unhappiness over recent world news. A few nights previously was the infamous "Crystal Night," November 10, 1938.

On this night, hundreds of Jewish businesses, shops, and homes had been smashed and burned in Germany. Jewish synagogues had been destroyed, along with Jewish holy books, and thousands of Jewish people had been beaten or shot, women raped, and defenseless children attacked. In an inferno of broken glass and destruction, thousands of Jews had been gathered up and deported to parts unknown.

Subsequently, we learned that these very Jews were being accused of inciting the violence and were being fined millions of marks as punishment.

Mr. and Mrs. Frank, Henk, and I discussed the latest news. Mrs. Frank was particularly vocal in her bitter response to these barbaric events so near and yet so far away.

Mr. Frank, with his usual nervous, quiet manner, kept shaking his head, expressing hope that perhaps the sickness of Jew-hating had run its course like a raging fever, and that this detestable behavior would subside, giving decent people a chance to see their folly in standing behind such bullies and sadists. After all, Germany prided itself on a cultured, civilized tradition. Didn't people remember that many of these same Jews had come to Germany with the Romans thousands of years before?

As soon as Margot and Anne were called to the dinner table,

we curtailed our discussion of these dreadful things. We lightened up our voices and spoke only about cheerful and pleasant subjects. Subjects suitable for innocent and impressionable children's ears.

A few months had passed since our last dinner in the Frank home. We could see how much Margot and Anne were changing. At nine, little Anne was developing quite a personality. The color in her cheeks was bright; her conversations came in a rush. She had a rapid, high-pitched voice. Margot was getting even prettier, approaching adolescence. She continued to be the more introspective of the two girls; quiet, sitting with a straight back, hands folded in her lap. Both girls had very good table manners.

We learned that Anne liked to be in plays at school. Anne talked about her many school friends, speaking of them as though each were her best and only friend. She was obviously a child who liked the company of her peers. She talked about her visits to the homes of these girlfriends, and their visits to her home. Together, Anne and her friends made excursions around Amsterdam, having little sleep-over parties. Anne was crazy about the movies, too. So were Henk and I. We talked about pictures we'd all seen, comparing which stars we liked most.

Margot got remarkably high marks at school. She was becoming an outstanding student and didn't mind the arduous hours of studying that were necessary to maintain such high standards. Anne also did well in school, but was turning into a social butterfly.

Mrs. Frank dressed her little girls quite prettily. They always wore freshly starched and ironed little print dresses, many with hand-embroidered white linen collars. Both girls' dark hair was always freshly washed, and combed to a sheen. This was just how I would care for my children when the time came, I thought.

At dinner, we savored the delicious desserts offered by Mrs. Frank. My love of sweets was as passionate as the children's. It was a joke that I could never refuse a second helping. Mr. Frank must have been the family storyteller, because before Margot and Anne were sent off to do their schoolwork, he promised to join them for a story when they'd finished it. Anne was very happy about that.

AROUND THIS TIME a new refugee joined Travies and Company. He was an old business acquaintance of Mr. Frank's. He was to be our adviser/expert in the spice business, as Mr. Frank was rapidly expanding the company. His name was Herman van Daan, and although he was by origin a Dutch-born Jew, he had lived for many years in Germany. His wife was a German Jew. He too had left Germany with his family when Hitler came to power. The name of the spice business was Pectacon.

There was nothing about spices that Mr. van Daan didn't know; with one sniff of his nose he could name any spice. Never was he without a cigarette dangling from his mouth. He was a tall, large man, well-dressed, who stooped slightly when he walked. He had a manly, plain-looking face and scarcely any hair left, although he was only in his middle forties. Mr. van Daan always had a moment for a joke.

Van Daan was quite an agreeable sort, and had no trouble fitting into the routine of Travies and Company and Pectacon. Never could he start his work without strong coffee and a cigarette first. When Mr. Frank and Mr. van Daan put their heads together, they came up with successful ideas for marketing our products and finding new customers.

THE FRANKS began holding open house at their home, with coffee and cake, on an occasional Saturday afternoon. Henk and I were sometimes invited to these gatherings. There were usually seven or eight other guests, all Germans, mostly Jewish refugees who had fled from Hitler's Germany.

Although these people had not all known each other beforehand, they had much in common. Mr. Frank liked the idea of introducing these refugees to Dutch people who were interested in their lot, in why they had fled, and in their welfare here in Holland. Mr. Frank always introduced Henk Gies and me as "our Dutch friends."

Mr. van Daan often came and brought his pretty, coquettish wife, Petronella. Another couple who came quite often were a Mr. and Mrs. Lewin. Mr. Lewin was a pharmacist having difficulty finding work in Amsterdam. They too were German, although Mrs. Lewin was a Christian. Both the Lewins and the Van Daans had taken apartments in our River Quarter.

Another man frequently invited was a dental surgeon named Albert Dussel. He was a handsome man, a charmer who resembled the romantic French singer Maurice Chevalier. Dussel brought along with him his strikingly beautiful wife, with whom he had just recently fled Germany. Her name was Lotte, and she was not Jewish.

I liked Dr. Dussel. He was a very appealing person. When I learned that he had been taken in by my dentist on the Amstellaan, and that he was hoping to establish a practice of his own sometime in the future, I decided to see him for my own dental work. As I'd hoped, he turned out to be an excellent dentist.

At these Saturday gatherings we all sat around a large round dark oak table in the Franks' living room. The table was filled with coffee cups, creamers, Mrs. Frank's beautiful, polished silver, and delicious homemade cake. Everyone talked at once. Everyone knew every detail of the latest developments around the world, and especially those concerning Germany. When Czechoslovakia was occupied by Hitler in March of 1939, our voices rose in angry discussion. It was one thing that the Sudetenland had been annexed in September, 1938, to "preserve peace," but this invasion was an outrage.

At some point during each Saturday get-together, the Frank

girls would enter the room. The adult conversation would suddenly halt while the girls were introduced around and said their good-days. Anne smiled easily—an infectious smile that illuminated her whole face. Margot was showing signs of becoming quite a beauty, with very good skin and the beginnings of a shapely figure. They were offered slices of cake and stood together, Anne barely reaching Margot's nose, each wolfing down the cake. The room remained rather quiet until the girls had departed and the door had been closed. Then our voices immediately would rise to a roar.

Always the conversation eventually returned to life in Germany before those present had had to flee their homeland. Difficult as things now were, our German friends were careful about their complaints. When times were hard for the adults, the children never knew. This was very much the Dutch way with children too. All these people were hard workers who had put together decent lives. None of them had imagined that they would be forced to tear up their roots and flee their homeland and begin again in middle years in a foreign country. Fortunately, they had come to Holland, as free and tolerant a place as any that existed.

Cigarette smoke would rise in puffs. The discussions would never really end, but just taper off as the dinner hour approached. Henk and I would be among the first to say our goodbyes and descend the two flights of steps to the Merwedeplein below. We'd sometimes almost collide with Margot and Anne, rolling up on their trusty black bicycles, their cheeks rosy from the fresh air. They'd lean their bicycles against the railing on the front stoop and rush upstairs. Henk and I would briskly cross the grassy square and be on our way.

# CHAPTER FOUR

THROUGHOUT EARLY 1939, and especially after the occupation of Czechoslovakia, we grew more concerned about Hitler. We knew he could not be trusted. The mood during the spring and summer was watchful and nervous. Holland had mobilized its troops to keep them alert. Some people felt total apathy toward world events and cared about nothing but their Sunday card game, but others reacted to the world situation as if it were a splinter under a fingernail. It wouldn't go away; the pain was always there. We lived our lives more intensely.

Late that summer, Queen Wilhelmina formally announced to the world the Netherlands' absolute neutrality.

The tension forced Henk and me to take a look at our situation. A deep bond of true love had developed between us. Neither of us had made a formal commitment because we had such modest incomes, almost no savings, nothing to use to buy furniture and begin a life. Poorer couples like us often had to have long engagements.

But we decided to throw caution to the wind. Time was passing, and neither of us was getting younger. I'd turned thirty; Henk was approaching thirty-four. We decided that as soon as we could find an apartment, we would get married. We began the almost impossible task of finding a place to live right away.

In hunting for an apartment, or rooms in someone else's apartment—any kind of decent lodgings—Henk and I seemed to crisscross the whole of the city of Amsterdam. There was nothing to be had. Henk, with a more patient character, never showed that he was chafing under the frustration, but in me it brought out my stubborn side. The more I met with failure, the more determined I became. I swore to myself that if there was a place for us hidden away somewhere in our city, I would somehow find it. I didn't care how many bicycle trips it would take in icy winds and snowy darkness, or in the chill of early morning before going to work.

Unfortunately, all my determination was not making it any easier for Henk and me to be together. Amsterdam always had a tradition of sheltering people who had run from tyranny of one sort or another. Despite the tight immigration laws, the city was now bursting full of refugees, both political and religious. Everyone was squeezing someone extra into an attic room or an unused basement. Families took in lodgers, and sometimes the lodgers took in lodgers. The city's population had outgrown its housing. There just wasn't any more room.

As we continued our unsuccessful quest for an apartment, the event we had all been fearing finally occurred. On September 1, 1939, Hitler's army marched into Poland. On September 3, England and France declared war on Germany. Holland sat right in the midst of these three countries.

But once Poland was swiftly conquered in the *Blitzkrieg*, not much happened. We began to call the war a "sit-down war" or "Sitzkrieg." Then, on November 8, our hearts actually lifted with hope for the first time in a long while, when news came over the radio that there had been an attempt on Hitler's life. Yes, the attempt had failed, but for the first time in so long the evidence indicated that somewhere "good" Germans still existed. If there were some, then perhaps there were more. If there could be one attempt on Hitler's life, then perhaps there might be another. And this one might succeed. Dared I begin to hope?

I wanted Hitler to be put down, murdered, anything. Then, as I reflected on my gnawing feelings, I realized how much I had changed. I had been brought up never to hate. Murder was a terrible crime. And here I was, full of hate and murderous thoughts.

AN ICY WINTER set in upon Amsterdam. The canals froze over. Ice skaters quickly appeared on them. Snow came early. On November 30, the Soviet Red Army attacked Finland. But as we greeted 1940 and the new decade, the radio was strangely quiet. Nothing much seemed to be going on again. I wondered what the New Year would bring. Once again Henk and I became determined to find a place to live and a way to begin a married life together during the coming year. And perhaps then we could even start a family of our own.

BUSINESS KEPT improving at Travies and Company. More workers were needed in Mr. van Daan's growing spice business. We realized that we had outgrown our rooms at Singel 400. In January 1940, Mr. Frank told us that he had found new offices with abundant space for the company to continue to grow. The new building was not far from our present location, on the Prinsengracht, another canal curving through old Amsterdam.

The new building was at Prinsengracht 263. It was a narrow, gabled red brick building that had originally been built in the seventeenth century. It was very much like many of the old buildings in this part of Amsterdam. Having moved west, we now bordered on a working-class quarter known as the Jordaan, coming from the French word for "garden"—*jardin*. All the streets there were named for flowers. Our new office was on a street of small factories, warehouses, and other small businesses like ours.

The place was sprawling, with three doors on the ground floor facing the canal. The first front door led up a steep old wooden stairway to storage rooms that we didn't have any need to explore or to use right away. The next door led via a short stairway to a landing with two frosted-glass doors. The one on the right side, with the word OFFICE on it, was the entrance to my workroom, with places for other office girls. The door on the landing's left side led to a passage with the entrance to the office of Kraler and Van Daan on the right. At the end of this passage were four steps and another short landing, with a frosted-glass door giving entrance to the private office of Mr. Frank. The third door at the front of the building led to the street-level work area.

Waiting to greet us was a big, fat black-and-white tomcat with a slightly battered face. The cat took a long look at me. I took an equally hard look at him and quickly got some milk. I hated to think of the fat Amsterdam rats hidden in this old, damp, sprawling place. This cat would be our office mascot and would keep the rat population under control at the same time.

The company had changed some personnel. Willem had left us and was replaced by new workers for the workroom, an older man and a young boy, an apprentice.

Soon afterward, Mr. Frank called me into his office and introduced a young girl whom he had been interviewing. She had brownish-blond hair and was quite a lot taller than I. She wore glasses, and I could tell right away that she was painfully shy. Her name was Elli Vossen. Mr. Frank had just hired her to work in the office. She was twenty-one years old.

I took Elli under my wing and put her at the desk across from

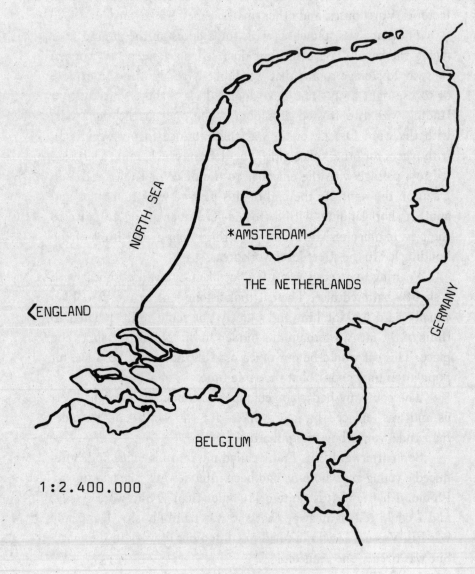

NORTH SEA

*AMSTERDAM

THE NETHERLANDS

ENGLAND

GERMANY

BELGIUM

1:2.400.000

THE NETHERLANDS

me. Mr. Frank liked her, and so did I. Right away Elli and I were a good team, and became friendly. We began to eat our lunch and take walks together, and talk to each other about this and that. She was the eldest of six sisters and one brother.

Shortly after we moved, Mr. Frank took a middle-aged Dutch gentleman into the company. His name was Jo Koophuis. He had had various business dealings with Mr. Frank over the years, and was a personal friend as well. Mr. Koophuis was a frail-looking, pale-faced man, with large, thick glasses, a pinched nose, and a delicate look. He was a quiet person whose personality immediately inspired feelings of trust and kindness. Mr. Koophuis and I quickly established a warm rapport.

Jo Koophuis, Elli Vossen, the other office girls, and I began to share the front office. Kraler and Van Daan continued to share another in the back. In fact, these men seemed to have formed two teams: Koophuis and Frank specializing in the household products and the financial business, and Van Daan and Kraler dealing in spices, especially spices used for sausage-making.

On and off, various other women were hired for the office to work along with Elli and me. They were usually pleasant young girls who did their jobs and left. I had become the senior office worker. It was up to me to make sure our responsibilities were always completed, that our work was done with efficiency and order and was always neat and clean. It was.

MARGOT FRANK turned fourteen in February of 1940, one day after I turned thirty-one. During dinner at the Franks' that winter we realized that we were seeing a young lady rather than a girl. Her figure had filled out quite a bit. Thick eyeglasses now covered her serious dark eyes, and her attention was always on bookish matters and never on frivolity. Regardless of the glasses, Margot continued to grow prettier, her skin smooth and creamy.

Anne was not quite eleven that chilly winter of 1940. She clearly looked up to her older sister. Anything Margot did or said was sponged up by Anne's darting eyes and quick mind. In fact, Anne had developed the skill of mimicry. She would mimic anyone and anything, and very well at that: the cat's meow, her friend's voice, her teacher's authoritative tone. We couldn't help laughing at her little performances, she was so skilled with her voice. Anne loved having an attentive audience, and loved to hear us respond to her skits and clowning.

Anne had changed too. Her thin legs seemed to be stretching out longer and longer from beneath her dress; her arms, too. She was still a small, thin girl, but seemed to be entering a preadolescent growth spurt, the arms and legs suddenly too long for the body. Still the baby of the family, Anne always wanted an extra bit of attention.

Anne had grown less sickly during the past year or so. Margot, unfortunately, had not, and continued to suffer from minor sicknesses—stomachaches and the like. The children now always spoke in Dutch, with no accent, and even Mrs. Frank's Dutch was coming along. Sometimes, in order to give Mrs. Frank a chance to practice her Dutch, we would switch the conversation from German to Dutch on our visits and guide her along, trying to make it fun for her to improve. The new language had come hardest for Mrs. Frank, probably because she was at home so much. It had been much easier for Mr. Frank, out in the world of Amsterdam all the time, and the children had taken to it like ducks to water.

THE SPRING of 1940 burst upon us. The earth thawed; the flower stalls were full of moist tulips, jonquils, daffodils. As tight-fisted as we were with our pennies, a few could always be spared for a handful of cut flowers. The silky air and the lengthening days gave us all feelings of hope for the situation in Europe. Perhaps, just perhaps?

Henk and I spent every free moment together. As spring grew lovelier, Henk grew even more handsome and delightful in my eyes. His jokes seemed funnier; his arm around my shoulder grew firmer.

On April 6, news reached us of another attempt on the life of Hitler. This news made me almost want to shout with joy. This attempt had been close. Perhaps, I yearned, the "good" Germans would not miss a third time?

But then Hitler marched right into little Denmark and, with equal effortlessness, into Norway. Barely a shot had been fired in either place. Everyone in Holland had the same fear. We waited to see what would happen next. Fortunately, we were spared. And so we continued to enjoy the spring.

# CHAPTER FIVE

ON A THURSDAY night in May, I crept into my bed across the room from my sister, Catherina. The night was unusually balmy. Our customary late-night talk had ended when we scolded ourselves, remembering that we both had to be up early the next morning, another working day.

Deep in the night, interrupting my heavy sleep, I heard what sounded like a persistent humming noise. I thought nothing of it, pulling sleep more tightly around me, but then the noise was mixed with a faraway muted sound of thunder. Neither interruption had made much of an impression on me, when suddenly I became aware of Catherina shaking me awake. Downstairs, someone was turning the static-filled dial of the radio. My heart began to pound.

We ran downstairs to join the family and try to figure out what was happening. Radio reports were confusing. Were those German airplanes? If so, why were they heading in a westerly direction? People had run out into the streets to see if anyone knew. Some had climbed onto the roof. The faraway explosions were coming from the direction of the airport.

Dawn broke; the confusion continued. No one went back to

sleep. We were all too upset. Word came that German soldiers dressed in Dutch uniforms were parachuting out of airplanes. Also, that bicycles and guns and equipment were coming down from the sky. No one had ever seen or heard anything like it.

We all milled around. First one set of information would pass from mouth to mouth, and then another. Finally, Queen Wilhelmina spoke on the radio and told us, her voice heavy with emotion, that the Germans had attacked our beloved Holland. We were being invaded; but we were fighting back.

It was Friday, May 10, 1940. No one knew quite what to do. Most people like me went to work just as we did every other day.

The mood in the office was forlorn and shocked. Mr. Frank's face was white. We crowded around the radio in his office and listened through the day for developments. It seemed that our brave Dutch Army was fighting on, though outnumbered, and that we were making a stand. It was not the time for discussion. We silently did our work. There was nothing to do but wait and see.

Henk raced over from his office at lunchtime. We huddled together, afraid to imagine what might happen. Several times in the course of the day there were air-raid sirens. Dutifully, we waited until the all-clear sounded, as there were no shelters in our quarter. However, no bombs fell, and I saw no fighting, no men in uniform.

More rumors were circulating: that German soldiers were parachuting dressed as nurses, farmers, nuns, and Dutch fishermen. Instructions came periodically over the radio to stay indoors; to pour out all alcoholic beverages to keep women safer from the German soldier, should he come. People ran to shops and bought as much food as they could.

An eight-o'clock curfew went into effect. We were told to tape over the glass in our windows, that this might protect us from splintering and flying glass. We were told to buy blackout paper to cover our windows at night. I did this.

All the time my head was against the radio. The information

was confusing. Were our Dutch troops holding back the onslaught? Was it true, as rumor had it, that the Dutch Government had sent a ship to IJmuiden to take Jewish people to England? Was it also true that many Jewish people had committed suicide? And that others had sailed off to England in boats they had purchased?

This confusion went on for several days, through the weekend. Any bit of information spread like fire. We heard that fighting was going on heavily around the town of Amersfoort, that the farmers had been told to evacuate and the cows had been left in the pastures. That the cows wailed and cried because they had not been milked and their udders were bursting.

Then, the worst news yet: that the Queen, her family, and the Government had fled in the night on a ship to England. They'd taken all the gold from the Dutch treasury with them. A wave of dejection went through us all. The monarchists wept with shame and feelings that they had been deserted. Then it was said that Prince Bernhard, Princess Juliana's husband, had come back incognito to Holland and had rejoined the Dutch troops in Zeeland.

As suddenly as it had started, it was finished. At seven in the evening of May 14, General Winkelman came onto the radio and announced that the Germans had obliterated Rotterdam with bombs dropped from the air; that floods were spreading across sections of Holland through opened dikes; that the Germans had threatened to bomb Utrecht and Amsterdam if we continued to resist. In order to spare further loss of life and property, the General explained, we were surrendering to the Germans. He asked us all to remain calm and wait for further instructions.

Like the lowest thieves in the night, the Germans had attacked us. Now, suddenly, our world was no longer ours. A strange air of limbo settled over us all. We waited to see what would happen. All the while, rage smoldered inside. Nothing worse could happen to us; we were no longer free.

Some people burned anti-Nazi newspapers and English books and dictionaries. Others began to wonder about their friends and neighbors. Suddenly it became important to know who might have had Nazi sympathies all along and who might be a spy. And what had we said to those people we now distrusted?

We began to see German uniforms here and there in the street. The German Army paraded through Amsterdam looking triumphant, in uniforms and helmets. People stood on one another's shoulders, many in clusters, as the Germans made their grand march through the spring sunshine in tanks and motorized vehicles over the Berlage Bridge on their way to Dam Square.

The Dutch watched, most faces set, unreadable, quiet. From out of their ratholes appeared Dutch Nazis, who were cheering and waving and welcoming. Some, like Henk and me, turned away and would not look. To us there were only two sides: those who were "right," those loyal Dutch who, no matter what, opposed the Nazis, and those who were "wrong," who collaborated or sympathized. Nothing in between.

LIFE WENT ON almost as usual. Business at Travies and Company continued to prosper. We worked quietly all day long. Four times each hour bells rang through the building, the bells from the Westerkerk (West Church) down the street. This church was a plain red brick building with tall gables. It was said to be the place where Rembrandt's bones were buried. The bells rang with a rich resonance, muted somewhat by the many elm trees up and down the street along the canal.

When we had first moved to the Prinsengracht, I'd noticed these bells every fifteen minutes. I would pause from my work, look out the window for a moment, and usually watch the sea gulls swooping down into the canal to pick up food. Then I would return to whatever work was on my desk in front of me. Very quickly, though, after we'd been there for several weeks, I'd often not even notice the bells anymore, they became so much a part of the atmosphere.

One day Mr. Frank took me aside and, a pleased look on his face, told me that he had read an advertisement for rooms that were for rent in our quarter at 25 Hunzestraat. Were we interested?

The following morning before going to work, I met Mr. Frank and together we went to a brick building much like all the others on Hunzestraat, a quiet street only two blocks from the Franks' apartment on Merwedeplein. The rooms were on the ground floor. Mr. Frank rang, and we waited. A small, pretty lady, dark and plump, answered. Her name was Mrs. Samson. Mr. Frank made the appropriate introductions and we all shook hands. We realized that Mrs. Samson was Jewish. Then she showed us the rooms and told us why they were suddenly free. She was a talker and words came easily.

It seemed that Mrs. Samson had a daughter who was married and lived in Hilversum, a few miles outside Amsterdam. On the day of the German attack, the daughter, son-in-law, and children had decided that they would try to escape to England and had run, like so many others, to the harbor city of IJmuiden.

When Mrs. Samson's husband, a photographer who made portraits of children in school, had come home that night and heard about his daughter and two small grandchildren, he was very upset because he had not seen them before they went. He decided to go to IJmuiden to try to find them and say goodbye.

He did not know that his daughter and her family had been unable to get onto one of the crowded ships that day and had been forced to return to Hilversum. While searching for them, Mr. Samson had gotten onto a ship and had been unable to get back off. Word reached Mrs. Samson that somehow, accidentally, he'd sailed for England.

Now she was alone in the apartment. She had no idea if she'd ever see her husband again. She was frightened about being alone. That was why the rooms were for rent.

On the spot I told her that we would like to rent her rooms. Henk and I would move in right away. She expressed relief. It would be better to have young, strong people in those rooms during times like these.

Henk and I moved into Mrs. Samson's rooms. When we first moved in we told her that we were married, but rather quickly, as we got to know her, we told her that it wasn't true, but that soon, we hoped, we would be married. These unusual times were quickly making for unusual arrangements.

During the day we could hear the airplanes' droning sound as the Germans flew above us. News came that Luxembourg and Belgium had fallen almost as quickly as the Netherlands had; that Germany had successfully invaded France and that fighting continued; that a man named Winston Churchill had replaced Neville Chamberlain as Prime Minister in England.

In Belgium, King Leopold III had surrendered to the Nazis and was now in their hands. Slowly, we began to realize that it was better that Queen Wilhelmina had not gotten into German hands, that it was perhaps good that she was safely in England. She spoke movingly to us Dutch on the BBC radio, saying that she would lead the Free Dutch Government from England until the Germans could be vanquished. She told us to remain calm, and not lose heart, to resist the Nazis any way we could, and that somehow, someday, we would be a free nation once again.

At the end of May, an Austrian-born Nazi named Arthur Seyss-Inquart, who had become the chancellor of Austria after Germany annexed the country in 1938, was now appointed Reichskommissar of the Netherlands by Hitler. Seyss-Inquart was a stocky, quite everyday-looking man who always wore glittering glasses and walked with a limp. Naturally, we despised him right away.

In June, the swastika flew from the top of the Eiffel Tower in Paris. The German Army had surged across Europe like a flood. It seemed unstoppable. Hitler's victorious armies occupied most of Europe, from the frozen Arctic lands of Norway to the wine-growing regions of France, from the farthest eastern reaches of Poland and Czechoslovakia right to the lowlands at the edge of our own little Holland, on the North Sea. How could England stand alone against such might? Mr. Churchill roared over the radio that it could and would. The British were our only hope.

Near-normality continued in Amsterdam as summer came. Often it seemed as though nothing had changed. The chestnut trees filled out; the summer daylight continued until ten at night. Henk and I, with our meager belongings, slowly set up our little home together in two rooms, fully furnished, with shared use of kitchen and bathroom.

For the first time I began to cook whole meals. I realized that I had a knack for cooking. Henk was happy; so was I. It was almost as though nothing had changed—until my eye would light on a German soldier sitting in an open-air café, or German policemen, known as *Grüne Polizei*, or "Green Police," because of their green uniforms. Then the reality of our domination would return. I would set that impenetrable look back on my face and continue on about my business.

The Germans were trying to win us over with niceness. I was not taken in by their friendliness, by their confident aura. I simply avoided any contact whatsoever. This was not difficult, since there didn't seem to be a great many soldiers among us.

The official radio now played nothing but German music all

day. The movie theaters showed only German films, so naturally
we stopped going to the movies. It was decreed against the law to
listen to the BBC. This had no effect on us, as all hope and encouragement came from the BBC.

Then, in late July, Radio Orange, the voice of the Dutch Government in Exile in London, began nightly, and was like a drink
to the thirsty. As the newspapers had stopped printing anything
but the German news, we knew nothing about what was going on
in the outside world and longed for any information. So each night,
although listening was illegal, we'd all gather around our radios
for Radio Orange.

Despite their constant anxiety, our Dutch Jews so far had been
treated no differently from anyone else. In August, Jewish refugees
from Germany were told to report to the aliens office to register,
which they did. No harm came to them. They were registered, that
was all.

The movie theaters showed an anti-Semitic newsreel called
"The Eternal Jew," but as we'd stopped going to the movies, neither Henk nor I saw it. Books that the Germans didn't like were
removed from our libraries and bookshops. It was said that they
were also making changes in school textbooks to suit their ideology.

In August, Hitler began to send hundreds of bombers across
the Channel to England. First one wave would come, then another.
Daily, we'd hear the endless hum of aircraft off in the distance.
Sometimes we'd hear the RAF flying in an easterly direction, and
our hearts would quicken. The BBC spoke of bombings over Berlin. Hope would surge. Then the German radio spoke of London
burning and that the British were almost at the point of capitula-
tion. Our hearts would sink, our rage churn.

In September, Hitler's Luftwaffe began to fly massive raids at
night. The droning of these harbingers of death formed a background to my nightly sleep. As ordered, I covered our windows at

night with sheets of blackout paper. The nights at home felt stifling; our rooms were pitch black with no moonlight entering.

Thousands of Dutch were working in German factories across the border. Other Dutch workers had gone to German companies in Belgium and France. Everywhere brightly colored posters sprung up inviting Dutch workers to come to Germany to work. These posters always showed pink-cheeked idealized Aryan faces.

The swinish Dutch Nazis, known as NSBers, joined up with the German Nazis. They received special treatment and privileges. We gave these snakes a wide berth. Not always did we know who was "right" and who was "wrong." So we never spoke about the war to anyone if we were not sure. Sometimes now when I went shopping I would find the shops half-empty. The Germans had begun to take our food and ship it to their Fatherland.

Jewish despondency deepened when in the autumn of 1940, Dutch Jews in the Civil Service and in other public and government positions, like teachers and professors and postmen, were ordered to resign their jobs. An outcry went up. Others, like Henk, had to sign an "Aryan Declaration," which was an archly written statement that said essentially, "I am not a Jew." We were shocked at these edicts, shocked, enraged, and ashamed because so many dignified and learned people had been dismissed in such a shabby way.

None of this changed life at Travies and Company, except that we renamed our office cat Moffie—a nickname we called the Germans. A Moffen was a biscuit in the shape of a fat little pig. Because our cat was known to steal food from other houses in the neighborhood, just as the Germans were doing with our food, Moffie seemed appropriate.

Mr. Frank and Mr. van Daan did their best to hide whatever fear and dejection they felt. Everyone behaved as normally as possible with them. By decree of October 22, 1940, however, our company had been ordered to register along with all other businesses owned by Jews or having one or more Jewish partner.

It started insidiously, and as the long, dark winter settled over us, the noose around the Jewish neck began to tighten. First, all our Jews were made to register with the census office. The charge was one guilder. The joke became that the Germans were doing it for the guilder. Then it was whispered that in The Hague, not thirty-five miles from Amsterdam, signs were appearing on park benches and in public places saying Not for Jews and Jews Not Wanted Here. Could such a thing be true in the Netherlands?

The answer became clear as outbreaks of anti-Semitism occurred in Amsterdam. Violent fights broke out between Jews and Nazis in the old Jewish Quarter near the marketplace. The Germans used this as an excuse to raise the bridges around the quarter, post soldiers, and seal off the quarter with signs. On February 12, 1941, the Dutch Nazi newspaper reported that Jews with sharpened teeth had ripped open the necks of Nazi soldiers and sucked their blood like vampires. The depths of the Nazi lies and depravity shook us all.

Then, in our very own quarter in South Amsterdam, there were several violent altercations between Jews and Nazis. One of these occurred at a favorite ice cream parlor, Koco's, on Rijnstraat. It was said that some Jews had poured ammonia on the heads of German soldiers.

Four hundred Jewish hostages were seized from the old Jewish Quarter in February. Then rumors circulated that told of humiliating tasks that these people were made to do, like crawl around on their knees at the feet of Nazi soldiers. Then they were gathered in a *razia*—a Dutch word for "roundup"—at gunpoint and shipped away by truck. They were shipped to a place called Mauthausen, a prison camp. Quickly, word came that these men had met with "accidental" deaths. Families were notified of death by heart attack and tuberculosis. No one believed these stories of sudden accidental death.

The Dutch are slow to anger, but when they finally get fed up, their anger will burn white hot. In order to show the full measure of indignity we Dutch felt about the treatment of the Jewish people, we called a general strike for February 25. We wanted our Jews to know that we had great concern for what was happening to them.

On February 25 all hell broke loose! All transportation and industry ground to a halt. At the forefront of the strike were our dockworkers, and all other workers followed suit. Before the German occupation, Holland had had a great many different parties and political groups. Now, suddenly, we were all one: anti-German.

The February strike lasted for three marvelous days. I heard that the morale of Dutch Jews rose tremendously; everyone felt the solidarity that the strike inspired. Dangerous, yes, but wonderful to be doing something against our oppressors. But after three days the Nazis reasserted themselves with brutal reprisals.

Henk and I hadn't been to the Frank home for quite some time. We felt deep anxiety for our Jewish friends. I was eaten by a feeling of terrible regret. How had we been so naive as to think that our neutrality would be respected by an immoral man like Adolf Hitler? If only our Jewish friends had gone to America or Canada! Henk and I felt special pangs of regret for the Franks, with their two young children. Mrs. Frank, in fact, had two brothers who had gone to America.

When we did again see the Franks, we noticed that since the occupation Margot's poor health had been aggravated by anxieties. She was sick quite often, but she managed not to let anything interfere with her studies. Her sweet, quiet nature covered up her fears.

Meanwhile, Anne was evolving into the most extroverted person in the family. She spoke candidly about all kinds of things. She was aware of everything going on in the outside world. She was very indignant about the injustices being heaped on the Jewish people.

In addition to all Anne's many interests, like famous film stars and her best girlfriends, a new subject had gotten her attention: boys. Her talk now was spiced with chatter about particular young people of the opposite sex.

It was as though the terrible events in the outside world were speeding up this little girl's development, as though Anne were suddenly in a hurry to know and experience everything. On the outside, Anne was a delicate, vivacious not-quite-twelve-year-old girl, but on the inside, a part of her was suddenly much older.

OUT OF THE BLUE I received a summons to appear at the German Consulate. I was filled with fear and foreboding.

I dressed with great care, and Henk and I went together to the German Consulate on the Museumplein. It was a patrician building on a street near the Rijksmuseum. The place exuded a sinister feeling.

Henk and I approached the door and were told to stop. We were asked the nature of our business. I showed the summons I had received. After a careful look, we were directed through the doorway and down a corridor to a particular door. I held Henk tightly by his arm.

The doorway was ajar. Before we could enter, we were again challenged. Again, I showed the summons. I could hear loud, ominous voices just inside the door. A voice inside me said that something very unpleasant was about to happen. My hand gripped Henk's arm even tighter.

I was told to enter. Henk started to enter alongside me, but the guard reached out a hand and told him, "Wait."

I went in alone.

Inside, the official made no polite conversation when I presented my summons. He simply demanded my passport and looked at me as though I were a speck of dirt. I handed him the passport, my heart pounding. He took it and left.

I waited for what felt like an interminable amount of time. All the while terrible thoughts raced through my head: That they would send me back to Vienna. That I would never again see my dear Henk. That they would try to get me to join the Dutch Nazi Party. That something would happen to my relatives still living in Vienna.

Once an official came in from the back office, looked me up and down, said nothing, and went away again. More time passed. Another official came into the room and looked me over. I had the idea that they were looking me over to try to figure me out. Most German girls my age who had been living in Holland for some years were housemaids. I didn't look like a housemaid. I knew they were puzzled by me.

Finally, the first official returned with my passport in his hand. He asked if it was true that I had refused to join a Nazi Girls' Club. I recalled the visit of the young girl many months before. I replied, "Yes. It is true."

With an icy look in his eye, he handed me my passport. Coldly he said, "Your passport has been invalidated. You must return to Vienna within three months."

I opened my passport. On the page that showed what date my passport was valid, he had put a big black "X." My passport was now indeed invalid.

Not knowing what to do, I went to the Aliens Department of the police, where in the past I had gone each year to register. The Department was on the O.Z. Achterburgwal. There I had always been treated nicely through the years. I asked the policeman in charge of the office for aliens what to do. I told him what had happened at the German Consulate and showed him my passport.

He listened sympathetically and examined the big "X." He shook his head sadly. "We're living in an occupied country. We can't help you anymore. We have no power."

He thought for a few more seconds and scratched his head. "The only thing I might suggest is that you go back to the German Consulate and make a scene. Start crying and say that you really didn't mean it when you refused to join the Nazi Girls' Club."

My back stiffened. "Never."

"Then the only other alternative I can think of is to marry a Dutchman."

I told him that I was planning to do just that.

He shook his head. "On second thought, you'll need your birth certificate from Vienna in order to marry."

I told him that I still had several relatives in Vienna. Perhaps they could help? He continued to shake his head. He pointed out the date written beside the large "X." "It can't happen. You have only three months to get your birth certificate. Even in normal times it would take probably a year or more to get a legal document sent. And these are not normal times." A sad look crept across his round Dutch face.

I ran home and quickly wrote to my Uncle Anton in Vienna. "Please send my birth certificate!" I begged him, and I quickly posted the letter.

And so the waiting began.

As I waited to hear from my uncle that spring, the Germans continued to advance. The radio was full of announcements of General Rommel's victories in North Africa, also that the Germans were on the verge of conquering Greece and Yugoslavia, and that Romania, even with a pro German government, was also occupied, just as we were. I, and others like me, clung to every bit of good news we heard from the BBC and Radio Orange—any defeats, all acts of successful sabotage by underground resistance forces that were slowly emerging in Holland and everywhere else.

The Greeks surrendered in April, 1941. The newspapers showed the swastika flying above the Acropolis as it had flown in France.

At the same time, a rash of new anti-Jewish edicts sprang up. Suddenly, Jews were prohibited from staying in hotels, or going to cafés, movie theaters, restaurants, libraries, even public parks. Worst of all, Jews were told to surrender their radios to the police. At their own expense, they had to put them in good working order, and then bring them to the police. To be without this lifeline to the outside world was unfathomable; the radio was the source of all news and hope.

Finally, Uncle Anton wrote. But his letter said only that he needed my passport in order to obtain my birth certificate. "Send it right away."

I should have known. This was impossible. If I sent my passport to Vienna, it would immediately be apparent that it had been invalidated. I couldn't let Uncle Anton know that. Just the fact that he had been in touch with someone who had refused to join a Nazi Girls' Club might put him and my other relatives in danger.

Naturally, Mr. Frank knew everything that was going on with me. Regardless of his own problems, he always had a sympathetic ear to listen to my troubles. I had always confided in Mr. Frank, so I told him the latest troubling development that had come with Uncle Anton's letter. Mr. Frank listened quietly, thought the situation over; then together we examined my invalid passport, shaking our heads in despair.

Then one of Mr. Frank's eyebrows arched. "I have an idea," he announced. "Why don't you make a photocopy of the first page of the passport? This one only, the page that shows your picture and the official German stamp with the swastika. Then, send that to your uncle in Vienna. Tell him to take it to the City Hall. It shows that you have a passport. Then tell him to say that you can't send your complete passport as you can't walk around without it these days in Holland."

We exchanged a look of two conspirators. "Perhaps it will work?"

I did as Mr. Frank suggested. Time was running out for me. Henk and I were like two squirrels waiting in a cage, both doing our best to hide how we felt from the other. To be made to leave Holland was, to me, a fate worse than death.

Every day, as I waited for news from Uncle Anton, new edicts were issued against the Jews. Now Jewish doctors and dentists could not treat non-Jews. I ignored this and continued my treatments with Dr. Dussel. Jews were not permitted to bathe in public swimming pools. I wondered where Anne and Margot Frank and their friends would go to cool off in the summertime.

Jews were ordered to buy the *Jewish Weekly*, in which these new edicts were published. Perhaps the Germans thought that this way we Christians wouldn't know what was happening to the Jews. But word of every new measure spread like fire. Also, little underground anti-German leaflets and newspapers had started to circulate. They were quite illegal, but offered fresh air and an antidote to the poison of lies and persecution everywhere around us.

A letter came from Uncle Anton. It said: "I've gone to the City Hall with the photocopy of your passport. Everywhere there are young people giving the Nazi greeting. They kept sending me from one person to another, one place to another. Finally, I left in despair. But don't give up hope. I'm going to try one more time, and if I still have no results, then I'm going to go personally to see the Mayor of Vienna!"

These words frightened me greatly. If Uncle Anton started an inquiry, it would turn out that I was someone who had refused to join a Nazi Girls' Club, that my passport had been invalidated. Uncle Anton was in danger just for helping someone like me. This was terrible. And even worse, there was so little time left.

Finally, in June, when it seemed that all was lost, a third letter from Uncle Anton arrived. I held my breath and opened it. It said: "I went into the City Hall to try again. This time there was an older woman in the office. I told her I had a niece in Amsterdam who wanted to marry a Dutch boy and could she please get her birth certificate from Vienna. Then this elderly clerk broke into a smile and told me, 'Listen, I have so many wonderful memories of Amsterdam because I've spent many enchanting vacations there. Wait here.' She left the room and quickly came back with your birth certificate. So here it is, my dear niece. May God bless you and your Dutch boy. Uncle Anton."

Out fell my neatly folded birth certificate.

Everyone at Travies and Company was happy about my news. Everyone's spirits lifted. I thanked Mr. Frank effusively. After all, it had been his idea. He brushed off my gratitude. "I'm very happy for you and Henk," he told me.

Elli gave me a hug, and everyone gathered around to see the document. I felt like whirling round and round with joy.

Quickly, Henk and I ran down to Amsterdam's City Hall to set a date for our wedding. Our happiness quickly drained out of us, however. We were told that when a Dutch person marries a foreigner, the foreign person's passport must be turned in to the City Hall clerk. We were in shock. My passport had a big "X" and was invalid. If the clerk was a Nazi sympathizer, I would be deported.

With our hearts in our throats, we made an appointment to be married on July 16, 1941. We would throw our fate out into the wind.

THE SUN was shining down on July 16—a beautiful storybook summer day in Amsterdam. I dressed in my best tailored coat and hat, Henk in a fine gray suit. As it was our wedding day, we treated ourselves to a ride on the streetcar, the number 25 to Dam Square. All the while my mind was on only one thing, the big "X" and the cancellation in my passport. I could not relax, and neither could Henk.

As the streetcar approached the busy square crowded with flocks of pigeons, bicycle riders, and people on their way to work,

I knew one thing for sure. No matter what happened, even if I was turned over to the Germans to be deported, or worse, I would never go back to Vienna. Never. It was impossible. I would go directly into hiding. I'd become an *onderduiker*—a Dutch term that means one who "dives under," goes underground, into hiding. I would never, never go back to Austria!

Mr. Frank had shut down Travies and Company for the day. As Henk and I waited to be called at the City Hall, some of our friends arrived. Among them were my adoptive parents; Mrs. Samson, our landlady; Elli Vossen; Mr. and Mrs. van Daan. Mrs. van Daan wore a fancy fedora hat and a short tailored suit.

Because Margot Frank and Mrs. Frank's mother were both sick, Mrs. Frank had stayed home to care for them. Anne and Mr. Frank arrived together. Mr. Frank looked handsome in his dark suit and hat. Anne looked very grown-up indeed in her little princess-style coat and matching hat with a ribbon around the brim. Anne's hair had grown longer, and it looked shiny and full from brushing.

Our friends were all as nervous as cats as we waited. If a group of people could all hold their breath at once, that's what we did. They all knew the perilous situation.

Anne's eyes flicked nervously back and forth from Henk to me. She stayed close to her father, hanging on his hand. Perhaps we were the first romantic bride and groom she had ever seen in the flesh. I could see as she looked at Henk that she thought of him as a gallant, dashing figure. Perhaps she thought of me in the same way? A wedding was the number one romantic occasion for a girl of twelve.

Our party was one of several that stood and waited. Names were called; more people arrived. Finally, our names were called. Henk and I stepped forward toward the desk. Our friends pressed in behind us like a wall. The clerk reached out his hand and asked for the official certificate.

Henk handed it to him. The clerk glanced at it, made a nota-
tion, looked up, and said, "Please, may I have the passport of the
bride?"

A great fist grabbed hold of my heart and squeezed. This was
the terrible moment. I knew it; Henk knew it. Our friends knew it
too. There was absolute silence.

I'd been holding my passport so tightly it was stuck to my
hand. I unstuck it and handed it over. All eyes were on the official,
trying to read his political leanings from his nondescript face. He
opened the passport and thumbed through the pages. But all the
while, his eyes were on Henk—not on me, not on the passport.
Without looking down at it, he said, "It's all right."

The fist ungripped my heart, and a feeling like a thousand
tingling little shocks went through my entire body. My knees were
weak; my throat squeezed shut.

My head roared as our little group moved into the next room
where the official ceremony was to take place. As we had almost no
money, we had taken the least expensive ceremony. Henk and I
stook flanked by two other couples about to be married. The official was saying to all three of us brides, ". . . you must follow your
husband . . ."—the usual legal promise a wife had to make. But I
heard nothing. Nothing but the thumping of a delicious drum in
my mind. It beat, "I'm Dutch! I'm Dutch! I'm Dutch!" with a
glorious boom.

The thumping drum was suddenly interrupted. There was a
pull at my sleeve. It was Henk. All eyes were riveted on me, waiting. A second passed. Henk's warm blue eyes filled in the blank for
me: "Yes." I quickly ad-libbed, "I do, I do."

A collective sigh of relief came from the crowd.

Our little party marched out onto the street. The sweet summer sun poured down. Joy erupted. Anne jumped up and down,
forgetting her young-lady poise. Our friends' eyes shone moistly.

Everyone hugged everyone; there were kisses, strong handshakes among us all, and even with strangers who were attracted by the excitement. We found a street photographer and engaged him to take photographs of us for a memory book.

I was in such a state of euphoria that I broke the Dutch tradition that the bridegroom carry the marriage certificate. I was so happy that all that afternoon, I kept the certificate gripped as in a vise. My dream of becoming Dutch had come true because of Henk. But I was happy because Henk was my ideal; my love for him was true.

Anne was impressed with my gold ring. She looked at it dreamily. I'm sure she was imagining that someday she too would marry a tall, handsome man like Henk. Because times were hard, we had only one ring, although the custom was for a couple to have two. Henk and I had barely scraped together enough money for one gold ring. He had insisted that I should wear it. We agreed that later, when hard times were over, we'd buy another ring for Henk to wear. For the time being, one would do.

Our friends teased me about forgetting to answer the official question about whether I would marry Henk. I told them that all I had been able to think about was that at long last, I was Dutch. "Quite a victory against the Moffen, wouldn't you say?" Our friends laughed.

The group broke up. Henk and I had to be off to my adoptive family's home for a family get-together. Mr. Frank informed us that he was throwing a party for us the following morning at the office.

"It's not necessary," I told him.

He wouldn't accept my protests.

"I'll be coming," Anne announced, radiantly smiling.

The next morning the office became a party place. One of the traveling agents for the firm had brought liverwurst, sliced beef, salami, cheese. Everything was laid out on plates. None of us had seen so much meat in a long time. "Too much food," I told Mr. Frank.

"Nonsense," he said, smiling, so pleased to have something to celebrate in these grim times.

Anne wore a bright summer frock and was in a happy mood. She helped to lay out the meats on the plates, to cut the bread, to put out the butter. We were all still in a state of elation. Because there seemed to be so little any of us could do against our oppressors, my victory was all that much sweeter.

Anne and Elli passed around plate after plate of food. We all ate until we were stuffed; we drank until we could drink no more. We made toasts. I was deeply touched by the presents that were given us. It was not easy to get nice things these days, but everyone had found a way. Anne presented me with a silver plate from her family and the office staff. Mr. and Mrs. van Daan gave us crystal glasses with etched clumps of grapes. From Mrs. Samson, a ceramic box with a silver top in the shape of little fish. There were others.

I noticed how Anne kept her eyes on Henk and me; she was so enthralled by our romantic love story. She treated us almost as though we were two movie stars rather than two perfectly ordinary Dutch people who had simply married.

# CHAPTER SIX

ALL SUMMER a rash of anti-Jewish edicts were published, one after another. First, on June 3, 1941, it was ordered that a large black "J" was to be added to the identity cards of all persons who had registered during the census as having two or more Jewish grandparents. Everyone in Holland, Jew and Christian alike, had been forced to carry an identity card at all times.

People whispered that perhaps we Dutch, especially Jews, had been fools for answering all questions on the census honestly. Now, as though we had been tricked, the Germans knew exactly who and where all the Jews of Holland were. When the "J's" were ordered, a penalty was established: any Jews who failed to register would be imprisoned for five years and also would have all their property confiscated. The lesson taught by those who had been sent to Mauthausen and had either vanished or died was vividly in everyone's mind.

Some of the anti-Jewish orders were laughable. Jews were no longer allowed to keep pigeons. Others were devastating—Jewish bank deposits and valuables were suddenly frozen from transfer or use. Jews could not do what they pleased with their own savings and valuables. A slow strangulation was taking place, we began to realize: first isolation, and now impoverization.

Throughout all this, Jewish children had pretty much been unmolested. Now they were forbidden to mix with their non-Jewish schoolmates. Now Jewish children had to go to all-Jewish schools and be taught only by Jewish teachers. Anne and Margot Frank had been crazy about their school. I knew that both of them would be heartbroken.

All-Jewish schools began springing up in Amsterdam to accommodate the new edict. In September, 1941, Anne and Margot began to attend the Jewish Secondary School. Lashing adults with the brutal whip of hate was one thing. We'd seen that these German swine were entirely capable of that. But to hurt defenseless children was even worse.

Henk and I were eaten up with frustration when it came to the plight of our Jewish friends. To their faces we acted as normal as possible, as they did to us. But at home, at night, the frustration and anger of the day left me drained dry. Although neither of us could account for a feeling of bitter shame, it churned and gnawed in us both nonetheless.

AUTUMN CAME, and the days began to shorten. The Germans had invaded Russia that June, and they continued to sweep across that vast country as though nothing could stop them. It rained often, and the sky seemed always filled with clouds and mist. It was becoming harder to get what one needed at the shops. At the Pectacon Company, we had started to stock what were known as *ersatz*, or substitute, products, since we could not always get the real spices and products that we were used to selling. *Ersatz* products were usually quite inferior substitutes.

Our salesmen crisscrossed Holland and continued to bring

orders to the Prinsengracht. Some of these orders came from the German military stationed in various garrisons around Holland. Once every week or two these salesmen would return to the office in Amsterdam with their orders, which we would then fill and ship.

But when salesmen returned to the office, they also brought stories of their travels. They brought news of conditions in other areas of Holland. They told us that life was going on, despite the occupation, everywhere across Holland, but that everywhere Dutch resources—our coal, our meat, our cheeses—were being plundered and taken across the border into Germany.

I had met Mr. Frank's friend Mr. Lewin, a German refugee, several times at the Franks' Saturday get-togethers. Mr. Lewin could no longer work as a pharmacist because of the Nazis. Mr. Frank had given this man some of the empty storage rooms to use as a laboratory. I had no occasion ever to go to these unused rooms, but from time to time Mr. Lewin would stop at the offices on his way in or out and talk about his experiments. Sometimes he'd show skin creams he had made in his makeshift laboratory to sell.

So far, the edicts that had been squeezing Jews out of various professions and businesses hadn't touched Mr. Frank or Mr. van Daan or Travies and Company or Pectacon. What Mr. Frank had done with his savings and valuables when the banking edicts had been issued had not been discussed with us, naturally. He was always himself, never missed work, never complained, and kept his private life at home.

We were all nervous about what would happen next and whether any of these edicts would create problems for Mr. Frank and Mr. van Daan or any of our customers. Like ripples in a pond, the effects of the German persecution of the Jewish population seemed to be widening and deepening. None of us knew what was yet to come. Being Jewish had to feel these days as though one were standing on shifting sands—and for some, quicksand.

Mr. Frank was a shrewd man. Whatever his thoughts and perceptions about his personal position as a Jew, I knew he would be clever. And so one day he told Henk that he had some personal business to discuss with him. He and Henk went into Mr. Frank's private office.

Mr. Frank explained to Henk, alone in the office with the door shut, that his position in the company was creating a danger for everyone. He explained that he had thought it through very carefully and had decided that he would resign as managing director of Travies and Company. The corporate papers would be legally changed. In his place, his good friend Mr. Koophuis would be substituted.

Mr. Frank would remain in the capacity of adviser, but in reality would continue to run the business as usual. The only real change would be from the legal standpoint.

Mr. Frank explained further that another trusted Christian figurehead in the Pectacon Company would be, he believed, a further strengthening of the Christian look of the company. Would Henk consider becoming director of Pectacon, the spice company, with Mr. Kraler as managing director?

Henk was delighted that his old Dutch Christian name could lend a protective front to Mr. Frank's firm. Henk was happy to help Mr. Frank, a decent man whom Henk admired. Henk could trace his Dutch Christian ancestors for more than five generations. If this wasn't enough Aryan background for the Nazis, he told Mr. Frank, nothing ever would be.

The proper legal papers were filed with the proper authorities. On December 18, 1941, Mr. Otto Frank disappeared from the directory of Travies and Company. To his staff he became an adviser. New stationery and business cards were printed. The Pectacon Company became Kohlen and Company.

Life on the Prinsengracht continued, of course, without a

pause. Mr. Frank came to work every day. He sat at his desk in his private office and made all the decisions and gave all the orders. Nothing changed except that when a check had been made out, or a letter had been typed, the place for a signature would remain blank. Mr. Frank would then pass whatever it was that needed signing over to Mr. Koophuis or Mr. Kraler for a totally Christian signature.

In December of 1941 our spirits rose. After being attacked in Pearl Harbor by the Japanese, the Americans had declared war against the Japanese, and Japan's allies, the Germans and Italians, had declared war against the Americans. It was almost unbelievable: America, with all its manpower and airplane factories, was now allied with England against our oppressors. That great country, America, was now with us in this fight against Hitler.

We were further uplifted by news from Russia. Although Hitler had swept across Russia like a flash flood all through the summer and autumn, we were suddenly hearing on Radio Orange and on the BBC that the cold and muddy winter had come to Russia, and the Germans were bogged down, making no further progress. The BBC predicted that Hitler's armies would be crushed, just as Napoleon's armies had been. The German broadcasts, however, always making statements contradictory to the BBC, claimed that Leningrad and Moscow were on the verge of toppling. It would happen any day. Naturally, we longed for the BBC to be closer to the truth.

In January, 1942, Jews from little towns near Amsterdam were ordered to move immediately into the city. These people were told to give the police lists of their possessions that they were taking to Amsterdam. Then they were to have their gas, electricity, and water turned off, and to give the police the keys to their homes.

We heard that these people were given no time to find places to live, no time to dispose properly of their possessions, to take care of homes some had lived in for a lifetime. They simply came to Amsterdam with bundles, with pushcarts, sometimes a whole family's possessions in an old baby carriage. Amsterdam was filled with people as it was. Where were these people expected to go?

Mrs. Samson's daughter came from Hilversum with her husband and two children, aged five and three. Suddenly, there they were at Mrs. Samson's door. They were disoriented, frightened. Mrs. Samson became as upset as they were. What to do? Where to put everybody? There were only four rooms, including ours, in the apartment.

Henk and I talked it over and told Mrs. Samson that we would gladly leave and let her have her rooms back. We didn't tell her that we had no idea where we would go. She kept repeating, "No. No. No." So we all thought again, and finally concluded where three could live, so could seven.

The daughter, son-in-law, and the children shared a bedroom. Mrs. Samson had another bedroom. Henk and I had our own bedroom. We shared the sitting room like one big family. It was a squeeze, but it had to do. At dinner the son-in-law did his best to make jokes. He had been a violinist, but was now unable to work. Somehow, his humor infected us all with laughter, but underneath, this family was eaten up by fear and nervousness.

Henk and I removed ourselves as much as possible. There was nothing we could do to help the situation. We pretended that we did not see their fears and anxieties. Many nights we would go around the corner to visit friends on the Rijnstraat. These friends had rented Henk a room in their house for many years before he'd left to live with me. Often we would come to the Rijnstraat in the early evening and all sit around their radio listening to every bit of news from the BBC and Radio Orange. We were like thirsty children, drinking every word spoken in these faraway broadcasts.

Sometimes Winston Churchill would woo us with his passionate speeches, fill us with spit and vinegar and the strength to endure the occupation for another day, another week, another year, however long until "good" could triumph. The radio reported new kinds of bombers being built in America, that these bombers would be in the air in two years. "Now!" we'd exclaim. "Now—we need them *now*. We can't wait two years."

And in fact, things were quickly growing worse. The Germans began rationing our food. Special stamp cards with signatures were issued to each of us to go along with our ration cards. Each period of four weeks or eight weeks, we would receive a new ration coupon and our stamp cards would be signed by the official in charge. In the newspapers were lists of what could be bought against which coupon. Not only food was listed, but also pipe tobacco, cigarettes, and cigars. When I shopped, I could usually find what I needed, but sometimes I'd have to try two or three different shops rather than the usual one in the neighborhood.

We were being forced to use *ersatz* coffee and tea, both of which had the aroma of the real thing but no taste whatsoever. Henk could not always get enough cigarettes. He missed having a cigarette always waiting in his pocket. Now he had to think twice before he had a smoke. We were particularly angry about these shortages because we knew that the Germans were taking food and goods that belonged to us Dutch and shipping them off to Germany.

As more and more Jews were banned from their jobs, the Germans began organizing labor camps for unemployed Jewish men. The labor assignments were often "to the East." No one really knew where. Poland? Czechoslovakia? The whispers said that those who refused when they were called up for labor would be sent to Mauthausen to receive harsh punishment. If one obeyed and went when ordered, it was said that one would have to work very hard, perhaps, and receive very small wages, but "decent" treatment was promised.

We heard that many of the Jews who were being called up for labor would do desperate things in order not to have to go. We heard that some spread egg white on their hands before the physical examination and then would let their urine pass over their hands, hoping to create in the urine what would pass for kidney disease. Some might bring to the examination a bottle of urine from a diabetic. Others swallowed huge chunks of chewing gum, which, if caught in the digestive system, would look in an X-ray like an ulcer. Others would drink enormous quantities of coffee and take scalding hot baths before the physical exam in order to appear too sickly to make good laborers, and thus be disqualified.

Jews were no longer allowed to marry non-Jews. Jews could no longer ride on streetcars. Jews had to shop only at certain hours and at certain shops. Jews couldn't sit in their own gardens or at cafés or in public gardens in order to get some fresh air.

Our Saturday-afternoon get-togethers at the Franks' had stopped. So had the occasional dinner Henk and I had attended with the Franks and their girls. These laws were succeeding in isolating and separating our Jewish friends from the rest of us. Everywhere now in our neighborhood, so full of Jewish people, were anxious-faced Jews getting poorer and poorer daily, many scratching around for ways to feed their children. They whispered among themselves, then stopped whispering when people came near. They were suspicious always, and always now with downcast eyes. I felt an ache for these demoralized people whenever I saw them.

In the spring of 1942 came yet another edict. This one was printed in the Dutch newspaper, not just in the *Jewish Weekly*. From one week hence, all Jews were ordered to sew a yellow six-pointed star the size of an adult's palm onto their clothing above the heart. This meant *all* Jewish men, women, and children. Each star cost a clothing coupon from the ration book and 4 cents. On the yellow star was printed JOOD—"Jew."

On the day that this order was to begin, many Dutch Christians, deeply rankled by this humiliation of our Jews, also wore yellow stars on their coats. Many wore yellow flowers, as emblems of solidarity, in their lapels or in their hair. Signs appeared in some shops asking Christians to show special respect for our Jewish neighbors, suggesting, for instance, that we lift our hats to them in a cheerful greeting—anything to show them that they were not alone.

Many Dutch did what they could to show their solidarity. This edict, somehow so much more enraging than all the others, was bringing our fierce Dutch anger to a boil. The yellow stars and yellow flowers those first few days were so common that our River Quarter was known as the Milky Way. The Jewish Quarter was laughingly called Hollywood. A surge of pride and solidarity swelled briefly until the Germans started cracking heads and making arrests. A threat was delivered to the population at large: anyone assisting Jews in any way would be sent to prison and possibly executed.

Mr. Frank came to the office as usual. No mention was made of the yellow star affixed by neat stitches to his coat. No attention was paid. We looked through it as though it were not there. To me, it was not.

Although Mr. Frank gave the impression of everything's being normal, I could see that he was worn out. Now, because he was not allowed on the streetcar, he had to walk many miles to the office each day, and then return home on foot at night. It was impossible for me to imagine the strain that he, Mrs. Frank, Margot, and Anne were under. Their situation was never discussed, and I did not ask.

One morning, after the coffee cups were gathered up and washed, Mr. Frank called me into his private office. He closed the door. He locked eyes with me, his soft brown eyes looking deeply into mine with an almost piercing directness. "Miep," he began, "I have a secret to confide to you."

I listened silently.

"Miep," he said, "Edith, Margot, Anne, and I are planning to go under—to go into hiding."

He let me take this in.

"We will go together with Van Daan and his wife and their son." Mr. Frank paused. "I'm sure you know the empty rooms where my pharmacist friend Lewin has been making his experiments?"

I told him I knew of these rooms but had never gone into them.

"That is where we will hide."

He paused for a moment.

"As you will be working on, as usual, right next to us, I need to know if you have any objections?"

I told him I did not.

He took a breath and asked, "Miep, are you willing to take on the responsibility of taking care of us while we are in hiding?"

"Of course," I answered.

There is a look between two people once or twice in a lifetime that cannot be described by words. That look passed between us. "Miep, for those who help Jews, the punishment is harsh; imprisonment, perhaps—"

I cut him off. "I said, 'Of course.' I meant it."

"Good. Only Koophuis knows. Even Margot and Anne do not know yet. One by one I will ask the others. But only a few will know."

I asked no further questions. The less I knew, the less I could say in an interrogation. I knew when the time was right he would tell me who the others were, and everything else I would need to know. I felt no curiosity. I had given my word.

# CHAPTER SEVEN

As THE SECOND anniversary of the German occupation grew close in the spring of 1942, Hitler's might was not lessening. All our hopes rested with the Allies—our allies. Underneath, we were haunted by the memory that when the Spanish oppressor had come to little Holland in the sixteenth century, he had stayed for eighty years.

Our lives had totally changed. Children could be seen playing at parachuting soldiers, jumping from their stoops at the end of an old umbrella. In villages were unwritten agreements that if an airplane was seen, each house opened its doors in order that all the children of the neighborhood could run inside.

At the last light of day, as though we'd been doing it all our lives, up went the blackout frames. We were getting used to queuing up at almost every shop and always buying a little extra if it happened to be available. Just in case. And always, now, our chairs were pulled up as close as possible to the radio.

Jews bore the most anxiety. Their freedoms had been snatched away one by one; their jobs, their mobility. So much free time and forced indolence was a heavy weight to carry. So much time to think, so much time for nasty thoughts and fears.

Because of the yellow star, Jews, who had once been undiffer-
entiated from other Dutchmen, were suddenly conspicuous. When
a child who was unused to Jews came into contact with one, he
would be surprised that the Jew didn't have horns or vampire
teeth—that he looked like the rest of us, instead of like a devil,
as the Germans said he did. Our Dutch heritage prohibiting the
making of differences between people had been violated. Worst
of all, our children's minds were being poisoned.

Nightly the drone of bombers overhead interfered with our
sleep. Sometimes, air raids, the warbling siren giving the warning,
and then the wait for the single tone that meant all clear. In our
neighborhood there was no shelter, so Henk and I got used to the
warnings and paid them no mind. We'd just pull the blankets a
little higher and snuggle a little closer to each other, deep in the
soft bedding.

Mrs. Frank's mother, Mrs. Hollander, died during the winter.
Her death was handled as a quiet family matter. Things being what
they were these days, people kept their own business to themselves.
Mr. Frank made an effort not to burden others with his difficulties.
His privacy was at all times treated with utmost respect.

Suddenly one day, Mr. van Daan came to me in my office and
said, "Miep, take your coat and come with me."

I put my work aside and did as he asked, wondering what he
had in mind for me.

Van Daan led the way down the Prinsengracht over the bridge
to the Rozengracht and onto a small side street. There he led me
to a butcher shop. I paused as he was about to enter the shop,
thinking I'd wait for him outside, but he motioned for me to follow
him inside.

It was strange for Herman van Daan to do such a thing. I
thought perhaps he had in mind something to do with his spices
for sausage-making that he wanted me to know. I followed him
inside.

I stood quietly beside him as he and the butcher engaged in conversation. I could see that they were on friendly terms. Mr. van Daan chewed on the cigarette that was never out of his mouth and chattered away, paying me no mind. Finally, he purchased a small quantity of meat and had it wrapped in brown paper to take home to his wife.

I wondered, Why is he going to a butcher near the office when he lives in another neighborhood—our neighborhood, in South Amsterdam—where there are plenty of butcher shops? I said nothing, he said nothing, and we returned to the office.

Several times in the next months, Mr. van Daan would ask me to come with him to this same butcher shop. I did as he asked, but I always wondered why he didn't just shop near home. Each time he'd engage in joking, friendly talk with the butcher and purchase some small cut of meat, and I'd always stand quietly aside until he'd turn to me and motion that he was ready to go back to the office. I hoped that Mr. van Daan would explain himself to me at some later date.

In late May, the BBC announced that the Royal Air Force had completed its first massive bombing of Germany. The city chosen was Cologne, close to the border of Holland along the Rhine River. We gasped when the BBC told of one thousand bombers participating in this raid.

Now my ears pricked up nightly when I heard the bombers droning above the thudding of the German antiaircraft artillery. Through the blackout shades I could see momentary flashes of searchlights arching across the sky. The bombers were heading for German industrial regions, for factories and other important installations. Save one bomb for Hitler himself, I thought.

Meanwhile the oppression of the Jews continued unabated. They now had to be in their own homes from eight at night until six in the morning. And under no circumstances were Jews to visit

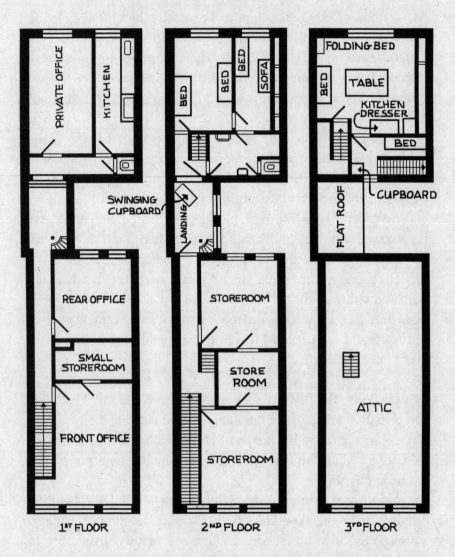

FLOOR PLAN OF THE ANNEX

homes or gardens or other accommodations that belonged to Christian people. Mixing between Jew and Christian had become a crime.

And then, the lowest trick of all. Bicycles belonging to Jews were to be handed in to the Germans by a certain date in June. The owner not only was to deliver the bicycle himself, but was responsible for its being in perfect working order. Spare tires, tubes, and patch kits were to be delivered as well. Nothing worse could happen to a Dutch person than the loss of his bicycle.

Now how could a Jew get from place to place? How could he get to work, if he still had work? How could young people like Margot and Anne Frank get along without their trusty black Dutch bicycles?

IT WAS the first Sunday in July, a warm summer night. Henk and I, Mrs. Samson, and the others had eaten our evening meal and were all engaged in our various activities. For me, Sunday evening meant doing small things to get ready for a new workweek.

These days anything unusual was immediately upsetting, and when there came an insistent ringing of our bell, tension rose in the apartment at the sound. Our eyes darted from one to another. Quickly, Henk went to the door and I followed him. There stood Herman van Daan in quite an agitated condition. Henk and I spoke quietly to him, not wanting to upset Mrs. Samson and her family.

"Come right away," Van Daan entreated in a hushed but urgent voice. "Margot Frank has received a postcard ordering her to appear for forced-labor shipment to Germany. She's been ordered to bring a suitcase with winter things. The Franks have decided to go immediately into hiding. Can you come right now to take a few things that they'll need in hiding? Their preparations aren't complete, you see."

"We will come," Henk told him. We put on our raincoats. To be seen carrying bags and packages would be too dangerous; we could hide much under our baggy old raincoats. It might appear odd to be wearing raincoats on a warm, dry summer night, but it was better than having bags full of possessions in our arms.

Henk made some explanation to Mrs. Samson so as not to alarm her and the others, and we left with Mr. van Daan. When Mr. Frank had confided in me about the hiding plan, I had that very night told Henk about our conversation. Without discussion, Henk had affirmed his unconditional assistance to the Franks and agreed that the plan was a sound one. But neither of us had expected the Franks to go into hiding this soon. Walking quickly but not hurrying, in order not to attract attention, we went toward the Merwedeplein. On the way, Van Daan told us that Mr. Frank had just told his girls about the hiding plan but not where the hiding place was.

"You can imagine," he explained, "they're in a state of great confusion. There's so much to do and so little time, and their damned lodger seems to be hanging about, making it all quite difficult."

Walking to the Franks', I suddenly felt a great sense of urgency for my friends. Conscripting a sixteen-year-old girl for forced labor was a new abomination the Germans were inflicting on the Jews. Yes, I thought, the sooner our friends got safely out of sight, the better. And how many more young girls like Margot have they conscripted? Girls with no father like Mr. Frank and no hiding plan? Girls who must be horribly frightened tonight. With these thoughts, I had to force myself not to run the rest of the way to the Merwedeplein.

When we arrived at the Frank apartment, few words were exchanged. I could feel their urgency, an undercurrent of near-panic. But I could see that much needed to be organized and prepared. It was all too terrible. Mrs. Frank handed us piles of what felt like children's clothes and shoes.

I was in such a state myself that I didn't look. I just took and took as much as I could, hiding the bunches of things the best way I could under my coat, in my pockets, under Henk's coat, in his pockets. The plan was that I'd bring these things to the hiding place at some later date when our friends were safely inside.

With our coats bursting, Henk and I made our way back to our rooms and quickly unloaded what we'd had under our coats. We put it all under our bed. Then, our coats empty again, we hurried back to the Merwedeplein to get another load.

Because of the Franks' lodger, the atmosphere at the Frank apartment was muted and disguised. Everyone was making an effort to seem normal, not to run, not to raise a voice. More things were handed to us. Mrs. Frank bundled, and sorted quickly, and gave to us as we again took and took. Her hair was escaping from her tight bun into her eyes. Anne came in, bringing too many things; Mrs. Frank told her to take them back. Anne's eyes were like saucers, a mixture of excitement and terrible fright.

Henk and I took as much as we could, and quickly left.

Early the next day, Monday, I woke to the sound of rain.

Before seven thirty, as we had arranged the night before, I had ridden my bicycle to the Merwedeplein. No sooner had I reached the front stoop than the door of the Franks' apartment opened and Margot emerged. Her bike was standing outside. Margot had not handed her bicycle in as ordered. Mr. and Mrs. Frank were inside, and Anne, wide-eyed in a nightgown, hung back inside the doorway.

I could tell that Margot was wearing layers of clothing. Mr. and Mrs. Frank looked at me. Their eyes pierced mine.

I made an effort to be assuring. "Don't worry. The rain is

very heavy. Even the Green Police won't want to go out in it. The rain will provide a shelter."

"Go," Mr. Frank instructed us, taking a look up and down the square. "Anne and Edith and I will come later in the morning. Go now."

Without a backward glance, Margot and I pushed our bicycles onto the street. Quickly, we pedaled away from the Merwedeplein, going north at the first turning. We pedaled evenly, not too fast, in order to appear like two everyday working girls on their way to work on a Monday morning.

Not one Green Policeman was out in the downpour. I took the big crowded streets, from the Merwedeplein to Waalstraat, then to the left to Noorder Amstellaan to Ferdinand Bolstraat, Vijzel-straat to Rokin, Dam Square, Raadhuisstraat, finally turning onto the Prinsengracht, never so glad before to see our cobbled street and murky canal.

All the way we had not said one word. We both knew that from the moment we'd mounted our bicycles we'd become crimi-nals. There we were, a Christian and a Jew without the yellow star, riding on an illegal bicycle. And at a time when the Jew was ordered to report for a forced-labor brigade about to leave for parts unknown in Hitler's Germany. Margot's face showed no in-timidation. She betrayed nothing of what she was feeling inside. Suddenly we'd become two allies against the might of the German beast among us.

Not a soul was about on the Prinsengracht. After opening the door, we carried our bicycles into the storeroom, then we left the room and shut the door. I opened the next door to the office and shut the door against the rain. We were soaked through to the skin. I could see that Margot was suddenly on the verge of crumbling.

I took her arm and led her past Mr. Frank's office and up the stairway to the landing that led to the hiding place. It was approaching the time that the others would be coming to work. I was now afraid that someone would come, but I kept silent.

Margot was now like someone stunned, in shock. I could feel her shock now that we were inside. As she opened the door, I gripped her arm to give her courage. Still, we said nothing. She disappeared behind the door and I took my place in the front office.

My heart too was thumping. I sat at my desk wondering how I could get my mind onto my work. The pouring summer rain had been our shelter. Now one person was safe inside the hiding place. Three more had to be protected by the rain.

Mr. Koophuis arrived at work and took Margot's bicycle somewhere that I didn't know. Soon after he left I could hear the warehouseman arriving, stamping the water off his shoes.

Late in the morning I heard Mr. and Mrs. Frank and Anne coming through the front office door. I had been waiting for that moment and quickly joined them and hurried them along past Mr. Kraler's office up the stairway to the door of the hiding place. All three of them were quite wet. They were carrying a few things, and all had yellow stars sewn onto their clothes. I opened the door for them and shut it when they had vanished inside.

In the afternoon when no one was around and all was quiet, I went upstairs to that door myself and disappeared into the hiding place, closing the door tight behind me.

Entering the rooms for the first time, I was surprised by what I saw. In total disorder were sacks and boxes and furnishings, piles of things. I could not imagine how all these things had been brought up to the hiding place. I had not once noticed anything being brought in. Perhaps it had been brought at night, or on Sundays when the office was closed.

On this floor there were two quite small rooms. One was rectangular with a window, and the other long and thin, also with a window. The rooms were wood-paneled, the wood painted a dark green, the wallpaper old and yellowish and peeling in places. The windows were covered by thick, white, makeshift curtains. There was a toilet in a large room, with a dressing area off to the side.

Up a steep flight of old wooden steps was a large room with sink and stove and cabinets. Here too the windows were covered with curtains. Off this large room was another rickety stairway to an attic and storage area. The steps to the attic cut through a tiny garret-type room, again filled with piles and sacks of things.

Mrs. Frank and Margot were like lost people, drained of blood, in conditions of complete lethargy. They appeared as though they couldn't move. Anne and her father were making efforts to create some order out of the multitude of objects, pushing, carrying, clearing. I asked Mrs. Frank, "What can I do?"

She shook her head. I suggested, "Let me bring some food?"

She acquiesced. "A few things only, Miep—maybe some bread, a little butter; maybe milk?"

The situation was very upsetting. I wanted to leave the family alone together. I couldn't begin to imagine what they must be feeling to have walked away from everything they owned in the world—their home; a lifetime of gathered possessions; Anne's little cat, Moortje. Keepsakes from the past. And friends.

They had simply closed the door of their lives and had vanished from Amsterdam. Mrs. Frank's face said it all. Quickly, I left them.

*Part Two*

# IN HIDING

# CHAPTER EIGHT

A FEW DAYS after the Frank family went into hiding, Mr. Frank asked Henk and me to go to his apartment on the Merwedeplein and play a little charade with his lodger in order to see what had occurred after their disappearance; to see if the Franks were being hunted. Early in the evening, right after dark, Henk and I made our visit.

When we rang the bell, the Franks' lodger, a middle-aged Jewish man, let us into the apartment. Setting looks of innocence on our faces, we inquired after Mr. Frank. "Mr. Frank hasn't come round to the office recently. We wondered if he's all right."

The lodger replied, "The Franks have vanished." Then he got up, left the room, and returned with a slip of paper in his hand. "I found this," he explained, showing Henk an address written on the paper. "I think it's an address in Maastricht."

We examined the address. Maastricht, the Dutch city on the German/Belgian border, would be along the route if one were making an escape. "Mr. Frank has family in Switzerland," ventured the lodger. "Perhaps they've fled to Switzerland?"

He shook his head. "People in the neighborhood are saying that Mr. Frank had escaped to Switzerland through the help of an old army friend. In fact, one neighbor said that they had seen the whole family drive off in a big car. Nobody knows for sure." He shrugged. The lodger didn't seem upset. People were no longer surprised when their friends simply vanished.

"I'll stay on here," he told us, his eyes drifting around the apartment. "If I can," he added. "I'm Jewish too, you see."

Without making a show of curiosity, I glanced around the apartment at the furnishings. I kept on the lookout for Anne's cat, Moortje, knowing that that would be the first thing she would ask about when we told about our visit to her home. I saw no sign of her.

We bade the lodger good night. "Please, would you let us know if you receive any word of the Franks' whereabouts?" asked Henk.

The lodger promised.


"WHAT ABOUT MOORTJE? Have you seen my cat, Moortje? Is the lodger caring for her or has he given her away?" demanded Anne, first thing, when I went up to the hiding place to get the morning shopping list. "And my clothes, my things—did you bring any of my things to me from home, Miep? Did you, Miep?"

Mr. Frank gently explained, "Miep couldn't bring anything from the apartment, Anne . . . don't you see?" As he went on to tell her why, I noticed a new composure, a new calm about Mr. Frank. Always a nervous man before, he now displayed a veneer of total control; a feeling of safety and calm emanated from him. I could see that he was setting a calm example for the others.

Anne hadn't finished with her questions. "What about my friends . . . who's there? Have any of them gone into hiding like us? Have they been taken in a *razia?*" The *razias,* or roundups, of Jews were still occurring.

Anne was emotional, longing for news. As she and the others gathered round, I related the story of my visit with Henk to the Merwedeplein. They wanted every detail.

"What about Jopie, right across the street from you?" Anne asked when I finished my tale. "Is she all right?"

Jopie was Anne's friend, a girl her age who lived across from us on Hunzestraat. Anne knew that I sometimes spoke to Jopie's mother, who was French. A couturiere, she was not Jewish, although her husband was. The husband was an antiques dealer. They lived above our milk shop, and sometimes I'd run into Madame in the street when I went for milk. She was always alone.

"Yes, Anne, I've seen Jopie's mother. She's still the same. Her family is still there."

Anne's face darkened. She wanted more news of her friends, she so missed her friends.

I made clear to Anne that I could not say anything about her other friends. That it would be too dangerous to try to find out these things.

"And what else is going on outside?" asked Mr. Frank, hungry for news from the outside world he no longer inhabited.

Seeing this hunger, I told them what I knew. I told about the *razias* which were taking place in different parts of town. I told them the newest edict was for Jewish telephones to be disconnected. That prices for false identity papers had gone through the ceiling.

"And Henk—is he coming up for a visit after lunch?" asked Anne.

"Yes," I affirmed, "when the men in the workplace are at lunch. He knows much more about what's going on around town. Much more."

Faces brightened at the news that yes, Henk would come. "And Elli will be up during lunch." Everyone was pleased that more visits would be forthcoming. They longed for each of us to come up as often as possible.

Jo Koophuis came often, always bringing a little something. He had a special warm way about him. Mr. Kraler came too, sometimes with questions for Mr. Frank about the business, sometimes with *Cinema and Theater* magazine for Anne, who liked news and photos of film stars.

Order was slowly being made in the hiding place. Things were being stacked out of the way, up in the attic with the old files from the office. A feeling of home was beginning to emerge—the old, trusty coffeepot; children's schoolbooks or a hairbrush lying about.

Anne had glued her movie-star pictures onto her bedroom wall—Ray Milland; Greta Garbo; Norma Shearer; Ginger Rogers; Lily Bouwmeester, the Dutch actress; Heinz Rühmann, the German actor. Other pictures she liked: a big advertisement for our company's jam-making process; Michelangelo's *Pietà*; a big pink rose; chimpanzees having a tea party; Princess Elizabeth of York; many, many cutouts of cuddly little babies. Anne liked cutouts of cute babies as much as she liked movie stars.

Anne and Margot were sharing the long, narrow room on the first floor of the hiding place. Next door, in the bigger room, Mr. and Mrs. Frank had made their bedroom. Upstairs was the living and cooking area, the place to spend the day, as it was one more floor above the office kitchen and any noise made would be less easily heard. But no noise was made during the day while the workers came and went below. No toilet flushed; no shoes on the creaky wooden stairs. Everyone was still and quiet, and waited for one of us to bring the news that the workers below had gone.

I noticed that Mrs. Frank continued during those first days to be very, very low. Margot too was very low, so silent and undemonstrative. Always kind, and always helpful, Margot had a way of making herself invisible. She never got in the way; she made no demands.

Each day I brought a few of the things that Henk and I had taken from the Merwedeplein the night before they'd gone into hiding. Quickly, I brought everything I had to the hiding place.

Each morning, first thing, when there was a lull at the office, I'd tiptoe upstairs and get a shopping list from Mrs. Frank. She would give me money or I would take money from the cashbox downstairs, to be replaced later. Then, before she could start her barrage of questions, I'd promise Anne that I'd be back later with the shopping, and at that time I'd sit and we could have a real talk.

As THE *razias* continued, Jews searched frantically for places to hide. Some made desperate, sometimes foolhardy attempts to cross the border to Belgium. Everyone was looking for a "safe address." A safe address, a hiding place, had suddenly become the most blessed acquisition. It was better than a job in the diamond trade, more valuable than a pot of gold. People scrambled in every possible way for information that might lead to a safe address.

Mrs. Samson's daughter and son-in-law, Mr. and Mrs. Coenen, had been desperately searching for a hiding place. They were in a panic for themselves and their two small children as the *razias* in early July continued and spread into many parts of Amsterdam. They managed at last to find one.

When they found their hiding place, they wanted to tell us, but Henk and I had quickly learned that the less one knew about others, the better. None of us knew what the Germans might do with you when they captured you, except that every kind of torture was acceptable to these barbarous people.

Noticing their preparations around the apartment, we realized that their departure was imminent. Knowing that they were in such a panic to get away, Henk warned them to stay away from the Centraal Railway Station. "The Green Police are patrolling the Centraal Station day and night. It's foolish to go near there."

Other than that, we said nothing to these frightened people, with their children understanding nothing that was going on around them. We asked them no questions, and they told us nothing.

One evening, we came home from work and they had vanished.

That day there had been a particular rash of *razias* around town. When Henk and I returned home from work, Mrs. Samson told us that her son-in-law and daughter and their children were so nervous and frightened that they had decided to go immediately to the safe-hiding address. Mrs. Samson was still very shaky from their departure. Henk and I thought she might be better in a safe place until the *razias* had ended, so we suggested that she go and stay with my adoptive parents. She agreed, and I quickly made the arrangements for her.

Just after midnight that night the doorbell rang. Henk and I were in bed and froze at the sound of the bell. Telling me to stay, Henk went to the door. I was too apprehensive to stay, and followed him to the door. There was a woman at the door. With her—one at her side, and one in her arms—were the tiny sleepy children of Mrs. Samson's daughter, Mrs. Coenen.

The woman explained that the children's parents had been captured by the Green Police at the Centraal Station.

She held out the little girl in her arms. I came forward and took her. She nudged the little boy toward us as well, and Henk took him into his arms. "I have orders to bring these children to this address." That was all she said; then she turned and left and, walking quickly, disappeared into the darkness. We were speechless. Our thoughts were the same: Who was she? Was she Jewish or Christian? Why had the Green Police let her take away two Jewish children?

We brought the children into the kitchen, made warm milk and buttered bread, and put them to sleep.

The next day Mrs. Samson returned, and found her grandchildren. She tried to learn from them what had happened, but neither of the children was old enough to tell her anything about their parents. Nothing could be learned. Their parents had simply disappeared into the hands of the Germans.

Now more than ever, we realized that it was very important to find a place for these children to go into hiding. Discreet inquiries were made. We discovered an organization of students in Amsterdam that had addresses where children could be brought. Very quickly, in barely a week, the little granddaughter was brought, through this organization, to a hiding place in Utrecht. Then the grandson was taken to hide in Eemnes.

Now the search began for a "safe address" for Mrs. Samson. With each day that passed, life was becoming more and more difficult for Jewish people all over Amsterdam. The sooner she could go, the better, to avoid a *razia*.

WE WERE ENCOURAGED to learn that ten Christian churches in Holland had banded together and issued a public protest in the form of a telegram sent to the highest German authorities. Together, these Christian churches expressed profound "outrage" at the German deportations of Jewish people. They called the measures "illegal" and accused the Germans of going blatantly against all Dutch morality and against God's "Divine Commandments of justice and charity."

These telegrams were totally ignored by the Germans.

One week after the Franks had gone into hiding, I went upstairs to get the shopping list as usual and found that Herman van Daan, his wife, Petronella, and their sixteen-year-old son had moved into the hiding place. The boy was named Peter. He was a good-looking, stocky boy with thick dark hair, dreamy eyes, and a sweet nature.

I knew that the Van Daans had planned to come into hiding

fairly soon, but they too had moved up the date of their disappearance because the new rash of *razias* was raging all across Amsterdam. In contrast to the Franks' sad arrival, the Van Daans were overjoyed to be safely ensconced in their cozy hiding place. They had much to tell the Franks about what nightmares had been taking place in Amsterdam; so much had happened to their Jewish friends in only one week since the Franks had disappeared.

Peter had brought his cat into hiding. The cat's name was Mouschi. He was a spritely, lean black tomcat, very, very friendly. Anne liked Mouschi right away, although she still missed her own cat, Moortje, and spoke longingly and often about her. Mouschi made himself right at home in the hiding place.

The new living arrangements in the hiding place were established. Mr. and Mrs. Frank stayed in their bedroom, and Margot and Anne continued to share the long, narrow room off the bathroom and dressing room. Mr. and Mrs. van Daan were sleeping in the big room one flight up from the Franks, and young Peter had taken the tiny room beside his parents, halfway under the stairway that led to the attic, an area still filled with piles of storage that hadn't been put away.

During the day, the Van Daans' bed was folded up against the wall. Their room served as the kitchen and the living room, where everyone spent the day. But they stayed off the floor below, which was right above the private offices and the kitchen of the office. Quickly the Franks and Van Daans were putting things in order, creating quite a cozy home under the circumstances.

The Van Daans told harrowing tales of how streetcar line number 8 had been used to transport Jews to the Centraal Station. Anne, Margot, and Mrs. Frank went gray as they listened. Some of the Jews sitting side by side on these transports had been their own friends and neighbors. Whole streetcars were now filled with Jews wearing yellow stars and carrying allotted bits of luggage.

Jews were being herded onto special trains at the Centraal Station. The destination of these trains was a place called Westerbork. Westerbork was a kind of holding camp. It was quite far away from Amsterdam, in Drenthe, not far from Germany. I heard that some Jews had thrown postcards and letters out the train windows, hoping some stranger would mail them. Some had been mailed and received by family or friends, telling where those who had left their homes had gone.

After the Van Daans' arrival, I began going to both Mrs. Frank and Mrs. van Daan to ask what I could get for them at the shops. When I did, Mr. van Daan handed me a list of meat cuts. I read the list and shook my head. Our existing ration coupons would simply not provide so much meat.

Mr. van Daan laughed, his usual cigarette dangling from his lips. "Remember the butcher shop off the Rozengracht where you came with me to shop?"

"Yes, I remember," I responded.

"Go to this man," he explained. "Give him my list. Say nothing and he'll give you what we want."

I looked at him skeptically.

"Don't worry"—Mr. van Daan laughed, his eyes twinkling—"this man had several good looks at you when you came with me. He knows your face. He's a good friend of mine. You'll see, he'll give you what you want if he can."

Finally, I understood what those strange visits to the butcher had been about. I couldn't help shaking my head and laughing too.

And just as promised, with no words spoken, this butcher looked into my face and gave me what he could of what Mr. van Daan had written on the list.

MOST DAYS Henk would come to the Prinsengracht at about noon to have lunch with me in the office. His office was on Marnixstraat, a seven-minute walk from the Prinsengracht. Only once or twice a week, on days when he had to go to a different office of the Amsterdam Welfare Bureau, would it be too far for him to come for lunch.

After Henk and I had finished our lunch, Henk would go upstairs into the hiding place to visit with our friends. Sometimes he'd stay for ten minutes, sometimes for thirty or forty minutes, while the workers from below were off having their own lunch. Henk would always sit on the edge of the dresser against the wall, his long legs stretched out at an angle. Immediately, Peter's cat, Mouschi, would come running from wherever he was and jump into Henk's arms. Mouschi was crazy about Henk.

Before anyone else could get in a word, Mr. van Daan would ask Henk for cigarettes. Henk would give what he'd been able to buy on the black market in the old Jordaan section, quite close to the office. Sometimes he'd bring Egyptian cigarettes called Mercedes, and other times he'd be able to find only Dutch-made cigarettes, which didn't taste too bad.

Van Daan would light up a cigarette and then would ask, "So, what's going on in town?" and "What news do you have of the war?" Then Henk would tell whatever news he had, and discussion would begin among the men, in the same way that my discussions were always with the women. Except for always-curious Anne. Anne was always at the forefront of all the discussions, men's and women's. She was the most curious of all the people in hiding and the most candid. She greeted all of us visitors with a barrage of questions and inquiries.

Now that the Frank family and the Van Daan family were in hiding, they could not get ration cards. With the seven of them to feed, we needed these ration cards desperately. To solve this problem, Henk had made some useful underground connections. He told the people in hiding to give him their identity cards. Trusting Henk fully, they asked nothing and gave all seven cards to him.

Henk took the cards and brought them to his underground sources to prove that he had seven people in hiding to feed. These illegal organizations then gave Henk stolen or forged ration tickets, which he turned over to me. I kept these tickets with me in the office, using them when I went out on my daily shopping tours for food.

Henk had a friend who owned a bookshop and lending library on Rijnstraat in our River Quarter. The shop was called Como's. Each week Henk would ask our seven friends in hiding what they would like to read. Then he would go to Como's and search out the various requests. He was usually able to find what was desired, and for a few pennies he would borrow a pile of books.

Then, generally on Saturdays, I would bring the new books up to the hiding place in time for the weekend, when there would be no visits because the office would be closed. At the same time, I would collect books that had been finished. So much reading went on in hiding that usually more than one pair of eyes had devoured each book.

Henk, Koophuis, Kraler, Elli, and I tried to space out our visits. Our friends were always thirsty for them. Each day was interminable for those shut into the four small rooms. The only breath of fresh air could be had in the attic, where there was a skylight that opened and showed a patch of sky and the tower of the Westerkerk. Up in the attic the laundry was hung to dry; sacks of food stood out of the way, along with old file boxes from the office. Peter liked to tinker with his tools in the attic, and had made a little workshop. Anne and Margot liked to go upstairs to the attic to read.

Our visits had acquired something of a routine. I, early in the morning, would be the first to visit, the first face after a long night locked in together. But this visit was business only, to get the list for groceries, see what was needed for the day. Then Elli would come for lunch, usually sharing a bit of the lunch Mrs. Frank or

Mrs. van Daan had prepared. Henk would come next, to discuss the day's news with the men.

Then, in the lull of the afternoon, I would bring up the groceries and make a real visit. As Frank and Van Daan were the experts in our business, Koophuis and Kraler needed to make many visits upstairs to ask questions and solve business problems. At the end of the day, after the last worker had gone, one of us would come up and let the people in hiding know that they could move about in a normal way, talk normally, not worry about every sound.

Those first weeks, none of us could get used to taking the first big step onto the steep stairway in the hiding place. Several times I hit my head hard on the low ceiling over the step, so that when I arrived upstairs my eyes would be filled with tears and my head would be splitting. All of us smashed our heads on the ceiling—all of us except Henk, the tallest of all, who never forgot to bend down to avoid a crack—and our head-hitting became a joke. Finally, someone nailed an old towel on that spot, and the head-hitting ceased.

ALMOST FROM the first, Anne had asked me, "Miep, why don't you and Henk come and spend the night with us? Please, it would be so nice for us."

"Yes, one of these days we'll come," I promised.

Everyone was keen to have us spend a night in the hiding place. I assured them we would come. Before we could keep our promise, we were informed that we were invited to a special event, a supper party, and that Henk and I were the guests of honor. The party was to celebrate our first wedding anniversary. The date was set for Saturday, the eighteenth of July. Naturally, we accepted.

When the night came, I remained after the rest of the office staff had gone. Henk joined me. Both of us had made an effort to look nice for the special gathering.

As we entered the hiding place, we were greeted by delicious aromas of cooking food. When we climbed the flight of steps and entered the Van Daans' room, there was a beehive of activity. The table was set; our friends were delighted to welcome our arrival.

Anne presented to me a special menu she had typed up for the occasion. She must have gone down the night before to the private office to use the typewriter. The menu said: "Dinner, offered by 'HET ACHTERHUIS' on the occasion of the one-year existence of the marriage of Mr. and Mrs. Gies, Esquire." Anne had taken to calling the hiding place Het Achterhuis, or "The Annex." She then listed the courses we would be served, with her own little comments. The soup she called "Bouillon a la Hunzestraat," for the street on which Henk and I lived. We read the menu with pleasure.

The next course was to be "Roastbeaf SCHOLTE," which she had named after our butcher. Then, "Salade Richelieu, Salade Hollandaise, one Potato." She then went on to explain of the "SAUCE DE BOEUF (JUS)" that we should use "very small amounts because of the lowering of the butter allowance in the ration tickets." She listed "RIZ a la Trautmansdorf"—that is, rice done as in a cozy little village in Germany—and "Sugar, Cinammon, Raspberry juice" to be served along with "COFFEE with sugar, cream, and various surprises."

I promised Anne that I would treasure her menu as a keepsake always, and Mrs. van Daan announced that it was time for dinner to be served. Henk and I were given seats of honor. Our friends seated themselves around us—nine of us squeezed around the table, nine different unmatching chairs jammed together.

Then the dinner began. It was delicious. I learned that Mrs. van Daan had seen to the cooking. I said to Mr. van Daan, "I didn't know your wife was such a fine cook. The food is sumptuous."

Van Daan smiled proudly. "Didn't you know that my wife is a gourmet cook?"

"We know now," Henk replied.

WHEN THE SUMMER heat became extreme, it was not very nice up in the hiding place. Because of the necessity of the curtains at all times of the day and the blackout shades at night, there was not much fresh air. During working hours, only the left window was slightly open, to give the impression that the men from the workplace were working there. Hence, even under the best of circumstances the place was always a little stuffy. When the temperature rose, the stuffiness increased. Fortunately, because of the big, beautiful chestnut tree behind the hiding place, the rays of the sun were blocked out, and the place was not as hot as it might have been.

As the disorder began to be turned into order up in the hiding place, our friends found more and more ways to keep busy during the day. No one was ever idle when I'd appear silently from below. Whether reading or studying or playing games or scraping carrots or doing sums, our friends' minds were occupied all day. During the day, everyone sat wearing only socks, no shoes, to avoid making noise.

When I arrived, they all showed me their friendliest and most agreeable side. Even though they were living on top of one another, my friends were always polite to me and to one another in my presence. Right away, teamwork had developed between them, and any task was quickly done. All their different personalities were learning to blend, to form a kind of balance.

Margot and Peter were quite withdrawn, always part of the background. Mrs. van Daan was temperamental, flirty, chatty. Mrs. Frank, kind and orderly, very quiet but aware of everything that went on around her. Mr. van Daan was the joke-teller, something of a pessimist, always smoking, and somewhat restless. Mr. Frank was the calm one, the children's teacher, the most logical, the one who balanced everyone out. He was the leader, the one in charge. When a decision had to be made, all eyes turned to Mr. Frank.

THE SUMMER wore on, August came, and Mrs. Samson still had no "address." Through loudspeakers we heard Hitler's voice shrieking out at us about total victory being in sight. Regardless of how much we hated it, we could not argue. Yes, Hitler was holding Europe in his fist and squeezing. All would be lost if Hitler achieved victory before the Americans and British could ready themselves for a landing across the Channel. When thoughts like this, like pinpricks of anxiety, would pierce my mind, I'd banish them as quickly as I could. With such thoughts I would not have the strength to go on.

We could hardly believe that the *razias* could get any worse, but in August, they did. Jews sought anything that might buy a little more time, might offer some sort of exemption from deportation. Perhaps a position with the Jewish Council, the local group of Jewish leaders which acted as liaison between Jews and Nazis; a job in the diamond industry or a scrap-metal business; or a special shop which existed solely to cater to the needs of Jews—a Jewish bakery or grocery. Jews were no longer allowed to buy in regular shops, or were permitted to do so only during special hours.

Jews would try to delay deportation by using false statements claiming that they were physically disabled or that they had been diagnosed to have some mental deficiency. Anxiety and uncertainty mounted daily among the ordinary Jewish population. More and more Jews were being deported. Escape from a *razia* was becoming more difficult. When the target area of a *razia* leaked out and spread like wildfire, people would find a way to avoid being in their homes. Then, the next day, after the roundup had ended, people would go out to search for their families and friends to see who was still free.

Often husbands and wives were separated by a *razia*. One was dragged off, the other one left because he or she happened to be elsewhere. When a Jewish home was empty of human beings, after a week or so a moving company named Puls, which had the contract to collect Jewish possessions, would send a van around and quickly remove everything until the place was totally bare. Then, often within a matter of days, Dutch Nazis, the NSBers given high priority for new apartments, would move into the empty home.

August 6, 1942, became known as Black Thursday. A *razia* lasted throughout the day and into the night. We heard that Jews were picked up in the streets and dragged away. They were taken at gunpoint from their houses, ordered to lock their doors and surrender their keys and walk away from all they had. They were beaten. It was whispered that many Jewish suicides resulted from this *razia*. At night, when I came home from work, I'd hear stories with details about these *razias* from my friends and neighbors.

Recently, Elli had asked Mr. Kraler if her father, who was out of work and trying to support six children, could come to work with us at the Prinsengracht. We needed another helper in the workplace.

Kraler talked it over with Frank, who must have given the okay. Mr. Frank was still the official person when it came to making decisions. So Elli's father, Hans Vossen, came to work with us. His boss was Mr. Kraler, and his job was to mix different combinations of spices and grind them in the spice mills. Then he packed and shipped them.

Mr. Vossen was a thin man, almost as tall as Henk, about forty-five or fifty years old. One day, soon after he had started working with us, I came to work and found that Mr. Frank had had him taken into the secret of the hiding plan. To improve its security, Mr. Kraler asked Mr. Vossen to hinge a bookcase to the wall in front of the door to the hiding place. This bookcase, in which we kept empty account books in black-and-white bindings, concealed the door completely. One never would have known there was a door there at all. On the wall above it hung a map of the Grand Duchy of Luxenbourg that had been pasted up years before.

Mr. Vossen had placed a hook on the back of the bookcase, which could be fastened by our friends. When opened by them, it would permit the whole bookcase to swing out and away, so that one could enter the hiding place.

It was a wonderful idea. Elli told me later that it had been Mr. Frank's idea. Now suddenly, with so much frightfulness going on outside in the streets of Amsterdam, going into the hiding place was almost like entering the safety and sanctuary of a church. It was secure and our friends were safe.

Every time I pulled the bookcase aside, I had to set a smile on my face, and disguise the bitter feeling that burned in my heart. I would take a breath, pull the bookcase closed, and put on an air of calm and good cheer that it was otherwise impossible to feel anywhere in Amsterdam anymore. My friends upstairs were not to be upset, not to be privy to any of my anguish.

# CHAPTER NINE

JEWS WHO HAD so far avoided arrest were now afraid to go outdoors. Each day was filled with unbearable anxiety. Each sound heard was a possible arrival of the Green Police; each doorbell, tap on the door, footstep, squeak of a car, a *razia*. Many stayed in their homes and just sat. Waiting.

Mrs. Samson announced that she would be going into hiding, that she had found a "safe address." We were very glad. She wanted to tell us more, but we reminded her that the less we knew, the safer it would be for her, and for us as well. Henk made a request: "Could you wait a few days until Miep and I go on vacation? Wait until September; that way we can't know anything about your disappearance, and in case we're picked up and they beat us, we can say that we don't know where you went, that we were on vacation then."

Mrs. Samson said she would wait. We knew that this was a lot to ask of her, to wait even a few days, but we now had seven in hiding on the Prinsengracht to think about—that is, more than ourselves to consider. If something happened to us, it would create grave problems for them.

It was hard to know what was going on. In the official newspaper there was nothing but lies. The details of the war were grandiose. In August, the Germans claimed that they had captured the Russian oil fields at Mozdok, that they were announcing total victory. However, the BBC told us that yes, the Germans had captured the oil fields, but that they were of no value because the Russians had left them completely destroyed and useless.

Soon after, the Germans announced that the German Sixth Army had reached the Volga River, to the north of Stalingrad; that Stalingrad was within their grasp. Then Radio Orange reported the casualties the Germans had suffered and said that the Russians had sworn to fight to the last man, that the Russians were somehow hanging on.

The Germans described the Jewish deportations as "resettlement" and claimed that those taken were being treated decently, given proper food and shelter, that families were being kept together. But at the same time, the BBC claimed that Polish Jews in German prison camps were being gassed, that Dutch Jews were being used for slave labor, and that the Dutch Jews had been taken to camps very far from Holland, in Germany and Poland.

While we didn't know what was true, we did know that the Germans made those Dutch Jews taken for labor send postcards back to their families. The cards always said positive things about life in the camps: that the food was good, that there were showers, and so on. This was what the Nazi captors had ordered their prisoners to write.

Somehow, the Jews managed to transmit other information. For example, at the end of a card sent from one of the camps, a Dutchman would say, "Give my regards to Ellen de Groot." This was a common Dutch name and the Germans did not censor it. What the Germans didn't know was that in Dutch *ellende* meant "misery" and *groot* meant "terrible." So the message managed to tell of "terrible misery."

My head churned with the contradictory bits of information. I dreaded to think about the unpleasant rumors that were circulating, rumors of harsh treatment being doled out by the Germans to their helpless prisoners in these remote camps. For the sake of morale, I had taken to believing only the good news. I passed along all the good news to the hiding place and let the bad go in one ear and out the other. To go on, I had to believe totally that this war would come to a good end for us.

Because times were not normal, Henk and I couldn't take much of a vacation. We desperately needed a holiday, and managed to go for ten days to a little town outside Amsterdam. There, in the country, we walked and rested, but I couldn't keep my mind from wandering back to our friends in hiding.

When we returned to Hunzestraat, Mrs. Samson had gone without leaving a trace.

THE FRANK FAMILY and the Van Daan family managed to keep healthy throughout the summer. This was of the utmost importance, as the worst fear of all of us was that someone would get sick and we could not go to a doctor. This anxiety wore on all of us, especially Mrs. Frank. She was particularly careful always for the health of the children, always watching what they ate and wore, whether they were cold, whether there were any signs of illness.

Mr. van Daan's butcher friend was not the only merchant to help us provide the essential staples for our friends. Mr. Koophuis had a friend who owned a chain of bakeries in Amsterdam. When our friends went into hiding, Koophuis made an agreement with his friend to deliver a quantity of bread to the office two or three times a week. We paid for as much bread as we had coupons for. The extra bread would be paid for in cash after the war. As about the same number of people worked at the Prinsengracht as were in hiding upstairs, there was no cause for suspicion.

I had started to go to the same vegetable man in his little shop on the Leliegracht. The man had a kind way about him. I would buy whatever I could, depending on what he had that day. After several weeks, the man noticed that I always bought large amounts of vegetables. Without words passing between us, he began to put vegetables aside for me. When I came, he would bring them to me from another part of his shop.

I would put the food into my bag, take it quickly back to the office on the Prinsengracht, and put it between my desk and the window so that it could not be seen by anybody who did not belong to our group of insiders.

Later on in the day when it was safe, I'd take the groceries upstairs. Except for the heavy potatoes. These were brought by the kind greengrocer during lunchtime. I was always waiting for him in the kitchen, so that everything would work smoothly while no one else was about. He'd put the heavy load into a small closet I had shown him, and during the night Peter would go down and get the potatoes and bring them up. No words were ever exchanged about this between the greengrocer and me. Nothing needed to be said.

I was shopping for seven people in hiding as well as for Henk and myself. Often I had to go to several shops to get the quantities I needed, but I wasn't particularly conspicuous. These were not normal times. People were all trying to get as much as they could. There was nothing unusual about buying in bulk. Many shopkeepers were not so strict about coupons, either. Often if I had a coupon for, say, two pounds of potatoes and I wanted three pounds, I'd give the coupons and a little bit of money and they'd gladly give me the extra pound.

Milk was Elli's responsibility. It was usual in Holland for milk to be delivered to offices and homes. The milk was delivered daily. It was clear that the persons who worked in the office needed quite a lot of milk, so we were not afraid that the milkman might become suspicious. Every day, rain or shine, the milk arrived. Elli would take the bottles upstairs when she went up for lunch.

Mr. Frank told me Mr. Koophuis had originated the hiding plan, that it was Koophuis and Frank who had first thought it through. They had then taken in Mr. van Daan, inviting him and his family to join in hiding with them. Along with furnishings, much dry and canned food had somehow been secreted up into the hiding place. Sack after sack of dried beans, preserves, soap, linens, and cooking utensils had been brought at strange times in the evening. I don't know exactly how everything happened, but I believe that Mr. Koophuis had given instructions to his brother, who had a small cleaning business with a car, to bring large items. Mr. Kraler would have been aware of these deliveries.

Mr. Frank was the supervisor of the children's studies up in the hiding place. Rigorous studying was expected; assignments were corrected by Mr. Frank. Because Peter van Daan was not much of a student, Mr. Frank made a point of taking extra time and care with him. Otto Frank would have made a wonderful teacher. He was kind and firm, and always included a little bit of humor with his lessons.

The children's studies took great chunks of time each day. For Margot, it was easy. For Anne, although she didn't concentrate as hard as Margot, it was easy too. Anne was often writing in a little red-orange checkered cloth-bound diary that her father had given her for her thirteenth birthday on June 12, several weeks before the Franks had come into hiding. She wrote in her diary in two places, her own room or her parents' room. Although everyone knew that she was writing, she never wrote when other people were present. Obviously, Mr. Frank had spoken about this matter and given instructions for no one to disturb her.

As I heard from Mr. Frank, the diary was a constant companion for Anne, and also a source of teasing by the others. How was she finding so much to write about? Anne's cheeks went pink when she was teased. She would tease right back, always quick with a reply, but to be safe, she kept her diary in her father's old leather briefcase.

Anne thought her best feature was her thick, shining dark brown hair. She liked to comb it several times a day to keep it healthy and to bring out its sheen. When she combed her hair, she always covered her shoulders with a triangular shawl of fine cotton, beige with pink, light green, and blue roses and other small figures on it. This combing shawl, tied under her chin, caught the hair that broke off from her vigorous combing and brushing. She set her hair nightly in pin curls to turn up the ends. Margot curled her hair as well.

Both girls helped with the cooking and pot-scrubbing and potato-peeling and tidying-up. Both girls were learning or reading always. Sometimes Anne would spread out her movie-star photo collection to look at and admire the glamorous faces. She'd talk about movies and movie stars with anyone who would listen.

Each time I silently walked into the hiding place, I'd see each person engaged in activity. They looked like living cameos: a head lowered intently over a book; hands poised over a pile of potato peelings; a dreamy look on a face whose hands were mindlessly knitting; a tender hand poised over Mouschi's silky back, stroking and touching; a pen scratching across blank paper, pausing as its owner chewed over a thought, then scratching again. All of them silent.

And when my face appeared above the landing, all eyes would light on me. A flash of enthusiasm would widen all eyes. I would be sponged up by all the eyes with a voracious thirst. Then Anne, always Anne, would be upon me with a rapid-fire barrage of questions. "What's going on?" "What's in the bag?" "Have you heard the latest?"

As SOON AS Mrs. Samson had gone into hiding, Henk quickly put the apartment in our Christian name. We were afraid that leaving the apartment in Mrs. Samson's name, a Jewish name, meant that eventually a Puls van would come and take Mrs. Samson's furnishings away. Naturally we would return everything to Mrs. Samson and her husband when they returned.

Mrs. Samson had gone into hiding in September. Not long afterward, perhaps a month or six weeks, we received a letter postmarked in Hilversum, a town outside Amsterdam. Inside was a letter from a Mrs. van der Hart—a name that meant nothing to us. As soon as we read the letter, we understood. It seemed that Mrs. Samson was in hiding in a room of Mrs. van der Hart's house in Hilversum. Mrs. Samson was lonesome, and she had requested that Mrs. van der Hart write to us and invite us to visit.

We couldn't refuse. We made the short journey from Amsterdam to Hilversum by train. It took about forty-five minutes, including a fifteen-minute walk. We found the Hilversum address from the letter. There stood a big villa, the kind that only very affluent people owned.

We rang the bell and identified ourselves to the woman who answered the door. She was Mrs. van der Hart. She led us inside. Quickly she explained that at that time she lived in this house with her only son, a university student, twenty-one years old, named Karel. Her husband had gotten trapped in America when the war broke out in Holland. He couldn't get back, and she hadn't heard anything from him in two years. Mrs. van der Hart apologized for the state of the house. She explained that she'd always had servants before the war, but now she had to do everything herself.

She led us upstairs to a beautiful room, where we found Mrs. Samson living. Although she was lonely and frightened and restless from staying inside, she was being well fed and treated with kindness. We learned that this was to have been the hiding place for the family Coenen, Mrs. Samson's daughter's family—who, if they had not panicked and gone to the Centraal Station, might have been in that very room safely. Unfortunately, Mrs. Samson's daughter and son-in-law had disappeared into the hands of the Germans; their children were now in hiding.

We made our visit, told Mrs. Samson all the news about Amsterdam, and promised that we would come again. We made the early-evening train back to Amsterdam.

Around this time, an older Jewish man, a friend of Mr. Frank's whom we had met at one of the Franks' Saturday gatherings, wrote to us asking us to please come to see him at his home. He said it was very urgent.

Henk went alone to see this man. He returned home looking pale and drained. He was carrying two enormous gold-leafed volumes, a fine, beautifully printed edition of the complete works of William Shakespeare in English. Henk told me that the man, who was about sixty or older, was living in an apartment with his sister, a spinster older than himself, and his very old mother. Henk said that the man had immediately asked if Henk knew of a "safe address" for his mother, his sister, and himself. Henk shook his head sadly. "When he asked, I immediately thought, It's not possible for people this old to find hiding places; but I didn't have the heart to say that and instead said, 'I will look.' "

Then the man took the volumes of Shakespeare down from his shelves. The shelf was filled with beautiful leather-bound books. He then asked, "Mr. Gies, would you do me the honor to take something of mine into your home and keep it for me until after the war?"

Henk told him, "Yes, of course I will."

And so here was the beautifully bound Shakespeare. Henk and I were silent. What more could we say? We both knew it was next to impossible to find a "safe address" for people so old. Henk had promised he would try, and he did, but without any luck.

I knew how terrible Henk felt because of this old man. I had experienced a similar unhappiness about the same time when I'd passed a poor old Jewish lady sitting on a stone stoop right outside our apartment. The Green Police were coming to arrest her. Her eyes implored each passerby to help her. She was one of many Jews who seemed to be roaming the streets and sitting helplessly on stoops, since they were not permitted the use of park benches or public cafés.

Recently, the Green Police and SS had been making surprise *razias* during the day. This was the best time to catch the most defenseless Jews at home: the old, the sick, small children. Many had taken to the streets so as not to be in their homes if the Germans came for them. They often asked passersby if they'd seen any sign of a roundup or soldiers, and if so, where.

As much as I wanted to help this old woman and other people like her, I knew I had to be prudent. I had more than just myself to think about. So like so many others, I looked away. I went in and shut my door. My heart had torn.

ANNE AND the others had been after us to come and sleep upstairs in the hiding place. There was something always imploring about the way they asked, so one day I took some things from home with me to work, some nightclothes for Henk and myself.

When I announced to Anne and Mrs. Frank that we would finally come to spend the night, the enthusiasm was extraordinary. You'd have thought that Queen Wilhelmina herself was about to make a visit. Rubbing her hands together, Anne was filled with excitement. "Miep and Henk will be sleeping over tonight," she ran to tell the others upstairs.

Hoping to moderate her mood, I told Mrs. Frank, "We don't want any fuss."

Mrs. Frank smiled, put her hand on my shoulder, and squeezed. On my way out, I repeated my request to Mr. Frank, who was climbing downstairs: "Now, no fuss, please."

This is me (right) at age 12, 1921.

Me in 1933.

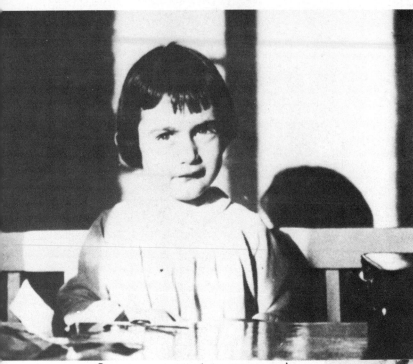

Anne Frank in 1933, at about the time the Frank family emigrated from Germany to the Netherlands.

Anne Frank and her classmates in 1935, shortly after I first met her. Anne is at center, circled.

Otto Frank at about the time I began working for him.

Anne around 1936;
and around 1937 in front of
the office at Singel 400.

Otto Frank and me in the office at Singel 400, 1937.

Jo Koophuis.

After the move to Prinsengracht 263. Seated in the foreground from left to right are Victor Kraler, Elli Vossen and me. Two other office workers are behind us.

An aerial view of the Prinsengracht as it looks today, with the Westerkerk at right.

Anne Frank, 1940.

My passport with the swastika stamp.

PERSONENBESCHREIBUNG

Beruf *Kontoristin*

Geburtsort *Wien*

Geburtstag *15. 2. 1909*

Wohnort *Amsterdam*

Gestalt *mittel*

Gesicht *oval*

Farbe der Augen *blau*

Farbe des Haares *blond*

Besond. Kennzeichen *keine*

Ehefrau

KINDER

| Name | Alter | Geschlecht |
| --- | --- | --- |
| | | |

Unterschrift des Paßinhabers

und seiner Ehefrau

Es wird hiermit bescheinigt, daß der Inhaber die durch das obenstehende Lichtbild dargestellte Person ist und die darunter befindliche Unterschrift eigenhändig vollzogen hat.

Amsterdam, den **13. Dez. 1938**

Der Deutsche Generalkonsul

I. A.

2

3

Margot Frank
and Anne Frank
in 1941.

OPPOSITE:
Top, Henk and me on our wedding day, July 16, 1941.
Bottom, Mr. and Mrs. Van Daan, and Victor Kraler.

THIS PAGE:
Right, Mrs. Samson (dark hat and coat).
Below, the wedding party.

THIS PAGE:
Left, the yellow star that Dutch Jews were ordered to wear.
Below, the order liquidating Pectacon as a Jewish business.

OPPOSITE:
Top, front view of Prinsengracht 263.
Bottom, rear view, showing the Annex, or hiding place, and the chestnut tree that shaded the building.

DER REICHSKOMMISSAR
FÜR DIE BESETZTEN NIEDERLÄNDISCHEN GEBIETE
DER GENERALKOMMISSAR
FÜR FINANZ UND WIRTSCHAFT
WIRTSCHAFTSPRÜFSTELLE

AMSTELSTRAAT 14
AMSTERDAM

den 12. September 1941.
Korte Vijverberg 5
B./N./HG 1o1

B v d. I. E.
29 NOV. 1941
MIDDERNACHT

 A b s c h r i f t.

Auf Grund des § 7 der Verordnung des Reichskommissars
für die besetzten niederländischen Gebiete vom
12. März 1941 (VO. 48/1941) über die Behandlung an-
meldepflichtiger Unternehmen bestelle ich Sie zum
Treuhänder der Firma

N.V. Handelsmaatschappij Pectacon,
Amsterdam-C, Singel 400,

mit der Aufgabe, die Liquidation des Unternehmens nach
meiner Weisung durchzuführen.

 gez. Bauer

Herrn
Mr. Karl W o l t e r s
A m s t e r d a m -N
Jan van Eijkstr. 31

Left, Edith Frank.
Below left, Peter Van Daan.
Below, Dr. Albert Dussel.

Anne in 1942.

The entrance to the hiding place. The bookcase in front of the doorway (right), and the bookcase moved aside to show the doorway and stairs.

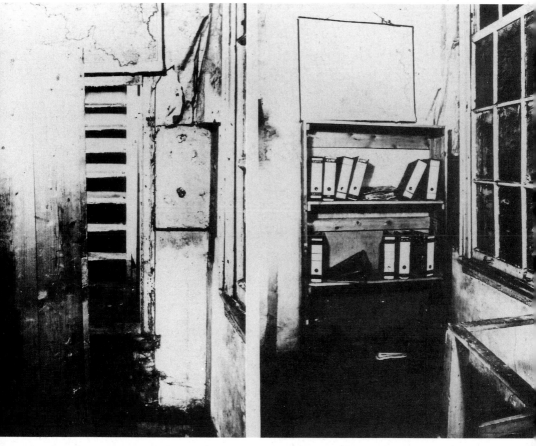

The Westerkerk tower seen from the window of the attic in the hiding place.
Anne's bedroom wall in the hiding place, with all her pictures still attached.

Above left, Anne's typewritten menu for our first-anniversary dinner in the hiding place. Above right, Herman Van Daan's shopping list while in hiding. This is typical of the lists that I took to the butcher to whom Mr. Van Daan had introduced me.
The map on the wall in the hiding place, showing the progress of Allied troops following the Normandy invasion.

Henk's and my identity cards.
Ration coupons and list from newspaper of what could be bought in 1944.

Above, Otto Frank's transit and repatriation papers, and below, his Displaced Person's card.

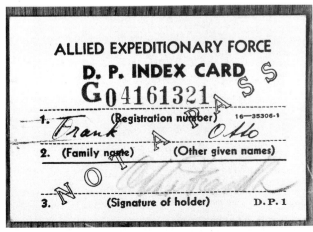

Prinsengracht 263 in October 1945. Standing, left to right, Koophuis, Kraler. Seated, me, Otto Frank, Elli.
The awful letter which told us that Margot and Anne were not coming back. The actual wording is: "With this I declare that Margot and Anne Frank, in the Schonungsblock no. 19 in Bergen-Belsen prison camp, died about end February, beginning of March (1945). I myself was a prisoner in the same camp in Block no. 1 and on friendly terms with above-mentioned girls."

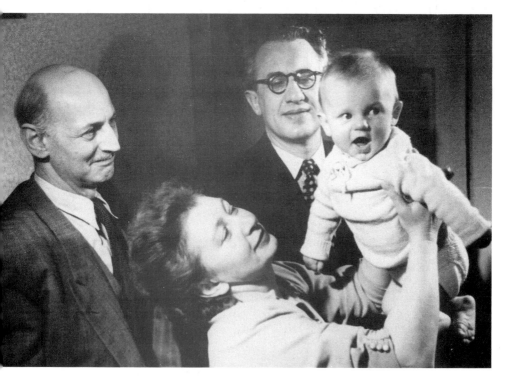

In 1951, with my son, Paul: Otto Frank, Henk and me.
Anne's combing shawl and a photo of Otto Frank on a desk that had belonged
to the Franks and which Mr. Frank gave to me before he died.

Reading Anne's book.

ANNE-MARIE O'HEALY

Henk and me
in Amsterdam,
1986.

JACOB DE VRIES

Miep Gies (right) and
Alison Leslie Gold,
2002.

A. GREENWALD

With a smile on his face, he shook his head. "No, no, of course not."

During the day I told Jo Koophuis of our plan. After work Henk came, and when the last worker had gone home at five-thirty, the end of the workday, Mr. Koophuis bade us good night. He locked the door of the building behind him. The office was quite silent with everyone gone. We made sure that the lights had been turned off; then we went up the stairway, pulled open the book-case, and went in. I closed it behind us.

Each of our friends greeted us happily as we made our way upstairs. "The last worker has gone," I informed them. Right away, there were voices, footsteps, the toilet flushing, a cabinet shutting. Already, it was noisy upstairs; the place had come alive.

Anne directed us toward the bedroom she shared with Margot. At Anne's insistence, Henk and I had been allotted their room. Anne and Margot were going into the room with their parents for the night. Anne pulled me to her bed, neatly made up, and told me she wanted me to put my things there. Amused, I told her that I'd be honored, and put my night things on her bed, and Henk's on Margot's bed.

Shortly, it was time for the radio broadcasts, and the entire group trooped down to Mr. Frank's office below to pull up chairs and gather around the Phillips radio on the table. The whole room bristled with excitement when the near-and-yet-so-far voice of Radio Orange came through the radio. "Here is Radio Orange. All things went well today. The English . . ." and on it went, filling us with hope and with information, our only real connection to the still-free outside world.

When it was time to sit down to eat, Henk and I were given seats of honor, as we had been at our anniversary dinner. All nine of us squeezed in around the table.

This time, Mrs. Frank and Margot had supervised the cooking. The food was tasty and filling.

With the blackout frames up and the electric light on, along with the heat from the cooking, the room became toasty-warm, cozy. We sat long over coffee and dessert, talking, our friends devouring the novelty of our presence. They seemed to be insatiable for our company.

As I sat, I became aware of what it meant to be imprisoned in these small rooms. As this feeling registered, I felt a taste of the helpless fear that these people were filled with, day and night. Yes, for all of us it was wartime, but Henk and I had the freedom to come and go as we pleased, to stay in or go out. These people were in a prison, a prison with locks inside the doors.

Reluctantly, we said good-nights, remembering that Mr. and Mrs. van Daan could not go to bed until we'd gone. Henk and I and the Frank family trooped down the stairway to the floor below. Here we said a second round of good-nights, and Henk and I got ready for bed in our little room, surrounded by Anne's movie-star faces on the wall.

I climbed into Anne's hard little bed, which was very toasty with blanket upon blanket, so many blankets that I couldn't imagine how Anne could ever be taken with a chill. The room was cool otherwise, and as I settled in as cozily as I could, I could hear every sound being made in the other rooms: Mr. van Daan coughing, the squeak of springs, the sound of a slipper dropping beside a bed, the toilet flushing, Mouschi landing on his padded feet somewhere above me.

The Westertoren clock struck at fifteen-minute intervals. I'd never heard it so loud; it echoed and reverberated through the rooms. The church was right across the back gardens from the Annex. In the office, the building blocked the sound. During the day, by the time I heard the ringing in my front office, the sound had been muted and cushioned by the entire building. It was soothing and distant.

All through the night I heard each ringing of the Westertoren clock. I never slept; I couldn't close my eyes. I heard the sound of a rainstorm begin, the wind come up. The quietness of the place was overwhelming. The fright of these people who were locked up here was so thick I could feel it pressing down on me. It was like a thread of terror pulled taut. It was so terrible it never let me close my eyes.

For the first time I knew what it was like to be a Jew in hiding.

# CHAPTER TEN

AT FIRST LIGHT I was still awake. Quite early I heard our hosts begin to stir, and each in turn made his way to the bathroom, which had to be used before the employees began to arrive down below in the workplace. The rain was pouring down outside.

Henk and I dressed quickly. We went upstairs together for breakfast, again around the table. Henk was the first to leave, as he needed to get out of the building and away before the workers began to arrive. I could see the looks of our friends, reluctant to let him leave them.

I sat as long as I could, being served more coffee, treated like the Queen once again. Anne grilled me about my impressions of the hiding life at night. "How did you sleep? Did the ringing of the Westertoren clock keep you awake? Could you hear the noise of planes on their way to bomb Germany? Could you sleep through all that?"

It was not easy to sidestep Anne's questions, but I did my best, not wanting to betray the experience I had undergone throughout the long fright-filled night.

Anne had a look of satisfaction on her face. She stared hard at me. It was not spoken, but we both knew that I had briefly crossed over from outsider to insider, that I too now knew what the long night was like in the hiding place.

"Will you come and sleep over again?" she asked.

The others also implored: "Yes, yes, spend the night with us soon again."

I replied, "Yes, we'll come and stay again."

Anne volunteered, "You can have my bed again. It feels safe to have our protectors so close."

I assured her that we were always close. "If not nearby in body, then close in spirit."

"At night too?" Anne asked.

"At night too," I replied.

She stared hard at me for a minute; then her face changed. "And you won't even have to get wet in this downpour in order to get to work."

HUGE *razias* took place in early October, 1942. October 2 was called "Black Friday." On that day word spread like wildfire through the Jewish Quarter that an enormous *razia* was coming. That day people waited in dread for the sound of the boots on the stairway and the piercing ring of the doorbell. Rumors had grown so horrible that there had been near panic in the Jewish quarters throughout Amsterdam.

This rash of *razias* had been malicious and widespread. Then, suddenly, they ceased. Weeks and weeks went by. New rumors spread that perhaps the deportation of the Jewish population was finished. Perhaps the camps were full, and the Germans had all the slave labor they needed.

It was a rainy and chilly autumn in Holland, and always gloomy. The BBC and Radio Orange told us of the rains in Russia that were slowing down the German Sixth Army. The English and Americans, led by General Eisenhower, had landed November 8 on the Moroccan and Algerian shores, and the great General Montgomery was pushing back General Rommel's divisions. Slowly, yes, but inch by inch. Naturally, the German-controlled newspapers shouted that the war was almost won. Soon, Germany would be ruling all of Europe, England, North Africa, Egypt, and on, and on.

Each time I went to shop I didn't know what I would find. Each time there seemed to be a little less in the shops and the queues were a little longer. The people were looking a little shabbier, too. But still, with just a little extra time and some searching, it was not difficult to purchase all that was necessary to feed our seven friends, and Henk and me as well.

Each time I entered the hiding place, every detail of life on the other side of the bookcase was pulled from me by Anne, Mrs. Frank, and Mrs. van Daan. The men quizzed Henk in the same manner. Anne asked often whether their apartment on the Merwedeplein had been emptied by Puls. Several times I'd ridden by on my bicycle and looked, but I could see nothing, just the same curtains that had covered the windows when the Franks lived there. I told her that I didn't know.

By chance one day I'd seen the Van Daan house emptied. Mrs. van Daan hadn't taken the news well; she had become distraught. I promised myself to guard against bringing news that would cause any upset. This wasn't easy to do. Anne would have made a great detective. She'd sense that something was being withheld and she'd pull and squeeze, probe and stare me down, until I'd hear myself revealing just what I had decided not to reveal.

The one most affected by bad news was Mrs. Frank. Slowly, as the winter approached, her attitude was becoming more and more dismal. All the rest of us were encouraged by the rumor that perhaps the *razias* were finished. We believed all the hopeful news told by the BBC and Radio Orange about the new Anglo-American offensives. But none of this seemed to hearten Mrs. Frank. No amount of encouraging news could penetrate her bleak outlook. As much as all of us argued against her view, she saw no light at the end of the tunnel.

DESPITE THE LULL in Jewish persecution, Jews felt no sense of safety. Although many were long gone, others still lived in dread, usually with no source of livelihood unless they worked in one of the ever-decreasing protected trades. It had been illegal for quite some time for a Christian to utilize the services of a Jew in the medical and dental professions, but I refused to discontinue being treated by Albert Dussel. He was an excellent dentist—in fact, a dental surgeon; and he was a man I liked.

During a visit to his office that autumn he asked me in a quiet, guarded voice, "Miep, perhaps you know of a hiding place for me?"

Shaking my head, I told him, "I don't." I promised that if I heard of any place, I would let him know.

The next day, when giving my news in the hiding place, I told Mr. Frank about my visit to Dr. Dussel, and that Dussel was searching for a hiding place. Mr. Frank listened to my news with interest; Dussel and his wife had been among the refugees from Germany who used to come to the Franks' Saturday-afternoon gatherings. I knew Mr. Frank was as fond of him as I was.

I thought nothing else about this exchange of information until several days later, when during my afternoon visit to the hiding place, Mr. Frank said he had something to discuss with me. I sat down and Mr. Frank said, "Miep, where seven can eat, eight people can eat as well. All of us have talked this over and we've decided that Dussel can come and join us here in our hiding place. But he must come first thing tomorrow morning."

Mr. Frank proceeded to explain why Dussel must come the

next morning. Mr. Frank didn't want Dr. Dussel to have time to tell anybody. Nor did he want him to have time to make elaborate preparations, which might arouse suspicion and cause danger to those already in hiding. I understood completely and told Mr. Frank I would pass his invitation along right away.

After work I went straight to Albert Dussel's apartment and told him that I had a hiding place for him. I gave him no details, just that I had a "safe" place for him to go into hiding. "But you must go tomorrow morning. This is the condition of this situation."

Dussel's face fell, and he shook his head sadly. "It's impossible," he said. "I have a lady I've been treating for a serious problem with the bone. Tomorrow is the final treatment. I can't let her down. I can't leave her suffering." He heaved a great sigh. "It's impossible, impossible. The following day, yes, but tomorrow . . . impossible."

I said no more and left.

The next morning, with a heavy heart, I went up to the hiding place to tell of my visit with Albert Dussel. Mr. Frank listened to what had transpired. I could tell that the subject was causing additional, unnecessary anxiety to all of them, to consider taking the chance of bringing in someone from outside. Mr. Frank said he'd discuss it with everyone and tell them the situation with Dussel.

Before leaving the office that afternoon I stopped upstairs in the hiding place, asking, "Well, have you reached a decision about Dr. Dussel?"

Mr. Frank announced gravely, "We have discussed it, and we have decided that a responsible doctor cannot leave a patient in the middle of a treatment. We respect him for it. Tell Dussel that if he is willing to come Monday morning, then there is a place for him." Mr. Frank continued, "We've come up with a plan. Miep, are you willing to help, despite the danger involved?"

I said I was.

Carefully, he told me the plan.

After work, I went back to Dr. Dussel and told him that I had a place for him and that Monday morning would be fine. I could see new hope in his eyes. "Monday morning is excellent. My patient is treated. I'm ready."

"Good; then here is the plan. Monday morning at eleven o'clock, you must be at the Main Post Office on the N.Z. Voorburgwal. Stay in the front and walk up and down as though you were pacing. Once you've established yourself to the contact, a man, he'll approach you and will say, 'Please follow me.' Then you will say nothing and follow this man wherever he goes. And," I reminded him, "carry as little as possible—nothing that would make you conspicuous. There may be a way for you to get things later, once you are safely in hiding. We will see."

Dr. Dussel thanked me profusely. I could tell that he was certain that my part in this was simply that of message-giver. He bade me goodbye "until after the war." He saluted me, and I wished him a safe journey. We could say no more. We both knew that danger lurked everywhere for a Jew on his way into hiding, especially during those last hours on the way to safety.

I could tell also that Dussel imagined that the hiding place was out in the country, as so many hiding places were.

Dussel's contact was Jo Koophuis. Dussel had never met Koophuis, so there was no possibility for Dussel to connect Koophuis with Frank. Nor had Dussel ever been to the Prinsengracht office. As most desperate Jews were willing to do, Albert Dussel was putting himself, his safety, perhaps his life into the hands of a stranger.

On Monday morning I sat working at my desk. At about eleven-thirty Mr. Koophuis came to me and said, "All is well. I've taken him through the hallway into Frank's private office. He's waiting there—he's amazed that he's been brought right into the center of Amsterdam rather than out of town. Miep, now it's your job."

I hurried into Mr. Frank's private office.

"Miep!" Dussel exclaimed, a look of shock on his face.

It was all I could do not to burst out laughing at the thought of the surprise to come. I said, "Give me your coat."

He took off his coat, now looking bewildered.

I put it over my arm. "Now come on," I said. "We go up-stairs"—and I pushed Dr. Dussel up the old steps leading to the landing where the bookcase stood in front of the hiding place. I opened the door behind the bookcase, went directly upstairs to the Van Daans' room, and walked inside, where all the people stood around the table smiling and waiting for him. Coffee was ready. A bottle of cognac. Dussel looked as if he were going to keel over. Seeing Mr. Frank was like seeing a ghost, because he thought that the Franks had escaped to Switzerland. Who could have imagined that they were right in the center of Amsterdam?

My heart was full, almost bursting. "Ladies and gentlemen," I said, "it's done." And I turned and left them all together.

BEGINNING RIGHT AWAY, I met once a week with Dr. Dussel's wife, a charming blond woman one year older than I, and delivered his thick letters to her. She would give me letters, books, parcels, and bits of dental equipment that he had requested. She was a Christian, and because she no longer had a Jew with her, she was in no danger.

I told Mrs. Dussel that I had to turn over the things she gave me to someone else, who was the one who delivered them to her husband. I pretended to know nothing about where Albert Dussel was hiding. However, Mrs. Dussel was a discreet and sensitive person; she knew better than to search out information. She never asked one question of me. We exchanged letters and parcels until the next week, when we would repeat the process.

Because Dr. Dussel had come into the hiding place, there was no place for Henk and me to come for another sleepover. So despite Anne's disappointment, her invitations had to cease. When Dussel came, Margot was moved into the room with Mr. and Mrs. Frank. Anne stayed where she was, now sharing her narrow room with Dr. Dussel. Everyone seemed very good-natured about the new arrangements, but the place had become rather cramped with eight instead of seven.

Quickly, though, it came to light that Albert Dussel had a fear of cats, so efforts were made to keep Mouschi separated from him. This wasn't always easy, because though Dussel was afraid of Mouschi, Mouschi understood nothing and made his usual effort to become friendly with this new member of his household.

Mouschi kept watch on everyone, including Dussel, from a toasty spot near the coal stove. The stove was usually flaming in the Van Daans' big room. Coal came up from the workplace below. There were drafty, damp areas throughout the hiding place, so often the occupants wore several layers of clothes, perhaps a shawl in addition. Despite the drafts and damp, it was cozy with the help of cooking heat and the coal fire. Unless the electricity ration was short, the lights brought cheer into the rooms.

As 1942 DREW toward its end, Henk and I made special efforts to stay dry and warm, as we realized that we could not get sick either. Fortunately, our health held up, as did the health of our friends in the hiding place. With the coming of winter, I became aware of a kind of flagging of energy up in the Annex. It wasn't easy to put one's finger on it, but it was as though some of the spirit had gone out of the people upstairs, and a kind of languor had taken over. I could see that Dussel's stuffy ways were getting on Anne's nerves, that Anne's capriciousness was irritating Dussel. The friendliness between Mrs. Frank and Mrs. van Daan had turned a bit starchy.

Peter was more than ever up in the attic, and Margot could sit in one place endlessly.

Little irritating accidents and sicknesses were occurring. Nothing dangerous: conjunctivitis for Dussel, a strained rib for Mrs. van Daan. Little aches and pains and complaints. It was to be expected. So many in those small rooms night and day; muscles not exercised enough, getting stiff; voices always muted; bladders unemptied for long periods of time; no outlet for Anne's abundant energy.

It seemed as though these little ills were a small price to pay for a safe oasis from the dismal life in German-occupied Amsterdam. We guessed that a large percentage of the Jewish population was no longer in Amsterdam, but had been deported to the east. Also, more and more Christian Dutchmen had to go to work in Germany to help in the production of German armaments.

EACH DAY that winter Henk and I would leave for work on our bicycles while it was still dark, as it didn't get light until nine in the morning. It then became dark again by four-thirty in the afternoon, so we rode home in the dark. Between work; the daily search, becoming longer each day, for the quantities of food I needed; visits to the hiding place; and keeping up a courageous front for our friends, I would return home quite wrung out at the end of the day.

Henk and I had become friendly with a young Dutch couple who lived across the street from us. The wife was pregnant at this time and due to deliver quite soon. Sometimes, despite the curfew, we'd visit together at night and listen illegally to the BBC at their house. We'd drink some coffee substitute and let the news on the radio pump some hope into us, replenish our emptiness.

One night both Henk and I felt particularly dragged-out. It had been a tiring, difficult day for us both. I had hidden away the last of some real coffee for a special occasion, and that night I impulsively took it out and told Henk, "Come."

With the coffee in one hand and Henk's big hand holding my other one, I dashed with him across the street after the curfew to see our friends. Their faces brightened at the sight of real coffee. We made ourselves as cozy as possible and gathered around their radio. Making each drop of rich coffee last as long as possible, we savored, in every way, the smell, taste, effect.

It worked like magic. Soon, we were animated and again full of spit and vinegar against the German oppressor. Once again we were no longer beaten down, just biding our time until the Allies could get to us.

Revived yet sleepy, we finally said good night and went home. The next day the husband came to tell us that right after we'd left, his wife had gone into labor, had been taken to the hospital by taxi, and had quickly had their baby. "Yes, the baby is fine. My wife is fine. What a cup of coffee you make, Miep!" he laughingly added.

I laughed too. We had made good use of our last real coffee.

THE OCCUPATION had slowly whetted my appetite for retribution, so that news that Germans were freezing to death by the thousands in the blizzards of Russia, and dying as well by the hundreds in the hot and desolate deserts of North Africa, had the effect of speeding up my pulse, and filling me with a quickening feeling of emotion.

The Germans bragged that they were eighty miles from Stalingrad, then that they were thirty miles from Stalingrad. They promised that any day the great city of Stalingrad would fall and the great country of Russia would be within Hitler's grasp. The BBC and Radio Orange told us that the soldiers of the Red Army had sworn that they would fight to the last man. It was obvious that the Russian casualties had been enormous. So had the German casualties.

Henk had taken apart our radio and was carrying it bit by bit upstairs to the attic of the hiding place. This meant that we now had no radio at home and had to either visit our friends in the neighborhood to listen to the news at night or hear it later second hand.

Elli and I began to plan to make a festive St. Nicholas Day for the hiding place. Although the Franks were Jewish, we knew that they were liberal about religious practice. All over the Netherlands, St. Nicholas Day, December 5, is more a day for children than a day of religious observance. We had in mind a day of festivity for Margot, Anne, and Peter.

Elli and I worked arduously over the rhyming, somewhat teasing little poems that are the tradition of St. Nicholas Day. Together, we racked our imaginations for little gifts that suited each member of the group in hiding. Since it was impossible to buy things in the shops, we were forced to use lots of ingenuity and do-it-yourself homemade ideas. In secret, we sewed, hammered, glued. Then we gathered all the little tokens and the poems and hid them in a big basket which we first covered in decorations that Elli had brought from home, leftovers from St. Nicholas celebrations in years past.

We hid the colorful basket until the appointed hour, when Mr. Frank could lead the entire group down the stairway for the surprise.

Elli left to go home, as did I. I thought about what to prepare for Henk's dinner, and I mused over how happy our friends in hiding would be while opening the big, festive basket of gay presents and funny rhyming poems. What a party they'd have!—particularly the children; especially Anne, thirteen-year-old sophisticated woman of the world until a party was announced, then ecstatic and excited like a joyous little girl of six.

Thinking about Anne, I recalled how I had recently noticed how pale and pasty her coloring had become. The others, too. Not a ray of sun or breath of fresh air had touched their skin in more than six months. I wondered how many times a Nazi had walked by Prinsengracht 263, never knowing, never suspecting. Then I banished those thoughts. Better to think good thoughts, how happy the children would be to come downstairs and find the basket of gifts and poems. Tomorrow Anne would recount to me every detail of the festivity. Together we could laugh and relive it.

# CHAPTER ELEVEN

WE WERE ALL SURE the war would be over in 1943. The weather was abysmal, dark, dank. People had been living under so much pressure that some had begun to crack.

Henk and I, all of us, followed the battle of Stalingrad. None of us had ever heard reports of such a bitter and bloody battle before. Inch by inch, the Germans were being beaten and left to freeze in the frozen snow. Good, I thought; let them all freeze, and Hitler as well.

The word "surrender" was being used for the first time over the BBC. The Germans were on the verge of surrender. We dared to hope, but no one could ever imagine the word "surrender" coming out of Hitler's mouth.

But surrender they did, on February 2. The following day, we gathered around the radios, tingling from head to toe with the news and squeezing each other's hands, when on the official German station the announcement of surrender was made, accompanied by the roll of tragic drums and the second movement of Beethoven's Fifth Symphony. What glee we felt! We hoped it was the beginning of the end.

But that good news was quickly followed by a disturbing surprise. Mr. Kraler solemnly told me that the man who had appeared
at the office, unannounced, one morning in February was the new
owner of Prinsengracht 263. Mr. Koophuis was showing him
around. The man with him was an architect who had been brought
along for advice.

Immediately, all my sense of safety disintegrated. This new
owner could do anything he wanted with the building. Naturally,
he would want to see all the rooms in his new acquisition. How
could this man not go up and look at what now belonged to him?

I braced myself for a terrible moment. My heart was leaping
out of my chest. If our friends were discovered now, what would
this man do? Was he *goed* or *slecht*—"good" or "bad"? I forced
myself to stay sitting at my desk and waited.

Finally, Koophuis, alone, a look of sickness upon his face,
came back into the room. I asked with my eyes. He shook his head.
"No, he didn't." He sank into his chair close by.

"I told him that I couldn't find the key when they asked about
the storage rooms in the back. I couldn't tell for sure, but he didn't
seem terribly concerned one way or another. He might come back
anytime and not be put off."

Our eyes asked the same impossible question. What to do
now? We were both racking our brains for any other place where
eight people could so comfortably hide, where two families plus one
more could remain together. We looked at each other with terrible
frustration. There was nothing to do now but tell Mr. Frank what
had happened. It was for Mr. Frank to decide; Mr. Frank was in
charge.

"How could the owner not tell us that the building had been
sold? How could he be so thoughtless?" Koophuis wondered aloud.
"Now a sword is hanging over all our heads."

•

MR. FRANK had no suggestions. Nothing could be done but wait to see what would happen, see if the new owner would return and if so, what he would want to see. This extra anxiety sat on all our chests. We waited, but the new owner did not return. We continued to wait through the winter.

Elli had signed up for a shorthand course by correspondence, but the actual student of shorthand was Margot Frank. Each time the lesson arrived, addressed to Elli Vossen, Elli would take it upstairs and Margot would get to work. Anne too was learning shorthand from these lessons. As both Margot and Anne had plenty of time to practice shorthand, they were becoming quite proficient. They were spending long afternoons, after the chores were finished, writing and rewriting the shorthand language. When the lesson was finished, Elli would mail it back, and then the next lesson would be sent. Elli was getting very high grades.

As this winter dragged on, none of us went very far from our coal fires. We all did our best to warm ourselves, to keep heat in. The small size of the rooms in the hiding place helped. Everything that could be burned was tossed into the little stove in the Van Daans' room. The Franks had another small, coal-burning stove in their room. All garbage and waste was burned after working hours at night. The ashes and other, nonburnable garbage were brought down by Peter and put into the garbage bin with the refuse from the workplace. There was so little garbage that it wasn't noticeable.

I'd begun putting aside blank accounting books for Anne, for lessons and for her own writing. Anne continued to be very secretive about her writing and always put her papers into her father's worn-out leather briefcase, which was kept in the privacy of his room. As the Franks believed in respecting the privacy of everyone, including children, and there was so little privacy in the hiding place in other ways, Anne's was always taken seriously and respected. No one would dare to touch her papers or to read her words without her permission.

ONE MORNING we arrived for work to find all our friends in a state. Noises had been heard the night before, and they suspected a robbery had occurred down in the warehouse. They were all at a terrible high pitch of anxiety. They were afraid that whoever had been breaking into the warehouse had been alerted by the sound of their footsteps.

There was particular concern that the radio in Mr. Frank's old office had been carelessly left dialed to the BBC station—a criminal offense. The chairs in the office were pulled up to the radio as well, creating a picture of a group that had been intently listening to the news. They were terrified that the thief would go and report the situation to the police, and the police would put two and two together and make a raid on the hiding place.

They'd gotten themselves up to such a pitch that even when the warehouse was explored, and no signs of a break-in or anything unusual could be found, they still were jittery and nervous about the radio, and everything else. I realized that our friends were having an infectious case of nerves.

Trying to calm them, we made light of the situation. Anything to let the air out of such bad nerves. We kidded and teased, and pretty soon they were kidding too, and laughing at their own supersensitivity to noise, making fun of their vivid imaginations.

IN MARCH the newest edict stated that for those Jews left, a new choice existed. The choice was between deportation and sterilization. Some chose sterilization and were promised safety as soon as they had been sterilized. They then received a red "J" in their identity card, rather than the ominous black "J." Those with red "J"'s were also freed from wearing the yellow star.

At this time, the Germans published an appeal to those in hiding, promising that anyone in hiding who gave himself up would be pardoned. Pardoned from what? we wondered. Naturally, none of us believed in this or any promise made by the German oppressor.

Our friends in hiding shook their heads at this information, more and more grateful as time passed for the luck they had in having such a safe hiding place. They could not imagine a better hiding place in all of Amsterdam.

In late March, there were again large *razias*. Now Jewish homes for the blind, the insane, the terminally ill were emptied out. I did my best to hide what I knew and saw from my friends in hiding. I never told of any horror I saw if it could be avoided. Even Anne's questions were not so probing. No one seemed to want to know any more than he or she already knew.

Then suddenly came a wonderful and dramatic event for the Jews left in Amsterdam. The official registration office which held all the papers saying who was a Jew and who was a half-Jew and who was a quarter-Jew and so on was set on fire. Rumor circulated that the fire was big, and the destruction great, but no one seemed to know just how big, nor how many registrations had been destroyed by this wonderful act of sabotage. If all the files were destroyed, then the Germans would have no way of knowing who was left to arrest. We waited to learn more. Unfortunately, it turned out that very few papers had been destroyed in the fire.

JUST WHEN the winter was approaching its end and April had finally arrived, illnesses struck us. Fortunately, they struck the helpers and not our friends in hiding. One day everyone was carrying on and the next, it seemed, no one was well. Both Elli and her father were struck down, and could not come to work for several weeks in a row. Elli had come down with a bad cold, and her father had gone into the hospital for tests.

Our dear Mr. Koophuis had never been really very healthy. He
was always dogged by a sensitive stomach, which had been getting
worse and worse. He'd begun to bleed internally, and his doctor
had sent him to bed, with the hope that good rest and less pressure
would be of benefit. Everyone in Amsterdam was living under pressure and anxiety with burning anger; little did the doctor realize
that Mr. Koophuis, concerned deeply for the safety of our friends
in hiding, had been carrying around an extra load of tension and
responsibility and pressure.

Henk, Mr. Kraler, and I made an extra effort to visit our
friends in the hiding place, because suddenly the visits of those in
ill health had ceased. To our friends, it was as though the sun had
gone behind a cloud, they so missed each and every visit. They
missed Elli's gossip and chatter and tales of the boyfriend she was
seeing. They particularly missed Jo Koophuis. He was the supplier
of jokes and affection and little gifts and goodies which improved
everybody's morale. Koophuis was the most uplifting to the spirits;
he'd leave his troubles behind him when he closed the swinging
bookcase. He brought with him only strength, encouragement, and
the ability to make all our friends feel so much better and brighter
than he'd found them. Now, though, his troubled stomach had
proved too much and he was forced into bed.

Henk and I did what we could to make up for the empty areas
of time left during the day. It was strange, but sometimes when I
felt I was at the end of my strength, I'd push myself just a little bit
harder, and tapping into a reserve of energy I didn't know I had,
I'd find that I could summon more strength and endurance as the
situation demanded.

Jo Koophuis came back to us more quickly than his doctor had
ordered, claiming to feel fine, though he looked thin and bloodless.
Mr. Vossen, however, was told that his stay in the hospital would
be longer. The prognosis was not good. So Mr. Kraler decided that

another man had to be hired for the warehouse. Mr. Frank agreed and told him to go ahead.

Kraler hired a man named Frits van Matto to work in the warehouse and take over Mr. Vossen's duties. As I was not involved in any way, I didn't pay much attention to this man. I first became aware of Van Matto when he began coming up to the office to take the orders from Elli. It was just a feeling, but there was something unsympathetic about this man; his presence left me with an un-pleasant feeling. Van Matto would make a special effort to get me into discussions with him. I stayed cool and aloof.

Van Matto tried even harder to be friendly when he realized I was on very good terms with Jo Koophuis, and that Mr. Koophuis seemed to like me a great deal. I could tell Van Matto thought that by buttering me up he could get on better terms with Koophuis. It didn't work. I couldn't help being cool to him. I couldn't say why, but something about him rubbed me the wrong way. It was just a feeling, but I trusted my feelings.

OCCASIONALLY, Henk and I would travel to Hilversum to visit Mrs. Samson in her hiding place. We would gather together a few little gifts—nothing fancy, as it was becoming more and more diffi-cult to get things. Mrs. Samson would practically devour us on these visits. She had never been a quiet person, and conversation would pour out of her in a torrent.

On one of these visits to Hilversum in the spring of 1943, the owner of the villa where Mrs. Samson was hiding, Mrs. van der Hart, told us that she would like to have a word with us. We went with her to her sitting room.

We noticed that she was rather distracted as she spoke, and upset. She asked us if we knew about the loyalty oath that Dutch university students had been ordered to sign by the Germans. The oath declared that the student would refrain from any act against the German Reich and the German Army.

We told her that we were aware of it and the fact that many students had refused to sign and that small student strikes were springing up around the various universities in Holland. The Germans had met this opposition in their usual way—arrests, imprisonments, and orders that any student resister must cease his studies immediately.

She got to the point of the discussion. "My son, Karel, has refused to sign the oath. He must go into hiding. He needs a place to—"

I cut her off. "No need to say more. Tell him to come to us immediately in Amsterdam. He can hide with us." Just as Mrs. van der Hart was hiding Mrs. Samson, we felt an obligation to reciprocate and hide her son.

Very soon afterward, in May, Karel came into hiding with us on Hunzestraat.

Karel van der Hart was a good-looking boy, thin, blond, medium height, pleasant. We gave him Mrs. Samson's old room. Right away, he was very happy with us. He very much liked my cooking, despite the limitations of rationing.

He confessed to us that his mother wasn't much of a cook. She'd had servants before the war, and since the war, with no servants, she had done her best, but the results were poor. Henk and I exchanged a look. Karel laughed. He knew what we were thinking: that when Henk and I were visiting Mrs. Samson, the food had tasted fine. "It's true," he explained. "For others, she cooks well, but when guests are gone, her cooking is . . . just not the same."

I made our rations stretch one more way. Henk and I looked at each other with amusement at the speed with which Karel could empty a plate of food. Naturally, we could not tell Mr. Frank and the others about Karel van der Hart's hiding in our home, because it put us in new danger. Anything that threatened us would have doubly upset them.

Right away, we established a routine with Karel. Henk and I

would go to work each morning. Karel would be alone in the house all day. This was a very lonely life for a young man, but what could we do? We didn't know what he did with his day besides read and play chess alone. We suspected that he went out sometimes for a stroll, but we didn't ask. Always, there was Karel's small chessboard lying open in the house, in the middle of a game that he was playing with himself. He could take all the time he wanted to think through a move. He had nothing but time.

IT WAS THE SEASON for spring cleaning, but even that was curtailed by the war. Soap was becoming more and more scarce. Thread and cloth were becoming more and more expensive. I had to think twice, three times before I patched the toe of Henk's socks. Could the piece of thread be used for something more necessary? Did our friends need it more than we did?

In everyone's life there was now a layer that was soiled, unfresh, frayed. A permanent look of shabbiness had taken over all of us who were moderately well off. A permanent look of dreadful poverty had come over those with even less than we had.

Sometimes, it took me twice as long to scavenge enough groceries for all of us. It was not unusual to wait in a long line at a shop, finally get to the counter, and find that there was almost nothing to buy: a few beans, some wilted lettuce, half-rotted potatoes—food that when I got it home was bad and made us sick. I had widened my circle and sometimes tried shops in neighborhoods that were out of the way, always hoping for a new source of food.

It had ceased to be interesting to eat. We were forced to make do with anything we had. This meant monotony and boredom and the same fare for days and days in a row. It also meant getting digestive problems, or being left half sick and still hungry after eating.

But never did I hear a complaint from the hiding place. Never a sign of boredom or disappointment as the food was unpacked and stored. Never was a comment made about how tired our friends were of eating kale, more than two weeks of kale, or some other food. Never did they complain to me about ever-decreasing rations of butter and fat.

Likewise, I never mentioned the pasty color my friends had taken on. The children's clothes were starting to fall apart, too; to fray, and simply wear out. In her own quiet way, Mr. Koophuis' wife had occasionally gotten hold of some secondhand clothes for the children, and had sent them to the hiding place with Mr. Koophuis.

Most in need, and most obvious, was little Anne, who was turning into not-so-little Anne before our very eyes. She was simply bursting out of her clothes, and her body was changing shape as well.

Her feet could no longer be squeezed into the shoes she had brought into the hiding place. It made me laugh when she tried, but inside I could have cried at the sight of those tender, growing feet that should have been running, dancing, and swimming.

This growth spurt was right on schedule; Anne would turn fourteen on June 12. Nature was moving her right along, despite the conditions forced upon her. We went all out to make her birthday as festive as we could—little sweets and goodies, books, blank paper, secondhand things.

Anne always showed the most joy and happiness when receiving or giving gifts and celebrating almost anything. This year, she was especially pleased with everything we had gathered for her. She made a great display of pleasure as she opened her gifts and read the birthday poems.

We were all making a special effort to be cheerful, and to fight any gloom. The extra effort was necessary because we had just received the news that Elli's father, Hans Vossen, had been diagnosed as having a fatal form of cancer. The doctors had no hope, and had given him not much longer to live.

We all rallied around Elli, and each other, in hopes that we could rise above the terrible specter of death stalking this kind friend, so precious to us all, one of our small inner circle.

# CHAPTER TWELVE

MR. FRANK told me he and Mrs. Frank had become aware recently that Anne was having a problem with her eyes. Without calling undue attention to Anne, they'd been keeping a close watch, afraid to think of the ramifications if something was seriously wrong with her always-moving, green-speckled eyes.

When he confided in me, I became fearful. Everyone's eyes were especially precious in this hiding life, since there was so much quiet time each day, time filled by reading, writing, studies. Now that I knew, I noticed that when Anne read or wrote, her eyes narrowed into a squint, straining to see. Mr. Frank told me she was also having headaches.

What to do?

Finally, the subject came out into the open and became a source of debate among everyone. The consensus was that Anne needed eyeglasses. But no one knew for sure. Our first serious medical crisis had erupted.

I thought about Anne's eyes and did a little research. Near the office I had seen an oculist's sign, no more than a ten-minute walk away. If I took Anne out and we were quick—in, out, back to the hiding place—I figured I could have her safely back upstairs within an hour. Then, after the oculist had prescribed for her, I could go back, make up some excuse as to why the young girl couldn't come back to fetch her own glasses, and bring them back to the hiding place.

It was daring and dangerous to take an unregistered Jew into the street, but it was pointless to dwell on danger. I was confident that I could escort Anne safely out and then back to the hiding place.

On a late-afternoon visit, I offered my suggestion to Mr. and Mrs. Frank. I didn't try to influence them; I simply told them my plan and waited for their response.

Anne's reaction was quite emotional. She went white around the mouth with fear. "I could take her right now," I offered, thinking that perhaps without time to be afraid, we could have it over and done before the danger of it really sank in.

I could see Mr. and Mrs. Frank exchanging looks, silently talking to each other with their eyes as only a married couple can do. Mr. Frank played with his chin. Mr. and Mrs. van Daan and then Dr. Dussel got into the discussion. Its tone was grave. After all, we were tossing about a very dangerous idea. Anne looked from one parent to the other. She admitted that she was scared to death by the thought, that she didn't know if she'd faint with fear just at the idea of actually being in the street. "But I'll go if you say," she added, looking up at her father. "I'll do what you say."

Mr. Frank told me they'd talk it over and tell me later what they'd decided.

"Fine," I responded.

The next day Mr. Frank told me that they had thought the matter through, and despite their concern for Anne's eyes, he shook his head mournfully. "It's just too dangerous to go outside. It's better if we all stay here together." Then he added with regret, "These things will have to wait until after the war.

"But . . . let's see . . ." he added, leaving the subject slightly up in the air.

Nonetheless, the possibility of Anne's going out into the danger of the street wasn't raised again. Especially afterward, because during another big raid on Germany, the antiaircraft fire was heavy. One plane was hit and crashed near the Muntplein, quite close to the hiding place. A terrible explosion occurred, and large fires could be seen burning.

In the Annex there was near-panic because of the plane crash. Although our friends tried to keep up a good face when I visited, they lived constantly with the feeling that they were about to be bombed, or burned, or crashed upon. This unrelenting terror left them all debilitated. They realized their total defenselessness should they be bombed. There was nowhere to go; there was no escape for them. With the terrible noise of the explosions seeming much closer than it really was, anxiety was reaching such a pitch that it left them drained and sick for days afterward. I was helpless to do anything to relieve their terror.

Not only did these bombings remind them of their total vulnerability, but after several more imagined robberies in the offices, an actual robbery finally took place. It wasn't much to speak of: the thieves had taken mostly ration coupons for sugar, which was so scarce these days, yet still available to the business for the jam-making process.

The thieves had taken our petty-cash box and several little odds and ends; but worst of all, and shattering to our friends' sense of well-being, was the fact that these scoundrels had broken right through the fortress of the door to the front office. Looking for booty, the thieves had penetrated right up into the offices, and perhaps to the very point of the bookcase that hid the entrance to the hiding place.

Again the radio dial had been left on the illicit BBC station, and this time no one in hiding had had any inkling that intruders were wandering just below. No one had been making any effort to be silent. Water might have been running, feet hurrying up the creaky stairway. Voices calling out upstairs might have been heard. It was brought home to our friends that their safe fortress was not so safe.

During these terrible times, the thieves could easily go to the police and report the presence of people in hiding. The Germans were paying hard cash for this information. A reward was given for each Jew who was found in hiding.

The times were such that a thief was safe and a Jew was not.

SUDDENLY, GOOD NEWS brought us all a tremendous surge of hope. Mussolini had crumbled. Our British and American allies had finally landed on European soil, and had begun to fight their way up to us from Sicily.

Our friends in hiding were euphoric.

Mr. Frank and Anne were the most optimistic that the war would be over very soon. Dr. Dussel and Mrs. van Daan were cautious but also optimistic. Mrs. Frank, Mr. van Daan, Margot, and Peter were the most cautious in their estimates of just how long it would take for the Allies to liberate us.

When the big radio in Mr. Frank's office had to be turned in to the Germans, Mr. Koophuis somewhere found a small radio in working order for the hiding place. No longer did our friends have to troop downstairs in order to listen to the BBC and Radio Orange. Our own radio, which Henk had been bringing to the hiding place piece by piece, still sat in pieces up in the attic.

The Franks and Van Daans had somehow stored a huge

amount of soap in the hiding place before they'd moved in. It had lasted more than a year. Now it was slowly running out and creating a problem for our friends, clean, orderly lot that they were.

Out in the shops, even with the ration coupons, soap was hard to come by, even synthetic soap, which seemed barely to have any effect at all except to leave a gray film on the water. Each day it was becoming harder and harder to get anything, and more and more of a scavenger hunt. Shops were just about empty more often than not, and if something was to be had, shoppers crowded in.

One particularly harried morning when I had quite a load on my bike already and was trying to finish my shopping, I was just about to make a turn when a careless motorcycle with a sidecar, carrying two German soldiers, collided with my bike. I jumped off before I fell off. Something boiled over inside of me.

It was unlike me to lose my temper, but the words angrily shot out of my mouth. "You contemptible, vile . . . vile men," I exploded—and was immediately aware that Dutchmen had been shot for much less. But I felt no concern for consequences, just fed up to the brim with these oppressors.

I was standing straddling my bicycle, shouting at the soldiers. The driver stopped the motorbike just ahead and turned and looked at me. The motor was making so much noise as I shouted that afterward—when I'd come to my senses—it occurred to me that they might not have understood me. Both German soldiers turned and gave a laugh, and rode away.

At the moment of the collision the streetcar had come by, and the motorman and passengers had seen the entire incident. Still burning with rage, I got back on my bicycle, and pedaled slowly in order to let the streetcar pass. But the motorman gave a sign to me, a gesture of taking off his hat, and waved for me to go first. He had understood the danger of the situation, as I, overcome with emotion, had not, and he had saluted me.

My heart was beating furiously as I realized what I had done.

Late that afternoon, bringing up a little parcel and a book, both for Dr. Dussel, I related the story of the German motorcycle to the hiding place. Everyone became agitated by the danger of my encounter. Later, I heard from Mr. Frank that the parcel I had brought was a highly illegal anti-Nazi book which he and the others had been very worried to know I'd carried. The punishment for possessing that book alone was imprisonment or death. "How could you put Miep in such danger?" Anne burst out at Dussel.

"No one would dare to tangle with our Miep," Dr. Dussel tartly replied.

But Anne was highly indignant. "When Miep is in danger, all of us are in danger," she scolded.

ONCE WHEN I was in the hiding place, Anne began to try on her clothes, imagining what she could wear back to school. She chattered a mile a minute, and we all smiled at the sight of her wrists and hands sticking out from stretched sweaters that reached only to her mid-forearm. Forget buttons; her shape had changed so much that it was impossible even to try to make buttons meet. Anne made it like a comedy to cover her frustration.

Anne was spontaneous and still childish sometimes, but she had gradually acquired a new coyness and new maturity. She had arrived a girl, but she would leave a woman. An understanding had developed between Anne and me. Sometimes, without words, I would sense how she felt, or what she wanted, as one woman to another. We had developed this kind of silent language as twice a day, day after day, week after week, I had been trying to satisfy her needs.

As Anne was growing up, she still sought my company and the company of the other visitors from below. Margot and Peter, through the course of the year, had not come closer to Henk and me. Anne always felt comfortable airing her thoughts to me. Margot and Peter made no requests, let me know no needs, nothing of themselves.

As she had when she was younger, perhaps even more so now, Anne still saw Henk and me as romantic figures. These unpleasant conditions had not changed Anne's nature. To a romantic young girl, I could understand how attractive Henk was—tall, handsome, authoritative. Henk never seemed to look threadbare; he oozed vitality. Everyone responded to his wry wit and fund of reliable information.

As for me, Anne often seemed to be studying me. I could see her admiration for my independence and confidence in the face of everything. She seemed to admire my femininity, too. No matter what I wore or how I fixed my hair, she was full of compliments and questions. She too tried new hairdos on her thick, glossy brown (nearly black) hair. She also tried to experiment with her clothes to add a little glamour or to make herself look older.

I felt a particular kinship with Anne, turning this important corner of her life and caught in these terrifying times. How much pretty things meant to young ladies of fourteen, who were just beginning to feel pretty themselves. And sadly, pretty things were the last thing we could come by. I believe that sometimes Anne felt pretty and sometimes she felt ugly.

I became determined to find something grown-up and pretty for Anne in the course of my searches. One day I stumbled onto just the right thing. I had found a pair of high-heeled red leather pumps. They were secondhand, but in good condition. I hesitated about the size: how awful if they didn't fit her. But then I thought, Buy! Take a chance.

I brought them up to the hiding place behind my back. I went to Anne and stuck them in front of her. Never have I seen anyone so happy as Anne was that day. And quick, on went the shoes, and they fitted just right.

She got very quiet then: she had never felt herself on high heels before. She wobbled slightly, but with determination, chewing on her upper lip, she walked across the room, and back, and then did it again. Just walking back and forth, up and back, more and more steadily each time.

DURING THE late summer and fall of 1943, the Germans had begun to round up non-Jewish Dutchmen between the ages of sixteen and forty. These men were being shipped to Germany for—as they called it—"labor service." Some were called up, and some were just going about their business out in the street when a military truck would pull up, Green Police with a rifle would jump down, and the man would be told to get into the truck.

This added a new element of tension to our lives. Henk was thirty-eight and as healthy and fit as anyone could be during these times.

One night when we were both home from our offices, exhausted, as we were every night, Henk told me that he had something quite important to talk with me about. I sat quietly and listened as he began to tell:

"One day I was at my office. I was in the washroom washing my hands. One of my colleagues whom I know very well, a pleasant fellow, came in and, after making sure that we were alone, asked me outright if I was willing to work with a Resistance group that had been organized in the office. He told me to think first, that the work was illegal and quite dangerous.

"I asked him some questions as to what the work was and who was involved in it. He told me that of the approximately two hundred and fifty men working in our department, perhaps eight had been asked to join. Then he told me several of the men who were involved. I was surprised that he trusted me this much—saying names, that is. Immediately, I said, 'Yes, I'll do it.' "

I listened, not wanting Henk to see the hard lump that had risen in my throat as he talked.

He continued, "The first thing he did when I agreed to join their illegal operation was take me to a doctor. This doctor works for the City of Amsterdam. We had a talk together. He made note of my name. He told me that if I got into trouble or had reason to believe I needed to disappear for a few days or longer, I could go to a particular hospital and mention the doctor's name along with my name, after which I would be admitted into the hospital and permitted to stay until things cooled down, or it was decided to send me into hiding."

I waited for Henk to give me details of his dangerous new work, but he didn't. Instead, he told me, "You see, Miep, the reason I'm telling you all this is that now, with the danger of the new call-ups, in case anything happens to me I want you to know what's going on, that I'm involved in secret Resistance work."

I couldn't help showing how worried I now was, simply as a wife, that something *would* happen to him. But as a fellow resister, I was happy that he'd found a new way to go against our oppressors.

He begged me not to worry. "If I don't come home one night, then wait for a message to be sent to you."

I looked at him with a look that said, "How could I not worry?"

"Worry only if you get a call from a hospital. That will be the only time to worry," said Henk.

We agreed that it was best to say nothing about this dangerous secret work to our friends in hiding. Henk didn't want to tell me any more either at that time, so I asked nothing. Nonetheless, a strange feeling gnawed at me and I caught myself inquiring, "Henk, how long have you been doing this work?"

"Maybe half a year," he replied. "I didn't want to tell you because I didn't want you to worry."

ALL SUMMER roundups of Jews continued in Amsterdam. During a Sunday, I think, at the very end of summer, on one of the most beautiful days we'd had all season, the Germans staged a huge roundup in our River Quarter, South Amsterdam. All the streets were blocked off. Truck after truck of German police went driving by. Before my eyes I could see the men wearing green uniforms sitting side by side in two rows in the trucks. The soldiers would pull up the bridges and stand guard at intersections so no one could get away.

All through the neighborhood could be heard the shrill, piercing whistles and then the sound of boots on steps, rifle butts pounding on doors, insistent ringing of doorbells, and the coarse, frightful voice demanding in German, "Open up! Be quick. Be quick!"

Henk and I were home that entire day. All day sorry-looking groups of Jews wearing the yellow Star of David, carrying knapsacks and suitcases, were pushed and marched in loose groups surrounded by Green Police past our street, right past our window. The sight was so anguish-making, so terrible, that we turned away and didn't look.

Late in the day there came a timid knock at our door. I went to the door and opened it. There stood an upstairs neighbor, a woman whom I knew just slightly. She was about forty, was always very chic, and worked in one of the finest, most expensive ladies' clothing shops on the Leidseplein, a shop called Hirsch. I'd very many times admired the clothes in the windows, but had never been able to afford their prices.

She lived with her old mother in the apartment above ours. They were Jews.

In her arms she carried a fluffy cat and a cat box. With a

pleading look in her eyes she said, "Please, would you take my cat and give him to the animal shelter, or . . ."—her eyes were dry and full of fear—". . . if you want, you can keep him."

Immediately, I took in the situation. I realized that she was being taken away by the Germans and had been given a very short time to get ready. I reached out my hands for the cat. "Give."

She put him in my arms. I thought, I'll never, never give this cat away to the animal shelter. Never. I told her, "I'll take care of him until you come back."

"His name is Berry," she told me, and quickly, she was gone.

I looked at the cat's face. He was almost all white, with some black on his back. He looked at me too. I held him in my arms and brought him into our apartment.

He made himself right at home. What a sweet cat! I thought. I loved him right away.

From that day on, Berry was like our child. Every day Berry would wait in the hallway for Henk to come home from work. And every day, when Henk came home, Berry would spring up and nip him very softly on his chin.

# CHAPTER THIRTEEN

ELLI AND I put aside office work—filing, invoicing—for Margot and Anne to help us with at night. Always, we would leave the girls what needed to be done in the back offices, and when we returned to work the next day, it would be neatly completed and waiting. But Margot and Anne were not supposed to come into the front office because the curtains there were never supposed to be shut.

The girls enjoyed helping us. They were a little like night fairies. While the place was shut and locked, they'd come down, do the filing or whatever work we'd left, and put it away, and there'd be no sign the next day that anyone had been there.

Other uses were made of the back offices after working hours and on weekends when it was safe. Dr. Dussel had begun to study Spanish, and would often seek out the privacy of Mr. Frank's office in order to study in peace. Privacy of any kind had become a precious commodity to our friends.

On weekends, because there was a small water heater downstairs in our kitchen, which couldn't be seen from the street, our lavatory became a fine place for a real wash with plenty of hot water. I suspected that our friends would sometimes come downstairs for a much-needed change of scene or just to be alone.

No one was very happy that winter was approaching again, the second winter in hiding. We'd all been so sure that the war would have been over by now. But we held high hopes that this winter would bring decisive progress for our allies.

As winter approached, Mrs. Frank began to act oddly. When I left the hiding place, she would follow me downstairs just as far as she could go—to the back side of the bookcase, in fact. It was as if she were escorting me out, but then, rather than bid me goodbye, she'd just stand there and look at me, with an expression of wanting in her eyes. I'd stand and wait for her to say what it was that she wanted of me, but she wouldn't say a word, just stand there awkwardly.

I began to feel very uncomfortable, standing face to face with her. My mind would ask, What does she want from me? It took a while, but finally I realized that what she wanted was to be able to talk with me in a confidential way, when no one else was around. So I began to leave myself some extra time and would go with Mrs. Frank into the bedroom that she and her husband shared with Margot. She and I would sit on the edge of her bed, and I would listen while she talked.

What she needed to talk about, which she couldn't talk about in front of the others, was that she was suffering under a great weight of despair. Although the others were counting the days until the Allies came, making games of what they would do when the war was all over, Mrs. Frank confessed that she was deeply ashamed of the fact that she felt the end would never come.

Sometimes, she would complain about Mrs. van Daan—something no one else had ever done about anyone in the Annex for my ears. If there were tensions and conflicts, they were never aired when one of us was visiting the hiding place. She desperately needed to talk about some of these things.

She'd complain that Mrs. van Daan was always impatient with her girls, especially Anne, complaining that the Frank girls were too free for her. It seemed that Mrs. van Daan was always bringing up her feelings about Anne and Margot at the dinner table. Mrs. van Daan would say things like "Anne's so fresh . . . outspoken. She's too free." This criticizing of Anne and Margot upset Mrs. Frank very much.

In a dark voice, she would express the fear-laden thoughts that she was secretly harboring.

"Miep, I see no end coming," she would say.

Once she said, "Miep, remember this: Germany will not come out of this war the same way it went into it."

I would listen with a sympathetic ear to whatever Mrs. Frank needed to say. And then, when I could stay no longer, I would have to break into the talk, because some chore or other was waiting. I would promise that we would talk again next time.

I would leave her sitting in that room wearing a look of gloom and depression.

By winter of 1943 it seemed as if all the Jews in Amsterdam were gone. Certainly, just about all the Jews in South Amsterdam were no longer to be seen. Either they had been deported or they were in hiding or had somehow fled. I dreaded to think about what had become of these people. So many unpleasant rumors circulated. As the Jewish apartments in our quarter were emptied of people, Puls movers would come and empty the homes of possessions and furniture. Quickly a new family would move in. We didn't know who these new families were or where they came from. We did not ask. We knew that some were NSBers who were high on priority lists for new apartments.

About the only way a Jew was seen now was floating face down in a canal. Sometimes Jews were thrown there by the very people who had hidden them, for one of the worst situations that could arise for us helpers was if someone in hiding died. What to do with the body? It was a terrible dilemma, as a Jew could not properly be buried.

The second-worst fear for people in hiding and for those who were hiding them was what to do if someone got sick. We faced that problem that winter when Henk and I returned home one night and found Karel van der Hart bent double with pain, his hands clutching his head. Henk and I looked at each other in desperation. Whatever happened, we knew we couldn't take him to a doctor or a hospital because his papers were not in order. We were on our own.

Karel was in such agony that I couldn't at first assess just where in his face this terrible pain was originating. Finally, I was able to pinpoint the pain in his forehead. He called the pain, "blinding, like a knife in my head."

Somehow, Henk and I got him to the couch and laid him down. I had no idea what to do.

As he wailed and writhed, I put some water on to heat. Then I got a mitten-shaped washcloth and sat beside Karel, soaking the washcloth in the hot water. Comforting him with one hand, I applied the heat to his forehead with the other.

I had no idea if I was doing the right thing, but again and again I applied the heat to his forehead. Henk stood in the doorway with an anxious look on his face. The pain continued. Slowly, the night was passing. The procedure seemed to be doing no good. Terrible thoughts were going through my head. Nonetheless, I continued to apply heat and pressure, and offer what comfort I could to the devastated boy.

Not one to give up, I had no intention of stopping, even when the first street noises could be heard from behind the blackout curtains, telling me that morning had come. Suddenly, Karel gave a particularly agonized cry, almost a bleat, and pus poured out of both nostrils. It poured like a river, and then it stopped. Karel started to blink his eyes and took a gulp of air. Then he raised himself on one arm and met my eyes with a sudden look of relief.

"It's getting better, Miep," he told me. "The pain is going away."

To this day I have no idea what was wrong with Karel. We were all fortunate that the problem disappeared as it did.

WINTER WAS especially cold and stormy. Always it was a fight with stinging rain and slippery streets and longer searches for food, the scarcities worse with each passing day. I could not relax my vigilance in my searches. Eleven of us had to eat. Because I was a lifeline, I felt myself to be a kind of hunter, ever hunting for my always-hungry brood. But slowly, I was turning into an unrelenting scavenger, and would make do even with scraps. I could not allow myself to get sick. I could not allow myself a holiday.

We were besieged with our worst fear, sickness. First, Mr. Koophuis was hospitalized again with his terrible bleeding stomach. Then I sprained my ankle trying to navigate with a terrible cold, and finally came down with flu. Fearing that I would be infectious to the others, I made myself stay at home in bed.

Fading into and out of sleep in my darkened room, my bed piled high with blankets, chills and shivers coming in waves, I thought of my friends in the hiding place. My worry for them was like a great stone on my chest. What will happen to them? I thought all day and night. What will be?

I knew that the Van Daans' money was running out and that Mr. Koophuis had privately sold some of their possessions and would be trying to sell even more on the black market, including

Mrs. van Daan's furs and pieces of her jewelry. I suspected that one and a half years of forced idleness and isolation was taking its toll on everyone's nerves.

I saw Margot and Peter fading more into remoteness. I could feel the sparks of unfinished conflicts left sizzling in the air when I would enter and everyone would put on a welcoming face. Anne was more often off by herself, writing in her diary, or up in the attic, alone and sullen.

The demons of anxiety were making me even sicker lying there. I couldn't stand idleness very long, and though not entirely well, I got up and resumed my duties at the first sign of recovery.

Then Elli's whole family were forced into isolation in their house because of diphtheria. So terribly contagious is diphtheria that Elli couldn't work for more than a month.

Amidst all the sickness, a gloomy mood had settled over the hiding place. I tried to think of what might lend a little cheer as the holiday season approached. I began to put aside any sweets that I could find, since in my mind, nothing cheered us up better than sweets. I scrounged up bits of butter and flour, careful not to let it be known that I was planning to bake a real cake.

It was out of the question to try to duplicate the grand St. Nicholas Day party we'd made the previous year. But Anne had other ideas. I learned the day after St. Nicholas Day that she had broken through her lethargy to begin a secret collaboration with her father. Together, Mr. Frank and Anne had composed rhyming poems for everyone and made their surprise presentation by filling the big party basket with shoes. Each shoe belonged to a different person, and each held an original, teasing, oftentimes very silly poem.

Right after St. Nicholas Day, Anne was put to bed with the worst cough and flu we'd seen yet. The coughing was a big problem during the day; it had to be muffled. Muted sounds of coughing and sneezing came from Anne's room until she was well again. When I visited, I'd always look in on her.

For Christmas, Anne proudly presented me with little creamy confections that she'd made herself for my famous sweet tooth. She too had been secretly hoarding her rations, in order to create such soft melt-in-the-mouth sweets just for me. Anne made me taste them right away, in order to watch the look on my face. She laughed, her eyes glistening, as I licked my fingers.

She'd beaten me at my own game, surprises, which only made me more determined to make the most beautiful cake possible for her and the others in return. My bits of butter and sugar were adding up. The last days of the year approached, dark, short, and gloomy, in occupied Amsterdam. The Allied bombings of Germany were ever increasing, so that the drone of aircraft was constantly in our ears at night.

Koophuis, Elli, Kraler, Henk, and I planned our surprise for a Friday night before New Year's Eve, when we would all remain after the workers had gone and present our friends with what each of us had scrounged up for them.

The workday ended, and Henk arrived from his office. Before he came in, he waited down the street until the last worker had mounted his bicycle and ridden away. We each carried our offerings up the steep stairway. Henk had located some black-market beer for our gathering. Each of us had come up with some goodies, and I'd baked my special spice cake, Anne's favorite.

The sight of our parade was like an elixir of pleasure. Before us, eight mouths began to salivate at once at the sight of the cake. Mrs. Frank put on some water for imitation coffee. Beer was poured as we all stood around the table. Anne noticed the message that I'd carved into the top of the cake and called it to everyone's attention. With beer and coffee, we all paused to toast the message: PEACE 1944!

ONE NIGHT Henk didn't come home from work. I'd dragged myself
home as usual. I lit the fire and put food in a pot to cook. I waited
for the familiar sounds of Henk's arrival: the door opening, the bicycle being dragged into the hallway, Berry leaping up to nip him
on the chin.

He didn't come, so I took the dinner off the heat and waited.
Even Berry, who usually roamed the gardens all day long until it
was time for Henk to come home, waited too. So I tidied this and
that, and waited, growing more and more nervous with each passing minute. Henk was so reliable. I had grown used to his predict-
able patterns, such as his coming home at about the same time
each day.

In recent months, bit by bit, Henk had told me more about
his Resistance activities. He had told me that his organization
would first investigate people who were in need of help. These people were often men who had refused to go as forced laborers to
Germany and had instead gone into hiding and could no longer
earn a living for their families or themselves.

These were men and women who were in danger and had to
go under to take the pressure off. They were people just like us.
They could have been us. It was Henk's job in the Resistance to
visit these illegal people by using passwords and special lists. He
would assess their needs, and then supply, through the organization,
whatever they most needed—ration cards, money. Since Henk was
a social worker for the City of Amsterdam, a caseworker who visited
people in need, he had a perfect cover for his activities.

As I waited for Henk that night, my nerves were getting the
better of me. I didn't know what to do, where to look, whom to talk
to. Henk had simply told me that I would get information if he
was arrested. Always, in case of capture, the less you knew, the
better.

As the evening wore on, I was beside myself. I could do nothing to suppress the terrible thoughts that were popping into my mind: that Henk had been arrested, that he was hurt.

I couldn't stand it any longer. I took my coat and went out into the icy night. At a nearby public telephone I called Henk's brother-in-law, who because of an importing business had some connections with the Amsterdam police.

He answered right away. "Henk's not come home," I blurted out.

To my surprise, my brother-in-law laughed. "So?" he replied. "He's sitting right here, having a drink with me. It's my birthday."

I felt relief. Then I felt foolish.

"Do you want to talk to him?" he asked me.

"No. Let him enjoy his drink. Please tell him to stay, and don't tell him it was me calling."

I went home and covered the food so that it would be waiting whenever he finally got home.


EVERYWHERE there were warning notices nailed onto signposts and glued to walls. Always with a black border, these announcements described executions of Resistance fighters by name and age and occupation. The threats against those who helped Jews were getting tougher.

Our friends loved stories about life outside the hiding place, and especially about the Resistance fighters. Henk, a wonderful storyteller, told all he safely could about the Resistance and any acts of sabotage against our oppressors. He would take Peter's cat in his lap and keep Anne, especially, hanging on his every word. Anne's eyes shone with enjoyment.

Naturally, Henk didn't tell our friends that he himself was doing the very acts of resistance that he was telling about. He didn't want to worry them. Nor did we ever tell them about Karel, hiding at home with us. We spared them information that would frighten them and cause them anxiety.

In FEBRUARY, I again fell ill, with flu and bronchitis. We all seemed to be taking turns with illness. Henk tried to make some longer visits to the hiding place to make up for my absence. Our friends needed our visits more and more.

Although no one complained, I knew that the stores of food staples the Franks and Van Daans had brought with them were running out. Whatever food I could find was now sometimes half-rotten. Regardless, I'd have to buy it anyway. We were all constantly getting stomach problems from bad food. Fat, especially butter, was growing impossible to come by. Mr. van Daan was always dying for a smoke, sometimes making do with imitation tobacco and sometimes with nothing at all, which was particularly hard on his nerves. Herman van Daan loved nothing more than a smoke.

When *would* the Allies begin their invasion? we all wondered. It had been in the air for months that they were planning an enormous invasion, a massive attack to liberate us once and for all. We expected it to come daily.

In February 1944, I turned thirty-five. But more important was Margot's birthday one day later. She was eighteen, and she needed the special attention. We all scrounged around for little gifts to give to Margot. Never did we forget any birthday.

In the hiding place, on the day of my birthday, Mrs. van Daan unexpectedly took me aside, asking me to come out into the hallway near the stairs. I braced myself to receive some grim news, but instead she looked into my eyes. "Miep, Herman and I have been wanting to find a way to express the inexpressible. But there are no words. This is just a small token of our appreciation and friendship. . . . Here . . ." She thrust a small package into my hands. "Open it!"

"It's not necessary . . ." I started to say, but she nudged me with her thumb. "Open it."

I did. Inside was a ring, the setting a diamond-shaped piece of black onyx with a twinkling diamond set in the center. A beautiful antique ring. But I immediately wanted to protest, thinking how many cigarettes and sausages this beautiful ring would fetch on the black market for the Van Daans, who were now dipping into their possessions, selling off everything they could through Mr. Koophuis.

Some firm, invisible hand pressed against my lips, keeping me silenced. Instead of being practical, I looked back into Mrs. van Daan's dark eyes and promised, "I'll wear it always—in friendship," and slipped it on my index finger. It fitted perfectly. Mrs. van Daan put her hand on my shoulder for an instant and squeezed, and then we went our separate ways.

AT THE END of February, another office burglary tied all our nerves in knots. This time, the offices had been rummaged in and the front door left swinging in the breeze. Terrible fear of this burglar mounted. Had the burglar heard the people in hiding? Was he the same burglar as before? Would he turn in what he might have discovered to the police and collect a reward?

The people in hiding didn't like Frits van Matto, the man who supervised the workplace. Though they'd never met him, for some reason they distrusted him and were always asking us about his activities. They were also nervous about the many desperate people who now roamed the streets of Amsterdam. Many had turned into thieves.

MARCH CAME at last, signaling the approaching end of the cold and dark days. For more reasons than ever before, we prepared to welcome spring. Coal shortages were everywhere, and sometimes even the electricity would go off for short periods of time.

Henk discovered that the people who had been providing the illegal ration coupons for our friends in hiding had been caught. Suddenly, this lifeline was cut. There was no way to avoid it: we had to tell them. Through his other underground activities, Henk managed to obtain five new ration cards. But five ration cards would be so little to try to feed eight. Henk promised to try to make better arrangements. Those in hiding took the news well, but naturally, they were fearful.

One day, as I was working through a small pile of invoices at my desk, the Westertoren bells rang out midday. I could hear the workers below slamming the door shut to go on their lunchtime break, and then all was silence. Henk was coming for lunch with me and I worked on, waiting for him to arrive.

Finally, I heard his step and looked up to see a very disturbed husband. He told me that he had to talk to me about something important. The sound of his voice signaled danger.

We went out and took a walk beside the canal. The ice was melting into great chunks. Henk immediately began to talk: "Two 'gentlemen' from Omnia came to our home this morning, just as I was about to leave."

Omnia was a German firm run by Dutch Nazis. It was in charge of liquidating Jewish property or businesses, or finding out why they hadn't as yet been liquidated.

"I invited these two unpleasant-looking men into the house. I had no choice. When they entered, I raised my voice in greeting, hoping that Karel would hear and stay out of the way. As they eyed the objects in the living room, they explained the purpose of their visit. It seemed that Mrs. Samson's son had several years before been dealing in some textile transactions and had been using his mother's address as his administrative office. Their purpose in the visit was to find out from me what had happened to him and to his business.

"I told them that as far as I knew, he'd gotten married and moved to another part of South Amsterdam with his wife. I had no idea if he was still there or if he'd been arrested. I knew nothing further about him. Which, as you know, is true.

"Then they began to search the house, opening drawers and looking through papers and into cabinets belonging to Mrs. Samson. All the time, my mind gnawed with fear that Karel was somewhere about. Their searchings were sloppy and rude. They found some papers that interested them among possessions of Mrs. Samson's that we had never touched or looked at, and they put them into their pockets.

"They began to ask me questions about myself. When had I married? How had I come by the apartment and the furnishings? I thought fast. Naturally, I couldn't tell them that when Mrs. Samson went into hiding, we had left her small bed/sitting room unchanged."

We had had the apartment registered in our name, so that no one could come and take away the "Jewish possessions"; so that they'd be safe for Mrs. Samson after the war. We'd even told our landlord—who, by that time, was a member of the NSB—that we had had some Jewish possessions transferred to the room of Mrs. Samson. At that time, he hadn't shown much interest, but as Henk spoke, my mind raced. I wondered if the landlord had gotten in touch with Omnia to report us. It was illegal to have Jewish possessions without authorization, but at least we were slightly protected by the fact that we hadn't hidden the fact from the landlord, even if what we'd told him had not been true. We had never touched our landlady's possessions, or even looked at any private papers around the house.

Henk continued, "I started to make up a story about how we

had acquired the furniture, but they weren't interested in listening. 'This furniture doesn't belong to you,' they announced. I began to argue, they half-listened, and then they replied, 'Okay, we'll accept that the living room may be yours, but the bedroom, absolutely not. You can't tell us that that's your furniture.' 'Yes, it is,' I repeated. They shook their heads and told me, 'We'll be back tomorrow at one o'clock, and if you don't admit the truth to us, we're going to send you to the prison camp at Vught.

"Then they left.

"Right away, Karel came into the living room. I asked if he knew what had just happened. He said, 'Yes,' he'd heard my voice and their voices, and had gone from room to room and then into the backyard, then had returned through the kitchen into the hallway and back into the bathroom. 'I was one room ahead of you at all times,' he told me with pride. But Miep, I'm determined not to let them take the furniture from the bedroom," Henk stubbornly added.

"Listen, Henk"—I spoke sharply—"we can again buy a bedroom set after the war, but if they take you away, I cannot buy another husband after the war. When they come tomorrow at one, you must admit that it's not our furniture and let them take it away. So let's have lunch. If we have to sleep on the floor, we'll sleep on the floor."

Henk silently agreed to do as I asked, and the next day at one o'clock he waited for these men to return. I too held my breath at work, waiting to know what had happened, not knowing if they'd taken him away, but finally Henk telephoned to say that they hadn't come.

Days passed and these men still didn't come. Shortly afterward, Henk saw one of them on the streetcar. The man ignored Henk, and Henk walked right by him too. Soon afterward, Henk again saw the man on the streetcar. Again, nothing was said. So we were left hanging, wondering if they would come back.

Just when it seemed that nothing more could possibly happen, one evening Henk and I came home and found Karel in a rather excited state, his cheeks pink, his eyes bright.

Right away he told us, "I went to a horse race today at the racetrack outside Amsterdam."

We suspected that he took little strolls around the neighborhood, but both of us were shocked by the information. We let him continue to speak. "There was a *razia* at the racetrack."

"Were you all right?"

He replied, "Yes, it was okay, they only asked my address."

"And what address did you give?"

"This address."

Now the blood rose into my cheeks. Henk demanded, "How could you do such a thing? Now they'll come here to look for you."

A look of sudden understanding passed across Karel's face when Henk said this. It was as though he hadn't made the connection before.

Gravely, Henk spoke: "You must go away. None of us are safe here any longer."

Karel understood and went to his room to pack his things. It was too dangerous for him to tell us where he planned to go. He simply left our apartment.

# CHAPTER FOURTEEN

WHEN THE OMNIA people did not come back to our apartment, and the police did not come to our address to look for Karel van der Hart, we decided that it was safe for him to come back into hiding with us. When we next went to visit Mrs. Samson in hiding in Hilversum, we found that Karel was living there too. He asked if he could come back to Amsterdam. We told him that we had already decided the same thing ourselves, that he should come back again into hiding with us on Hunzestraat.

On the train ride back to Amsterdam, we wondered out loud to each other, Is it really safe for Karel with us? We didn't know the answer to that question. Daily, people in hiding were being captured. There were raids and betrayals. The price for turning in a Jew or any person in hiding was going up all the time. Very soon afterward, Karel returned to Amsterdam and came back into hiding with us. We resumed our routine: one-player chess games, dinner for three.

Henk and I were at home on the day after Easter Sunday. It was to be a day off for everyone, and neither of us had rushed to get out of our warm bed. It was still quite early in the morning when we heard insistent ringing of the doorbell.

I ran to answer. It was Jo Koophuis in quite an agitated state, there to tell us that Otto Frank had phoned from the hiding place. There had been another break-in, and the situation seemed to be very dangerous.

Henk and I raced over to the Prinsengracht and let ourselves into an awful mess. A huge hole had been broken in the door. The place was in disarray. I hurried to the bookcase, whistled to them to unlatch it, swung it open, and dashed upstairs, Henk right behind me. Were they all right? My heart thumped as I ran.

At the top of the second stairway, I called out and entered a scene of terrible disorder. Never had I seen such a mess made by our friends. At the sight of us, Anne ran and threw her arms around my neck. She was in tears. The others gathered round us, almost as though they could be reassured only by a touch, by some contact with us. They were all trembling.

They all spoke at once to tell us how they had heard noises, had gone down into the office to look, had heard more noise, and thought people were in the building. So they had tried not to move for the whole night. Terrified every minute of the night that they were about to be captured, they were quite sure that the police had been roaming around the building, on the verge of entering the hiding place.

Henk immediately went downstairs to repair the door. I stayed with our friends, listening, comforting. Mr. van Daan kept saying, shaking his head, "I smoked up all my tobacco. What will there be to smoke later?"

"Come, let's put things back in order," I suggested, and together we all began to tidy up.

By the time we'd returned the place to order, Henk came back up from below. In a voice that was more severe than any I'd ever heard Henk use before, he entreated our friends never, never to go downstairs again. Especially when they heard a noise. "Stay behind the bookcase, no matter what. If you hear something, never go. Be silent, wait. Never go."

Not to frighten them, but to bring home his point, Henk reminded them that people in hiding were being caught all the time because they had gotten sloppy and careless and forgetful of the unrelenting danger to them.

Mr. Frank conceded, yes, it was necessary to stay upstairs, no matter what. He admitted that they'd acted without proper thought, and assured Henk that it would not happen again.

The next day, Anne reminded me of how happy I had been that day of my wedding when the ceremony had been completed and I was finally, safely Dutch. "I want to be Dutch too," Anne confided.

"When it's over," I promised, "you can become whatever you like."

SURROUNDED as we were by deprivation, the bursting forth of spring meant everything to us. Up at the hiding place, Anne would take me to the curtained window, the curtains now very soiled. She would point out each new burst of green on the great chestnut tree behind the Annex.

What an elegant tree it was, ablaze with rich green buds. Anne studied the progress of the buds each day, explaining to me how much bigger they were and how quickly they were ripening.

One morning, in a little less of a hurry than usual, I went about my normal chores. The air was balmy, though still chilly; clouds billowed across the sky, thick and lazy. I came to our vegetable shop on the Leliegracht.

I waited with several other shoppers, trying to get a look inside to see what it had to sell. Finally, my turn came, and rather than finding the man who'd given me extra quantities of vegetables, I found his wife. She looked distraught. I asked, "What's the matter?"

She whispered to me, "My husband's been arrested. They've taken him away."

My heart pounded. When one was taken away, means were employed to get that person to tell what he or she knew about others.

She continued, "He was hiding Jews. Two Jews. I don't know what they'll do to him."

Quickly, I purchased less than I needed and left.

I thought about this kind man who'd always given extra to me; who had, in fact, delivered heavy sacks of potatoes to the Prinsengracht. He must have known that I was feeding people in hiding, but he had never spoken about it. What would they do to him? What might he say to them when they did terrible things to him to make him tell what he knew about others? Would he tell about me?

The arrest of this man was a major catastrophe. Because he'd been so kind, I'd been able to keep feeding all eight in hiding. What to do now? Where to go? I walked nervously over to the Rozengracht, to another little shop downstairs in a cellar.

An old woman ran the little basement shop on the Rozengracht. I began to go there every day. I had an instinct about the woman, and made a plan in my mind. Each day I talked a little more with this old woman. Slowly, she began to brighten when she saw me, and then she began to talk about herself and her problems with her children. I would listen. I made a point of showing much compassion. She began to feel safer with me and told me more and more of her problems.

Now that I knew that she liked me, gradually I began to ask for a little more produce each time. She would give what I asked, all the while pouring out her heart. Once in a while, I'd go back to the shop on the Leliegracht and buy just a little, so that it would not appear strange that I didn't shop there at all.

All the time now we were counting the days of good weather, knowing that our allies would need good weather in order to make the landing we'd been expecting. In May, we counted many days of good weather, and still the landing didn't come.

In the hiding place, the conversation was always about the impending landing. A fervent excitement had been building in our friends. It was as though all would be well when the Allied invasion touched the Continent, wherever it might be. Our friends argued constantly with Henk and with each other over where they thought the landing would take place.

I longed for the landing soon, because the shortages were getting so bad that I was wondering for the first time just how much longer I could keep feeding everyone. Some days I would go from shop to shop and then to the black market, and still there wasn't enough.

And then it happened. The landing had begun in Normandy. On June 6, early in the morning, the news came over the BBC. Henk and I now had no radio and knew nothing, but the moment I started on my way to work I could feel a buzz in the air, like electricity. People were animated as they hadn't been in years. By the time I'd pedaled to the Prinsengracht, I too was glowing with the news.

Mr. Koophuis grabbed me by the arms and squeezed. "Yes, it's true." And when I went up into the hiding place, it was as if an electric current were running through the place. Everyone was glued to the radio, waiting for more and more information. The American General Eisenhower was going to speak later.

Each person now guessed how many days it would take to get from the Normandy coast to the Netherlands.

Henk ran upstairs at lunchtime, his cheeks pink with excitement. We gathered around the radio waiting for the American general to speak. For the first time, we all heard the flat American voice of General Eisenhower. He called the day D-Day, and as we wiped tears from our eyes, he assured us that total victory over the Germans would be coming within this very year, 1944.

DAILY, THE PINS in the map Mr. Frank had stuck up onto the wall moved closer to Holland. Anne turned fifteen in June. Once again, as we somehow did on all birthdays, we all came up with some little goody to make it a special day. Although she was changing, growing up, Anne was still the youngest and most vivacious among us.

Anne quickly used whatever paper I could put aside for her. I knew she needed paper for exercise books and for her diary-keeping. For this birthday, Elli and I put together a nice little bunch of blank copybooks, and I searched out some sweets on the black market for Anne's sweet tooth.

Right before the birthday, Peter, almost never conversational, took me aside and, pressing some coins into my hand, asked me if I could find some pretty flowers for Anne. I was surprised by Peter's request. As he stood there, I saw how strong-looking he was, how curly his brown hair was. Sweet boy, I thought, impressed by Peter's new tenderhearted side.

"It's a secret, Miep," he added.

"Of course," I answered him. Nothing more was said.

A few lavender peonies were all that I could find. I gave him the flowers. Red spots rose in his cheeks. Right away, Peter and the flowers disappeared into his room under the stairway.

One day in July, one of our traveling salesmen for Travies and Company appeared with an enormous crate full of dirty but fresh, ripe strawberries. "It's a gift for your office personnel," explained the salesman.

Saturdays were half-days on the Prinsengracht. As I worked, my mouth watered at the thought of the ripe strawberries. Finally, at midday, the workers below locked up and left. Just the inner circle remained—Victor Kraler, Jo Koophuis, Elli, me. Someone went into the hiding place to tell our friends that the workers were gone and they could now move around freely.

It's in my nature to be bossy, so when the idea struck me to turn the strawberries into jam right then and there, I took charge right away. Quickly I had all the helpers I would need. Those of us in the office stayed on, and our friends in hiding ventured downstairs into the back kitchen, which could not be seen from the street, each one asking me, "Miep, tell me what I can do to help."

Quickly, water was brought, strawberries were being picked clean of stems and dirt and washed off. Our operation was taking place both upstairs and down, and my jam-making team moved between the two kitchens. Everybody's spirits had risen for the occasion; the strong, sweet smell of stewing fruit pervaded everywhere. I noticed that everyone was walking around freely, talking normally, laughing and joking with the others. It was almost as though life itself were finally normal and we were all free to come and go as we pleased.

I was the expert jam-maker, so the group followed my instructions. No one took me very seriously, though, when I scolded anyone I saw eating strawberries rather than putting them into the water. Anne's mouth was so full of strawberries she could barely talk. Peter too, and Mrs. van Daan—and finally, the joke was on me, when I realized that though I had been scolding, my own mouth was also full of juicy fresh strawberries.

The air was so filled with sweetness that even the cats—Mouschi and Moffie—had curled up close together, enjoying the cozy, happy afternoon.

•

ONE BEAUTIFUL hot day that July, I finished my work early. The office was very quiet, almost sleepy. I decided to pay an unexpected visit to the hiding place. I thought I'd just go upstairs and talk with whoever wanted to chat. Visits made the time go faster for the people in hiding and were always savored.

I climbed the steep steps and, passing Mr. and Mrs. Frank's bedroom, I saw Anne alone over by the curtained window.

I went in. The room was dark, and it took a moment for my eyes to adjust, as the office downstairs had been much brighter. Anne was sitting at the old kitchen table beside the window. From her chair, she could peek out and look at the big chestnut tree and the gardens, and not be seen.

I saw that Anne was writing intently, and hadn't heard me. I was quite close to her and was about to turn and go when she looked up, surprised, and saw me standing there. In our many encounters over the years, I'd seen Anne, like a chameleon, go from mood to mood, but always with friendliness. She'd never been anything but effusive, admiring, and adoring with me. But I saw a look on her face at this moment that I'd never seen before. It was a look of dark concentration, as if she had a throbbing headache. This look pierced me, and I was speechless. She was suddenly another person there writing at the table. I couldn't say a word. My eyes were locked with Anne's brooding ones.

Mrs. Frank must have heard me come in, and I heard her soft step beside me. I could tell from the sound of her voice when she finally spoke that she'd summed up the situation. She spoke in German, which she used only when a situation was difficult. Her voice was ironic, and yet kind. "Yes, Miep, as you know, we have a daughter who writes."

At this, Anne stood up. She shut the book she was writing in and, with that look still on her face, she said, in a dark voice that I'd also never heard before, "Yes, and I write about you, too."

She continued to look at me, and I thought, I must say something; but all I could say, in as dry a tone as I could muster, was "That will be very nice."

I turned and went away. I was upset by Anne's dark mood. I knew that more and more her diary had become her life. It was as if I had interrupted an intimate moment in a very, very private friendship. I went back downstairs to the office, feeling distressed and thinking all the rest of the day, It wasn't Anne up there. She was so upset by my interruption, it was another person.

HITLER'S VOICE on the radio had become even more hysterical, his words often not making much sense. It was obvious to us all that he was trying to breathe new fury into his retreating troops. He shouted about new miracle weapons that his factories were producing which would soon inflict crushing blows on the advancing armies of the Allies. His voice had become hysterical, the voice of a desperate fanatic, rather than that of a leader of armies and men.

But despite the approach of the Allies, life in Amsterdam got worse. Sometimes, I'd sit at my desk in the office tapping the end of my pencil on the window ledge and staring into the canal below. Although there was work in front of me, I couldn't concentrate. I'd be thinking about my friends, so silent, yet so close above. I'd be feeling too weak to carry on. I'd think, My God, what else can I do that I'm not doing? Is there a shop somewhere I haven't tried? What's going to happen?

Worst of all, when I felt particularly weak, there was no one I could talk to about my insecurities. Naturally, I couldn't speak of them to those closest to me, Mr. and Mrs. Frank, nor could I speak of them to Mr. Koophuis, with whom I talked most often at the office. I could not even speak of them to Henk. Henk was doing his own illegal work, and I couldn't burden him further.

If I'd had a particularly bad day, I'd come home exhausted.

Sometimes I could see that Henk too had totally worn himself out. Neither of us would complain to the other. Instead, I'd cook the best dinner I could put together. Henk, Karel, and I would sit down and eat. Often Karel would chatter away, hungry for company after another day of total isolation. Henk and I would listen silently.

Sometimes Henk and I, in spite of the curfew, would go to our friends across the street. Together, we'd listen to the Dutch news from London.

We'd hear the familiar voice say, "Good evening. Here is Radio Orange from London. But first, a few messages." Then it would deliver such statements as "The bluebird is walking on the roof" or "The bicycle has a flat tire" or "The car is driving down the wrong side of the road."

We'd listen to these senseless words knowing that they were codes for our underground fighters and meant something important to them.

Radio Orange told us news of our own Princess Irene Brigade, which had been fighting alongside the Canadians since D-Day. We were proudly told about the two hundred and fifty Dutchmen flying with the RAF.

Toward the end of July, we learned of a very serious assassination attempt on Hitler's life. For several hours there were even doubts that Hitler was alive at all, but the German station immediately broadcast Hitler himself to prove that he was.

Then, a few days later, Radio Orange told us that General Bradley's U.S. Twelfth Army Group had smashed the German front. A few days after, it reported that General Patton's Third Army had taken Avranches. It seemed that the whole Western Front had been ripped apart and that the German resistance was near collapse.

News like this was my strong medicine.

Lying in my bed, I could hear the English bombers flying

toward Germany by night, and the antiaircraft explosions. By day, off in the distance, we heard the drone of the American bombers going in the same direction. Hearing them, I'd start to feel my strength come back. At night Radio Orange would tell us where those bombers had struck—Hamburg, Berlin, Stuttgart, Essen—and what kind of damage they had inflicted.

I could only hope that the collapse of the Germans and the end of this awful war would hurry. We all knew it was coming soon.

*Part Three*

# THE DARKEST DAYS

# CHAPTER FIFTEEN

IT WAS JUST an ordinary Friday morning, August 4, 1944. First thing in the morning, I'd gone into the hiding place to get the shopping list. Lonely after the long night locked in together, my friends were hungry for a good visit. Anne, as usual, had many questions to ask and urged me to talk a little. I promised that I'd come back and sit and we could have a real talk in the afternoon when I returned with the groceries. But conversation would have to wait until then. I went back to the office and got started with my work.

Elli Vossen and Jo Koophuis were working across from me in the office. Sometime between eleven and twelve o'clock, I looked up. There in the doorway stood a man in civilian clothes. I hadn't heard the door. He was holding a revolver, pointing it at us. He came in. "Stay put," he said in Dutch. "Don't move."

Then he walked toward the back office where Mr. Kraler was working, leaving us alone. We were petrified.

Jo Koophuis said to me, "Miep, I think the time has come."

Elli began to tremble and shake. Meanwhile, Mr. Koophuis'

eyes darted toward the doorway. No one but the man with the gun seemed to be about.

As soon as the man with the gun left our office, I quickly took the illegal ration cards, the money, and Henk's lunch out of my bag. Then I waited. It was about the time that Henk would come for lunch. After a very short time I heard the familiar sound of Henk's footsteps on the stairs. Before he could come inside, I jumped up, ran to the door, opened it, grabbed him by the arm, and said, "Henk, it's wrong here."

I shoved everything into his hands and gave him a little push. Henk understood me immediately and disappeared.

My breath caught in my chest, I went back to my desk, where the man with the gun had told me to stay.

After Henk left, Mr. Koophuis saw that Elli was very upset and was crying. He reached into his pocket and took out his wallet, handed it to Elli, and said to her, "Take this. Go to the drugstore on the Leliegracht. The owner there is a friend of mine. He'll let you use the telephone. Telephone my wife and tell her what has happened and then disappear."

Elli gave me a frightened look. I nodded my agreement with Koophuis. She took the wallet and dashed out the door.

Mr. Koophuis locked eyes with me and said, "Miep, you can also leave."

"I can't," I responded. It was true. I couldn't.

Jo Koophuis and I remained seated as we'd been ordered for perhaps three-quarters of an hour. Then another man came through the door into our room and called to Koophuis to come inside with him, and they went into Mr. Kraler's office. I continued to sit there, not knowing what was going on anywhere else in the building, too afraid to imagine what might be happening.

I heard a door open. The door to the storeroom was also open. Koophuis came back out, leaving the door open, so that I could see through the storeroom between Kraler's office and the front office.

At that moment, a German man followed Koophuis, and I heard him say in German, "Turn the keys over to the young lady." Then the man returned to Kraler's office.

Koophuis came to me, handed me the keys, and said, "Miep, see to it that you stay out of this."

I shook my head.

Jo Koophuis' eyes burned into mine. "No. See to it that you stay out of this. It's up to you to save what can be saved here. It's in your hands."

Then, before I could do anything but absorb his words, he squeezed my hand, then returned to Kraler's office, shutting the door behind him.

During this interlude, I thought two things. First, there was something familiar about the German's accent; and second, it struck me that they might have thought I did not know anything about the people in hiding.

A few minutes later, the Dutchman who had first entered our office, the man with the gun, came back into my room. Ignoring me, he sat down at Elli's desk across from me and dialed the telephone. I heard him asking that a car be sent.

He had left the door to the hallway open. I heard the German speaking sharply, then I heard Kraler's voice, and then the German's voice again. Suddenly, what had been familiar about this man's voice clicked in my mind. He was speaking German with a distinct Viennese accent. He spoke exactly like all my relatives, the ones I had left so many years ago.

This man came back into my office, but his tone was changing, and I could see that he no longer regarded me as an innocent. Obviously, he had figured out that I was also part of what had been secret. He came in and stood over me, saying, in a harsh voice, "Now it's your turn." He reached down and took the keys that Koophuis had given me.

I stood up, coming face to face with this man. I could feel his hot breath, we were standing so close. I looked him right in the eye and said in German, "You are Viennese. I am from Vienna too."

He stopped, frozen. I could tell I'd surprised him; he'd not expected this. He suddenly looked dazed, almost as if he were mixed up, and exploded, "Your papers. Identification."

I got out my identity card, which said "Born in Vienna. Married to a Dutchman." He studied my card. Then he noticed the man sitting across from me, making the phone call. He shouted at the man, who was in the middle of his call, "Get out of here."

The man hung up and slunk out like a little puppy. Then the Austrian went and closed the door to the hallway, shutting us in together.

In a fury, he flung my identification card at my head and approached me almost in a bent-over position, as though bent with rage. "Aren't you ashamed that you are helping Jewish garbage?" he snarled at me. He then began to curse me, shouting terrible words and saying that I was a traitor, that I would get a terrible punishment. He kept on cursing uncontrollably. I remained standing as tall as I could, not reacting at all to his words. The more he shouted, the more nervous he became. He began to pace from wall to wall. Suddenly, he spun on his heel and said, "What shall I do with you?"

At that moment, I began to feel that I was getting a little more control of the situation. I felt as though I'd grown a little in height. He studied me. I could hear him thinking, Here are two people standing across from each other who are from one country, from one city. One hunts Jews and the other protects them. He quieted down a bit; his face became more human. He kept studying me, and finally he said, "From personal sympathy . . . from me personally, you can stay. But God help you if you run away. Then we take your husband."

I thought, This isn't wise, but I couldn't help bursting out, "You will keep your hands off my husband. This is my business. He doesn't know anything about it."

He sneered at me and tossed his head back. "Don't be so dumb. He's involved in this too."

He went to the door, opened it, then turned around and said to me, "I'll come back to make sure you're still here."

I said to myself, You can do what you like, even drink poison, but I will stay here.

Then he said again, "I'll be back to check on you. One wrong move and off you go to prison too." He turned and shut me into the room alone.

I had no idea where he'd gone. I had no idea what was going on in the rest of the house. I was in a terrible mental state. I felt as though I were falling into a bottomless hole. What could I do? I sat down again. I was in shock.

Then, along the corridor past Mr. Kraler's private office and our office, down the old wooden stairway, I could hear the sound of our friends' feet. I could tell from their footsteps that they were coming down like beaten dogs.

I JUST SAT THERE, frozen. I'd lost track of time. At some point the two workers from downstairs in the workplace came up to me and said that they were so sorry, that they hadn't known. Then Van Matto came and said something, and I saw that the Austrian had given him the keys that he had taken from me. I can't imagine where the time had gone. First, it had been eleven or twelve o'clock when the Dutch Nazi had come. Then it must have been about one-thirty when I'd heard the footsteps on the inner stairway. Then, suddenly, Elli was back, and Henk had arrived, and I realized that it was five o'clock and the day had passed.

Henk said right away to Frits van Matto, "As soon as your assistants have left, lock the door and come back to us." When Van Matto returned, Henk said to Elli, Van Matto, and me, "Now we'll go upstairs and see what the situation is."

Van Matto was carrying the keys that he'd been given. We all went to the bookcase and turned it away from the door leading to the hiding place. The door was locked but otherwise undisturbed. Fortunately, I'd kept a duplicate key, which I went and got. We opened the door and went into the hiding place.

Right away, from the door, I saw that the place had been ransacked. Drawers were open, things strewn all over the floor. Everywhere objects were overturned. My eyes took in a scene of terrible pillage.

Then I walked into Mr. and Mrs. Frank's bedroom. On the floor, amidst the chaos of papers and books, my eye lit on the little red-orange checkered, cloth-bound diary that Anne had received from her father on her thirteenth birthday. I pointed it out to Elli. Obeying my gesture, she leaned down and picked it up for me, putting it into my hands. I remembered how happy Anne had been to receive this little book to write her private thoughts in. I knew how precious her diary was to Anne. My eyes scanned the rubble for more of Anne's writings, and I saw the old accounting books and many more writing papers that Elli and I had given to her when she had run out of pages in the checkered diary. Elli was still very scared, and looked to me for direction. I told Elli, "Help me pick up all Anne's writings."

Quickly, we gathered up handfuls of pages in Anne's scrawling handwriting. My heart beat in fear that the Austrian would return and catch us among the now-captured "Jewish possessions." Henk had gathered up books in his arms, including the library books and Dr. Dussel's Spanish books. He was giving me a look to hurry. Van Matto was standing uncomfortably by the doorway. My arms and Elli's arms were filled with papers. Henk started down the stairs.

Quickly, Van Matto hurried after him. Elli followed too, looking very young and very scared. I was the last, with the key in my hand.

As I was about to leave, I passed through the bathroom. My eye caught sight of Anne's soft beige combing shawl, with the colored roses and other small figures, hanging on the clothes rack. Even though my arms were filled with papers, I reached out and grabbed the shawl with my fingers. I still don't know why.

Trying not to drop anything, I bent to lock the door to the hiding place and returned to the office.

There Elli and I stood facing each other, both loaded down with papers. Elli said to me, "You're older; you must decide what to do."

I opened the bottom drawer of my desk and began to pile in the diary, the old accounting books, and the papers. "Yes," I told Elli, "I will keep everything." I took the papers she was holding and continued filling the drawer. "I'll keep everything safe for Anne until she comes back."

I shut the desk drawer, but I did not lock it.

AT HOME, Henk and I were like people who'd been beaten up. We sat across from each other at the dinner table, with Karel chattering as usual. We said nothing about what had happened until we were alone. Then Henk told me what he'd done after he'd come to the door and I'd given him the warning and sent him off with the money and illegal ration coupons.

Henk told me: "I went straight to my office with the money and ration coupons and my lunch. It's a seven-minute walk from the hiding place at normal times, but I got there in four minutes, even though I had refrained from running. I didn't want to do anything that would cast suspicion on me, in case they'd come after me.

"At the office, I took the incriminating materials out of my pocket and hid them in between some other papers in the middle of my file cabinet. My mind was racing. I knew I should do nothing but wait, but with every nerve in my body I wanted to do something. I found it impossible to stay there, and decided to go to see Koophuis' brother, who is the supervisor in a watch factory right around the corner from my office.

"I found him and told him of the situation. He was stunned too. We stared at each other, neither of us knowing what to say or do. At last, I suggested that perhaps we should go back to the Prinsengracht and stand across the canal, at the corner, and see if we could see what was going on. We agreed this might be the best thing.

"We quickly walked over to the Prinsengracht and stood on the opposite side of the canal, diagonally across from the hiding place. Almost as soon as we got there, a dark green German police truck pulled up in front of 263. No one was about, and the truck did not have its siren on.

"The truck had pulled up almost against the building, way up on the sidewalk. In our diagonal view, we could still see the doors to the building. Suddenly the door opened, and I saw our friends in a bunch, each carrying a little something, going right from the door into the truck. Because I was across the canal I could hardly see their faces. I could see that Koophuis and Kraler were with them. There were two men not in uniform escorting the group. They put the prisoners into the back of the truck and went around to the front and got in. I did not know for sure if you were with them.

"When the prisoners were all inside, a Green Policeman slammed the door shut, and right away drove up the Prinsengracht in the opposite direction from where we were standing. Then the truck crossed the bridge, turned completely around, and came right down the Prinsengracht on our side of the canal. Before we could make a move to be less conspicuous, the truck drove right toward us, and passed not two feet from us. Because the door was shut I could not see inside. I turned my face away.

"Then, because we didn't know who was still inside the office, nor what was going on, and how dangerous it was, we went back to our respective offices and stayed until the end of the day, when it would appear normal to return to the Prinsengracht."

Henk and I looked at each other. We both knew what was next, and neither of us had the heart to mention it. Finally, Henk slowly let his breath out. "I'll go tomorrow morning." The next day Henk went to tell Mrs. Dussel about the arrest.

"She took it very well," he told me later. "She was very surprised that all this time he was right in the center of Amsterdam. She said that she'd always imagined him way out in the country and that he wasn't the sort of man who much liked the country."

STILL IN SHOCK the next day, I went to work as usual. I had the most seniority now and took charge of the business. Having been with Mr. Frank since 1933, I knew the business inside and out.

That day, several of the company representatives returned from the road and had to be told what had happened. As Mr. Frank was extremely popular, they were very depressed at the news.

One of these representatives came to me and asked, "May I speak to you privately, Mrs. Gies?" I agreed and went with him into one of the empty offices.

"Mrs. Gies, I have an idea. We all know that the war is coming to an end. The Germans want to go home. They're tired. When they leave here, they'll want to take some things with them. That includes as much Dutch money as they can gather. What if you went to the Austrian Nazi from Vienna? He didn't arrest you and might listen to you. What if you went and asked him how much money he'd want to buy back the people they arrested yesterday? Only you can go."

I listened. As I looked at his face, I remembered that this man was a member of the NSB. In spite of that, he was friendly, and I recalled that Mr. Frank had been aware of this man's membership in the Dutch Nazi Party before he'd gone into hiding, since the man had worn a party pin under his lapel. I remember that Mr. Frank had commented, "This man you can trust. I know he's not a Nazi at heart. He must have joined the NSB because he was hanging around with a bunch of young men who joined. Being a bachelor and needing a social life, that's why he joined too."

Recalling Mr. Frank's words about trusting this man, I also listened to my heart, and I replied, "Yes, I'll go."

He explained more of his plan. "Mr. Frank was so popular, I know I can take up a collection among people who liked him so that we could come up with quite a little lump of cash to offer to the Austrian."

Immediately, I went to the phone and called the Austrian at Gestapo headquarters on the Euterpestraat in South Amsterdam. When I heard his voice on the phone, I told him who I was and asked in German if I could come and see him. "Something very important," I concluded.

"*Ja*," he replied. He told me to come Monday morning at nine o'clock.

That day I walked to Gestapo headquarters. The red-and-black swastika flew from the flagpole. Uniformed Germans were everywhere. It was a well-known fact that people who entered this building did not always leave it again. I entered the building and inquired of the soldiers on guard where this Austrian had his office.

I was told which office, and went directly there. It was a medium-sized room, filled with desks, all occupied by workers who were busily typing. The Austrian's desk was in the corner of the room. He sat behind it facing me when I entered. His name was Karl Silberbauer.

I went up to his desk and stood with my back to the typists.

I'd been thrown off by the fact that he wasn't alone, so all I did was stand there, briefly looking into his eyes. Any spoken words would have been audible throughout the room, so I just stood and didn't say a word. All I did was rub my thumb against the two fingers beside it, the index finger and the middle finger—the sign for money.

Seeing my gesture, he replied, "Today, I can do nothing. Come back tomorrow morning at nine sharp." And he looked down at his desk, dismissing me curtly.

Early the next morning I came back. No one was in the room except Silberbauer. I got right to the point. "How much money do you want to free the people you arrested the other day?"

He replied, "I'm very sorry. I can't do anything to help you. An order just came down. I can't deal as freely as I would like to."

I don't know what seized me, but I said, "I don't believe you."

He didn't get angry, he just shrugged and shook his head at me. "Go upstairs to my boss." He told me the room number and continued to shake his head.

Determined not to let my knees tremble, I forced myself up the steps to the room where I had been directed. I knocked on the door. No one answered, so I opened it.

As the door swung open, I saw a round table filled with high-ranking Nazis. Their caps were on the table, and in the middle of the table was a radio. The radio was playing an English broadcast. Right away, I recognized the BBC.

All their eyes burned into me. I realized that I had accidentally witnessed them committing a crime of treason, for which the penalty was death. I knew they would do with me what they would, so I had nothing more to lose. "Who is in charge?" I asked.

One of them stood up. Looking at me with a menacing face, he come toward me. His lip curled and he pushed me with his open palm against my shoulder. "*Schweinehund*," he snarled, pushing me out the door. Then he looked at me as though I were a lump of garbage, turned, and slammed the door in my face.

My heart was thundering. Fearing that any second I'd be grabbed by someone, I made my way back downstairs, back to the room of Silberbauer, where he stood waiting for me. He raised his eyebrow at me. I shook my head. "I told you, didn't I?" he said, glaring at me. "Now leave here," he ordered.

A small voice inside me asked, "What else?" I knew the Austrian was like stone. I had truly come to the end of my rope.

With measured steps, I walked toward the door to the building. Gestapo were everywhere in the corridors, like flies in fancy uniforms. Again the thought rang in my brain, People who enter this building do not always come out again. I put one foot in front of the other, waiting for someone to stop me.

Back out in the street, I was amazed at how easy it had been to walk back out the door.

PEOPLE IN THE office asked to see Anne's diary. My answer was always "No. It's not right. Even though it's the writings of a child, it's hers and it's her secret. I'll only return it back into her hands, and her hands alone."

I was haunted by the fact that some more of Anne's pages remained cast around on the floor in the hiding place. I was afraid to go back up there, as Silberbauer had already checked on me several times. He'd just pop his head in, saying, "I'm just making sure you haven't gone." I said nothing by way of reply. He'd seen what he wanted, that I hadn't gone anywhere. He'd turn and leave.

I was afraid to go behind the bookcase again. It was very hard for me to look at the rooms with the people gone. I couldn't face going back upstairs.

But I knew that after three or four days Puls movers were going to come to collect the Jewish possessions from the hiding place and ship them to Germany. I said to Van Matto, "Go with the Puls men when they come. Go upstairs and make believe you're helping them clean up. Pick up all the papers like this and bring them to me."

The next day, Puls came. A great truck pulled up in front of our door. I couldn't look as they piled the familiar things, one after another, into the truck. I stayed back from the window, still not believing that it was happening, trying to pretend that our friends were still going about their daily business so close above me.

Van Matto did as I asked, and when they'd left he handed me another pile of Anne's writings. Again, I read nothing, just put the pages together in a neat pile, and added them to the pages already in the bottom drawer of my desk.

Soon after the Puls truck had pulled away, the office was very quiet. I looked across the room, and taking large steps toward me was Peter's black cat, Mouschi. He came right over to me and brushed himself against my ankle. He must have run away during the arrest and hidden somewhere until now.

"Come, Mouschi," I said with determination. "Come into the kitchen and I'll find milk for you to drink. You'll stay here in the office now with Moffie and me."

# CHAPTER SIXTEEN

KNOWING THAT we were in danger now, we told Karel that it wasn't safe for him to hide at our home anymore. He would have to leave. He quickly gathered up his belongings and left, saying that he'd be back in Hilversum and could he return when it was safe again? We promised that we'd let him know when the heat was off, and that he could come back to us then.

With Jo Koophuis, Mr. Kraler, and Mr. Frank gone, there was no one left to run the business but me. Because I hadn't been arrested and because I was a Christian in charge, the Puls people had not disturbed anything in the office, or the expensive spice mills below. Suddenly, I realized why Koophuis had wanted me to stay out of the arrest. Regardless of how much I longed to have been arrested and taken away with my friends, I saw that I was needed to save the business. Since I knew the business backward and forward, I took charge. It was no problem keeping it going, except for the fact that signatures were needed for checks in order for me to continue paying the staff.

I went to the bank that our company used and asked for the

director. He received me in his office. He was a good-looking young man; married, he told me. I told him about the hiding and the arrests, and that I wanted to try to keep the business going for Mr. Frank, but that I had no proper signature for checks in order to pay the staff and the bills.

He heard me out, then told me, "Your signature will do. Just sign what needs to be signed and I will authorize payment. We'll give you as much as you need."

So in spite of the worst having come to pass, life went on at the Prinsengracht; orders for spices for sausage and pectin for jam-making kept coming, and we continued to fill them.

ELLI'S FATHER, Hans Vossen, died. His suffering from cancer had been great. It was almost with relief that I got the news.

Henk continued his underground work, even though he was in danger as well. So many Dutchmen like Henk were in hiding in their own homes or elsewhere because of the ever-increasing recruitment of men for labor by the Germans. So many people were in need of help.

Shortly after the arrest, Henk came home one night and told me he'd had a dangerous situation occur that day with one of his illegal "clients" which had made him very, very nervous.

"These people I was visiting, like many others in this neighborhood, left their downstairs door open. So I didn't ring downstairs, just went up to the first floor, one flight up. I would usually knock at the door and say the password, but before I did, I listened and heard a man's voice speaking German. I knew these people were expecting me. But I also knew that there was not supposed to be a man in the apartment; the man was in hiding out in the country, helping a farmer. I became very, very cautious.

"I continued to listen and continued to hear a man and a woman speaking in German. It occurred to me that it could have been the radio playing, or it could have been any number of inno-cent situations, but I couldn't take the chance, and left. I went back to the office and told my contact for my special work what had happened."

Shortly afterward, Henk's supervisor decided Henk was in danger. His usefulness was at an end. We agreed. The Nazis were too close on our heels. Henk had become more of a liability than an asset to the people he was helping.

Henk's supervisor eliminated the illegal cases from his normal caseload.

On August 25, France was liberated after four long years of occupation. The Allies were racing now. Brussels was liberated on September 3. And then Antwerp the day after.

We knew that we were next.

ON SEPTEMBER 3, the BBC announced that the British had entered the south of Holland, the town of Breda. A spirit of unrestrained optimism swept through Amsterdam, almost a kind of hysteria. On September 5, a day that came to be called *Dolle Dinsdag*, or Crazy Tuesday, parts of the German Army began to retreat.

These Germans were not the arrogant, healthy, well-uniformed young soldiers who had marched into Amsterdam in May 1940. They were bedraggled, shabby like us, and carrying with them what-ever money and valuables they had been able to gather.

Along with them, by train, by bicycle, by any means possible, also on their way to Germany, or to the east of the Netherlands, went the Dutch traitors who had collaborated with the Nazis for all these long years.

No one knew quite what was happening, especially the Ger-man soldiers themselves.

From hiding places, the red-white-and-blue Dutch flag was pulled out, its dust was shaken off, and it was flown with its orange band. People gathered in forbidden groups in the streets. Some had made little makeshift British flags out of paper, which children stood holding, ready to wave at the first sight of our liberators.

But that day passed, and then the next, and day after day, and still nothing happened. Slowly the German presence became obvious again, as if those who had left were returning. The announcement that the British had entered South Holland turned out not to be true. The euphoria of September 5 subsided somewhat, but people had no doubt that it was just a matter of days before we would be liberated.

We all continued going about our business in this state of limbo. Finally, on September 17, Queen Wilhelmina addressed the Dutch railway workers, who numbered more than thirty thousand, and asked them to go on strike—hoping thus to paralyze German military transport. Her speech was very moving, and with added inspiration, she entreated the workers to be prudent, to beware of reprisals against them. Her warning was meaningful. The penalty for striking at this time was death.

Another Crazy Tuesday occurred, with more confusion everywhere. That same day we heard on the BBC that the British and Americans had made a massive drop of men and supplies at Arnhem, and that Eisenhower himself was just west of the Rhine, right at the German frontier. The railway workers went on strike. The next day all transportation stopped.

Quickly, the striking workers went into hiding. The German mood was black with rage at the state of things. The entire country held its breath while we waited for our liberators to arrive.

One morning while all this was happening, I had a question that I needed answered and I phoned Mr. Koophuis' brother, who had been providing me with business advice. I asked him the question, some silly little thing, and he replied, "You should ask my brother that."

I was startled by his sarcasm. "How can I ask him? He's in the Amersfoort concentration camp."

He said, "No, he's on his way to you. Go outside."

I thought, what a terribly cruel joke, to say such a thing. But he said again, "No, go outside, Miep. It's true."

I dropped the telephone right out of my hands and ran outside. Elli thought I'd gone insane and ran after me, calling out to me with concern.

My heart pounding, I looked up and down the street, and there came Mr. Koophuis. He was on the bridge between the Bloemgracht and the Prinsengracht, waving his arms.

Elli and I ran to him. It wasn't like me, but I was shouting his name, and so was Elli. I reached him, and we hugged each other hard. All three of us were laughing and crying at the same time.

Together, we went back toward 263, all talking at once.

I couldn't stop looking at him. For a man who'd just been in a German prison camp, he looked better than I'd ever seen him. Thin, yes; but with color in his cheeks, and a brightness in his eyes that I'd never seen before.

I commented on how good he looked. He laughed and said, "The food at the camp was terrible. Just raw carrots, raw beets sometimes, watery soup. And . . . you won't believe this . . . for the first time in years, my ulcers are gone. All that raw food has cured my ulcers."

The good feeling of his return swept over me like a soft wave of relief.

Quickly I asked, "And the others, after the arrest . . ."

He shook his head. "We were all together at first, all ten of us, but quite soon Kraler and I were separated. I know nothing about them after that."

His safe and healthy return gave me great hope for all the

others. Jo Koophuis had been freed because of his health. The Red Cross had helped him return home so quickly.

We continued to wait for our liberators to arrive. The days passed slowly as we waited. As the month of September drew to a close, the weather became foul. Nothing had changed for us; the Germans had not budged. In fact, they were meaner and more vengeful than ever. Slowly, so slowly, our hope that the end had come began to fade.


TO PUNISH US for the railway strike, the Germans left civilian rail transport shut down. They ran the trains with their personnel for their own freight, but when it came to bringing food and coal for the population, their attitude was "Let them starve and freeze!" Quickly, shipments of food and fuel stopped. Only small amounts got to Amsterdam and Rotterdam from the Dutch countryside, carried by barge down the rivers. It became harder and harder for us to get food. Scraping together a simple dinner now took me hours and hours of going from shop to shop.

Just before the end of September, the British, to our horror, surrendered in Arnhem. All the jubilation and hope we had felt dissipated. Our allies seemed to be making no further progress. The Germans had dug in their heels. We were in a terrible mood of despair. Worst of all, another winter was coming. The weather was already grim and nasty with stinging rains, unusually cold. None of us had any strength to brace ourselves for what was shaping up to be a particularly unpleasant winter.

Hitler's voice still raved on the approved radio station, promising powerful secret weapons. Then Aachen fell to the Allies: the first German city to fall; the city where Edith Frank had waited with her girls while Mr. Frank had established himself in Amsterdam. The city was so close to Holland, and yet so far away.

So many thousands of Christian Dutchmen had been shipped to Germany in boxcars, just as the Dutch Jews had been, and so many thousands of adult men had gone into hiding that mostly women, children, and men over forty years old could be seen in the streets. It was pure luck that Henk hadn't been picked up. Somehow, his luck kept holding. Rumor had it that Hitler was conscripting boys as young as fifteen and men as old as sixty for his army.

The situation deteriorated rapidly when the rivers and canals froze up in November and barges could no longer bring food into the city. Black-market prices doubled, tripled, and multiplied again. For some weeks I had been leaving my bicycle at home when I went to work. It was now too dangerous. A German, seeing a functional bicycle, would just take it and ride away, leaving you standing. I couldn't risk losing my bicycle. We needed it for other things.

After Mr. Koophuis came back, he and I began to walk to the office together each day, and back again at night. The walk took more than an hour each way. Most days were gray and drizzling and desolate. Henk, because he worked for the city and had a permit which was respected by the Green Police, still took a chance and rode his bicycle to work. But soon he too stopped taking his bicycle and left it at home, because of a dearth of tire tubes and wanting to save it for other things. Now Henk too walked to work.

There was no coal to heat our houses, no gas to cook with, no streetcars, and on and off, no electricity. The Germans were supplying only themselves and hospitals with electricity and other essentials.

As there was no transportation, people had to go out into the countryside to search for food. People used anything they could find—handcarts, baby carriages, bicycles with wooden wheels, pushcarts, anything. We had been living on very little food before, and now the whole population began to live from hand to mouth, staying one step from starvation at all times, always weak and half-faint from lack of food.

I began to make trips out to the country too. Each time farther and farther. One day, I went along with the wife of one of the salesmen. We left before dawn and decided we'd go as far north as we could go and still be able to get back to Amsterdam by the eight-o'clock curfew. Because we both still had bicycles in working order and with real rubber tires, we decided to chance it and use our bicycles.

We got very far north, and began going from farm to farm. We were literally begging, offering money and objects that we had to sell, like sheets. We managed to pick up a few things—some potatoes, beets, carrots.

Knowing that we'd gone many, many miles north, we began to ride back as quickly as we could. Along the way, we passed two men who were pushing a cart. We felt sorry for them because we were going so much faster, and quickly left them far behind us. The weather was mild, for once, no rain, and we were making good time. We commented that these men would never make it back to Amsterdam by the eight-o'clock curfew going at the slow pace they had to go to push a wagon.

It was getting late, and we pedaled as quickly as we could. Suddenly, my friend got a flat tire. There was nothing we could do but get off and push our bicycles. Figuring that we'd never get to Amsterdam by eight, we decided we would be better off going to the next village and trying to find a place to sleep for the night, and then heading for Amsterdam again in the morning.

We asked people if we could please sleep in their barn, explaining that we couldn't make it back to Amsterdam in time for the curfew. None of them seemed to want strangers on their property, and everyone refused us. We were beside ourselves as to what to do.

Suddenly, the two men we'd seen pushing the cart appeared. They overtook us and we told them what had happened. They listened, then one said, "Here's what you should do. Take your bicycles and put them in our cart. You walk with us and we'll pretend you're our wives."

We looked at them suspiciously. The man continued, "You see, we work for the post office and we have special permits to be on the street after eight o'clock at night."

My friend and I looked at each other, still nervous. The man continued, "I don't want to upset you, but we're going to come to a German control station shortly."

Without one more thought, we quickly put our bicycles into the cart and leaned our own shoulders against it to help push.

Sure enough, we reached a German inspection station. The men told us to stay with the cart. "We'll go inside." And they went. We were very scared, because these Germans could do anything they wanted to, including taking all the food we'd found. The men were inside for quite some time, making us very nervous; but finally they came out smiling and said, "It's all right. We can continue."

Of course, we pushed even harder now. We hadn't even been asked for our papers. Inside the cart were beets and carrots that these men had found. Finally, we arrived at the Amsterdam harbor, Het IJ. It was after midnight. We had just missed the midnight ferry, and there wouldn't be another until one o'clock. Fortunately, the night was mild. We waited. We were so tired, we could barely stand anymore.

Finally, the ferry came. We crossed the harbor and walked through the silent streets until we came to the Berlage Bridge. There we said goodbye to our "husbands."

We pushed our bicycles and carried the food. My friend lived right nearby. In much danger, we didn't breathe until we'd shut the door to her house, bringing food, bicycles, and our weary selves inside. I slept there, woke at dawn, and pedaled the rest of the way home in the drizzly, gray light of dawn.

Henk and I had enough to stay alive on for several more weeks.

As THE WINTER began, people were becoming as thin as skeletons. Everyone, including us, was ragged and threadbare in every way. Children wore shoes with toes cut out or made from pieces of board or bits of leather and tied to their feet with string.

People were cutting down the beautiful, tall trees up and down the boulevards. The trees we all loved so much were being used for fuel. Cars ran on cooking gas, which was carried atop the car roofs in balloonlike enclosures, or else in contraptions that looked like potbellied stoves, with chimneys hanging down the rear of the car. Most bicycles still operable had wooden wheels.

During the dark winter nights, we made a little light from a piece of cotton thread floating in a small amount of oil in a glass of water. The thread burned with a minute, flickering yellow flame. This tiny source of light blew around the glass when gusts of draft entered the room.

Because people had taken to boiling laundry in the absence of soap of any sort, everything smelled sour and sweetish. Some of the poorest people began to be covered in red sores which came from scabies caused by lack of soap. There was also very little hot water. Because there was no transportation now, Karel could not get back to Amsterdam to hide with us again. We didn't know whether we were safe, but we had gotten word to him to come back if he wanted. But there were no trains.

Somehow, with no electricity, and no more coal, our business went on. Much reduced, but enough to keep us all going. We could still get imitation spices for sausage-making. Many businesses had shut down. Across doorways were signs saying CLOSED BECAUSE OF COAL SHORTAGE. I often wondered if there was really a business that had been shut down, or whether people were hiding inside, hoping that the sign would keep the German patrols away.

It seemed that most of our customers now were butchers. We were using filler made from ground-up nutshells and purchased in bulk, and bottles of synthetic scents from a chemical factory in Naarden, to make our imitation sausage fillings. When these two products were mixed, they looked and smelled almost like the real thing. Naturally, they had no taste, but the smell and consistency created the suggestion of sausage filling that would bind together with ground meat to make sausage.

These butchers were making sausage from God knows what, there was so little meat around. Never did we ask questions; it was better not to know.

One of our steady customers was a German-born man who was a chef. Despite his nationality, he was a good man. During the occupation, he had been forced to cook for the German soldiers. When he first started coming, Mr. Kraler had dealt with him. Now when he came, Mr. Koophuis would have long talks with him. He always paid in cash, and he told Koophuis that if any of us ever were unable to get food, we should come to him, and he would help us. The only trouble was that he worked in a town called Kampen, way off in the east of the Netherlands.

The time did come when we had no more food. Mr. Koophuis urged me to go and see this man to try to get some food. I went with the same woman I'd gone with before, the wife of one of our salespeople. No longer did she have a serviceable bicycle, so we borrowed one for her from our friends across the street.

Again we set off in the gloomy gray light of dawn. It was quite a long way to Kampen, and we rode all day. Along the way, we saw many of our countrymen going from farm to farm, trying to obtain food any way they could. The day was overcast, cold. The roads were filled with half-frozen snow and terrible ruts. Some people pushed broken bicycles or baby carriages. People were wrapped in all the clothes they had.

We came to Kampen and the military barracks where this man worked. He secretly smuggled us inside, right to the kitchen. It happened to be my birthday, February 15, 1945. He said, "Sit down; you can eat whatever you want."

I had been hungry for a long time now, especially for fat and protein, which had all but disappeared from my diet. "For your birthday," he said, and began to put rich foods before us. Porkchops, creamy butter. We ate and ate this wonderful meal.

The plan was that he would give us more food to take back to Amsterdam, and that we would spend the night with a friend of my friend, a minister who lived in a town nearby.

Neither of us could stop eating, so naturally we overate. Because we were no longer used to real food, we both began to grow very, very woozy. I became deathly sick to my stomach, and couldn't move, couldn't leave the barracks.

The cook began to get very scared, not knowing what to do with us. All he could think of was to put us into an empty prison cell. He half-carried me into this cell, all the time very much aware of the danger of being seen, then he said he'd be back to get us at five in the morning, and shut the cell door.

In the cell, there was nothing but an empty pail; no blankets, nothing. The pail was not empty long. I was sick all night—high fever, chills, agonizing cramps. I thought it was the end of me.

The night passed, and at five in the morning, the cook came back and spirited us away, half-carrying me to my bicycle. Throughout all my misery, I hadn't forgotten the food I was to take back to Amsterdam, and I carried it with me. Somehow I found the strength and mounted my bicycle, much food hidden under my clothes, and rode off with my friend, who was in much better shape than I.

Right away, we came to a bridge which was guarded by German soldiers. Usually, at places like this, everybody was stopped by the soldiers before being permitted to cross the bridge. Men often were physically searched and asked for papers; women were normally just asked for papers and inspected visually.

The meat and other food I was carrying were bulging from under my clothing, and bursting out of our bags. We were deathly afraid that we would have to turn everything over to the Germans. Since there was nothing else to do, we bravely rode up to the bridge, toward the soldiers on guard.

As we dismounted and looked, we saw the soldiers' sleepy faces. Instead of making a motion for papers, they just waved us through. We couldn't believe our luck.

We pedaled on and got to the minister's wife, who saw how sick I was and put me right to bed. I couldn't have gone on any farther. She cared for me, and by the next day I was well enough to get back to Amsterdam. We left at 5 A.M.

By the time we got to Amsterdam, we had again missed the curfew, and arrived at the bridge across the Amstel late in the night. To our surprise, there stood the Green Police with a new inspection station. At the sight of the green uniforms, we were filled with fear—not just for the food we had with us, but for our safety as well.

Again our luck held; they were inspecting for weapons. And with their Germanic precision, if they were looking for weapons, they didn't bother about other illegal things, like food. They searched us for weapons, found none, and told us to pass on.

I'd been gone several days, and I knew that Henk would be filled with terrible thoughts about my safety. I knew, though, that neither he nor I would say anything about our fears. These were the chances we all took every day. Risks and danger were with us always. There was no way to survive without taking risks. You just did it.

By MIDWINTER, the Germans had reduced our rations to 500 calories a day. Even though the BBC told us that Eisenhower had eighty-five divisions closing in on the Rhine, it meant nothing to us. Each frozen day was an obstacle to be surmounted: enough warmth not to freeze, the minimum calories to keep going. That was all we thought about.

Henk's mother died in December. She was fortunate to die in a hospital. Not all Dutch people were this lucky. People everywhere in Amsterdam were perishing daily of starvation. Sometimes they would just sit down at the side of the road and die. Sometimes they were so weak that they died of diphtheria, typhoid, or just the cold. Neighborhood soup kitchens had been set up, and each day people would line up in the cold to get a bucket of something warm to put in their stomachs.

All day people scavenged for bits of coal in the old coal yards. Railroad ties were dug up for the wood. If you had a wooden staircase standing in the garden or against the wall outside, you might wake up in the morning and find your staircase gone. Any houses left empty were stripped of wood from windows, stairways, furniture, anything.

Daily, all of us racked our brains for ways to get food. Henk came up with a plan for himself and me. Before the occupation, his father had fished for many years in farmland ditches near the little village of Waverveen, about seven or eight miles from Amsterdam. Like every other fisherman, my father-in-law had his own particular favorite fishing spot; he'd always fished, through the years, on a particular farmer's land, and had developed a friendly relationship with the farmer.

Henk's plan was to establish contact with this farmer. In doing so, it was necessary to tell a lie. Neither of us liked lying, especially to someone like this farmer, who was a devout Christian. But it was necessary. Henk paid the farmer a visit and told him that his father was quite ill and needed milk to build him up. Could he or I, his wife, come to the farmer and pick up some milk?

First, Henk got a real country meal, a meal he desperately needed. Then, impressed with Henk's sincerity—which inside made Henk feel very guilty indeed, as his father was quite healthy—the farmer told him to come every day and he would give him two bottles of milk at normal prices.

So every morning, one of us—first Henk one morning, then I the next—would get up at four-thirty and regardless of the weather, go an hour out into the country to this farmer's place. When I came for the first time I introduced myself to the farmer so that he'd know me. Each day when I arrived at the farm, there was a long line of people from Amsterdam waiting for milk. I would go to the end of the line, but the farmer would see me and call me out of the line. He'd say, "Come."

When others grumbled, the farmer would say, "No, she has to come up here first; she has a sick father-in-law." I felt terrible, for I thought the people in line must really have sick people at home.

And with this guilty feeling inside, I'd go to the front of the line and get the two precious bottles of milk, then ride another hour home in the dark. Always in terror of being stopped and having my bicycle taken, I used all my strength to ride quickly, but not in a way to arouse suspicion in anyone I passed. The icy wind slapped my face. Sometimes snowflakes made seeing almost impossible. My overcoat collar never would stay wrapped close enough around my ears. But the milk bottles rested safely in a sack in the front of the bike.

Piles of garbage lay uncollected now—frozen, thankfully, or they would have stunk. Hungry people scavenged through the garbage for any scraps, even before dawn.

•

AT LAST MARCH CAME, and then April, but still the winter raged. Some days were a bit warmer, and sometimes the sun shone briefly before the clouds closed again. Everywhere, as the earth thawed, there was a stench, whether the sickly smell of endlessly boiling tulip bulbs or pulpy sugar beets, or badly washed clothing hanging to dry, or bodies wrapped too long in ragged clothes.

All conversations centered on food. Food obsessions were affecting all our minds. Henk and I would get together some nights with our friends. Because we had no radio, our friends on Rijnstraat had promised to come and tell us when the war was over. So rather than go to listen to their radio, we'd often pull out our cookbooks and spend the evening copying down recipes that we would cook after the war. Sometimes, someone would read from Rabelais, scenes of eating and drinking.

Always, my fantasy would return to chocolate. Hot chocolate, frothy, like satin. The glands under my tongue would ache with longing.

PRESIDENT ROOSEVELT died on April 12, and Vienna, the place of my birth, fell to the Russians on April 13. Montgomery had crossed over the Rhine and was moving toward Bremen and Hamburg. The news was that all around us, Europe lay in ruins, the Germans defeated on all fronts. Like a great half-circle around Holland, freedom had arrived.

And still we waited daily, hundreds of good Dutch people falling dead of starvation while we waited, everyone weakened, all our minds distracted, fuzzy, unable to absorb or hold on to anything beyond our own next meal. Each day was just another day on the Prinsengracht, the long walk back to our River Quarter punctuated by feelings of faintness and waves of nausea, Jo Koophuis beside me. Always Henk and our cat Berry waiting for me at home, or I for them. How to stretch two potatoes into a meal for two grown people and one cat?

Mussolini was captured in Como, on the Swiss border, and then was killed. He and his mistress were hung up by their feet at a gasoline station in Milan. And then, on May 1, the German radio interrupted Bruckner's Seventh Symphony. Drums rolled; an emotional German voice announced that Hitler had died in the line of duty and his successor would be someone named Dönitz. The prayer I'd said so many times with my fist in the air had come true.

Somehow, it was not enough.

The warming of the temperature and the lengthening of the days eased two of our crushing problems, lack of heat and light, but the problem of food was more critical. My mind was never clear anymore: the daily search for food took all my strength and concentration. That and keeping the office going were so difficult. Each day was a fight to keep from sinking totally, as others were doing everywhere I turned.

May brought beautiful weather: blue skies, for once; patches of green appearing despite the devastation everywhere in Amsterdam.

On Friday the fourth of May, after one more ordinary day at the office, I came home. Berry was sitting in the kitchen next to his bowl, waiting for his drop of milk. I began cooking a meal made up of a few carrots and several small potatoes. I was cooking with slivers of wood, and it seemed to take forever for the water to boil. My mind was elsewhere when suddenly a burst of air rushed into the room and Henk with it. He took both my hands in his, looked into my eyes, and said, "Miep, I have good news for you. The Germans have capitulated. The war is over!"

The words were so thrilling to me that my knees went weak. I thought, Can it really be true? I looked back into Henk's clear eyes. It must be, I realized. Henk could always be trusted.

We sat down to eat our meal feeling such joy that we stopped being aware of the gnawing hunger in our bellies. The food tasted like the most marvelous meal I'd ever eaten. What would happen next? Henk and I asked each other. The Germans were still in our midst; they had lost the war now and must be furious. We mustn't be careless now, Henk warned me: being careless could cost a life, and how wasteful, now that the war was won. And our friends in the concentration camps, wherever they had been sent—we asked each other: could they also be free?

Eight o'clock came, curfew time. Suddenly, there was a loud knocking on the front windowpane. Henk and I went to look and there stood our friend from the Rijnstraat, who had promised to come and tell us when the end arrived. He was tapping and waving his arms. "It's over. It's over." We let him in and told him we already knew.

"Come on," he told us. "People are everywhere in the streets, eight-o'clock curfew or not. We are free!"

The streets were crowded with people. People were bringing out paper, wood, old clothes, anything to burn. We went to the Rijnstraat. Big bonfires were burning; young people were dancing around the fires. Old people were walking up and down the street, laughing and embracing each other. The feeling everywhere was exhilarating, lovely. Germans were nowhere to be seen.

We started back toward home. I knew we'd hardly be able to sleep this night. The sky was just beginning to darken. I noticed how beautiful the twilit sky was. Then, right above the rooftops, I saw a flock of pigeons swooping and circling. It struck me that it was a very long time since I had seen any birds in Amsterdam. How long had the sparrows been gone? How long had the swans not been in the canals? The ducks? Of course, I thought, birds could so easily get away; there couldn't have been food for them to eat either.

Under the Germans, it had been against the law to keep pigeons. These pigeons must have been kept hidden throughout the occupation. Now, at the news, they'd been set free. They were like confetti thrown against the sky.

There were pigeons again above the roofs of Amsterdam. They were free, and so were we.

# CHAPTER SEVENTEEN

OUTSIDE AMSTERDAM, at Schiphol Airport, food parcels came raining down. Small tins of margarine, real butter, biscuits, sausages, bacon, chocolate, cheese, and egg powder. Airplanes flew over us quite low, and for the first time their drone caused no tightening at the throat. People ran up onto the rooftops and waved anything they could get their hands on—flags, bed sheets.

On Saturday morning, everybody seemed to be out on the streets as I went to my office. In spite of the news and the festivity, it was still quite dangerous. The Germans were beside themselves with anger. I heard that at the Dam Square, across from the old Hotel Krasnapolsky, the German soldiers had gone berserk and begun shooting into the crowd, killing quite a few people. But nothing stopped the celebrating. People continued to make fires and dance.

After work, I came home and said to Henk, "Come, Henk. Let's join the celebration." I pulled on his arm.

He shook his head. "No," he said. "I'll stay here. I don't feel like joining in the jubilation in the streets. Too much," he continued, "has happened in my country in these five years. Too many people have been taken away. Who knows how many will never return? Yes, I'm happy it's over, but I want to stay in and be quiet."

I took down the blackout curtains. For the first night in five years, we could look outside and see the moon.

We heard that the German soldiers were assembling in various parts of Holland and then leaving. Suddenly, they were gone. More Allied planes came and dropped more food parcels. There was the feeling everywhere that a miracle had happened. We waited for the announcement that the dropped food would be distributed.

On the seventh of May we had a day off. Shouts rang out in the street that the Canadians were coming. I threw my apron down onto a chair and again ran out with everyone else from our neighborhood to wait for the liberators on Rijnstraat. People said they were coming "right away," but we waited and waited, and they did not come.

Finally, after three hours of waiting, we saw four small Canadian tanks cross the Amstel over the Berlage Bridge. After a short stop, they rode farther into town. The soldiers wore berets. Their uniforms were light brown short jackets and trousers which were pulled tight at the ankles.

The main force of the Canadian Army arrived on the eighth of May. This lasted the whole day. They came in many columns, but Henk and I had gone to our offices and couldn't watch the parade. We heard from our friends that the soldiers were very, very grubby. Nonetheless, the girls kissed them on their dirty faces. The Canadians waved, and gave out the first real cigarettes anyone had seen in years.

They marched into South Amsterdam, and continued on toward the Dam Square and the Royal Palace. Queen Wilhelmina had already returned to her beloved Holland, now devastated and almost starved. Our Queen was sixty-four years old now, the short, stout lady whom Churchill had called "the bravest man in England." Like our country, she had endured.

THE CELEBRATIONS continued for days. The Canadian and Dutch national anthems were played again and again. There were music and dancing in the streets; a barrel organ that had been found somewhere, old accordions played—anything that made music. Right away, people planted marigold seeds, so that the color that the Germans had forbidden, orange, the color of our Royal House, would grow.

People who had been in hiding came out onto the streets. Jews came out of hiding places, rubbing eyes that were unused to sunlight, their faces yellow and pinched and distrustful.

Church bells rang everywhere; streamers flew.

The liberators had brought us new Dutch bank notes which had been printed in England. All currency was wildly inflated, and there was nothing in the shops to buy.

To wake up and go through a whole day without any sense of danger was amazing. And right away, Henk and I and everyone else began waiting to see just who would be coming home to us.

Shocking, unimaginable accounts circulated of the liberation of the German concentration camps. Pictures were printed in the first free newspapers; eyewitness information, too. Through the occupation we'd heard rumors of gassings, murder, brutality, poor living conditions in these camps, but none of us could have imagined such atrocities. The facts had far surpassed even our most pessimistic imaginings. I couldn't read the stories and turned away from the photos. I couldn't allow myself to think about these reports. I needed to do everything I could to keep my optimism about our friends. It would have been unbearable to think otherwise.

Quickly, short-term repairs were begun—boards put across empty windows, bridges and tracks repaired in order that trains might run again. Everything was needed, but no one had anything.

Henk was assigned to the Centraal Station to greet returning people and provide them with referrals for help—help with money, ration cards, housing. He went every day and sat at a desk. People came back on military trucks, and then trains when some routes were returned to service.

Jews and others who had spent years as slaves of the Nazis had awaited their return to a liberated Holland. Now they began to come back, their faces shriveled so that it was impossible to tell their ages.

Jews from the camps all had blue numbers tattooed on their arms. Children who no longer knew their birthdays and names could not recognize their families because they had been separated for so long.

Some of those who straggled back to our River Quarter found other people living in their apartments. Others managed to get their apartment back because an NSBer had fled from it. Slowly, a small trickle of Jews began to return to our quarter. Lists of survivors of the concentration camps were posted daily.

I heard it said that where the Jews had looked like everyone else before, now, after what they had endured, those who returned looked different. But people hardly noticed because everyone had been through so much misery that no one had much interest in the suffering of others.

Every day Henk sat at his desk at the Centraal Station and processed people. To everyone he would ask, "Have you heard anything about Otto Frank?" or, "Have you seen Otto Frank and his wife, Edith Frank, or anything of their daughters, Margot Frank and Anne Frank?"

And always the head would shake, "No," and the next would shake, "No." Each, in turn, would know nothing of our friends.

•

A FEW DAYS after the liberation, I was at work in the office when suddenly the electricity went back on. Click, just like that, we had electric light again.

Right away, we learned that Victor Kraler was alive, that in fact, he had escaped from the hands of the Germans and had been in hiding in his own home through the final days of the Hunger Winter, cared for by his wife. When he came back to the office, he told us about his escape:

"Most of the people in the Amersfoort camp where we were first sent were political prisoners of one sort or another, black marketeers, Christians who had hidden Jews. I was transferred from Amersfoort concentration camp to various forced labor camps, the last one quite close to the German border. One morning in winter, the camp was called to a roll call. Then a whole group of Dutchmen was marched out of the camp.

"I said to myself, I'll drop behind the group, and did, falling into step with some old German soldiers. These men were old and tired, and had had enough of the war. I thought, I'll talk to them in German and find out where we're all going. So I asked, and they said, 'We're going to walk to Germany. We're moving the whole camp to Germany.'

"I thought, Before I know it, I'll be in Hitler's Germany. I'll never be able to get out of there. So I began to drop behind again.

"Suddenly, out of nowhere, Spitfire planes appeared and started to dive down and strafe the area. The guards were yelling out, 'Lie down! Hit the dirt!' We were beside a cornfield. I jumped down into the field, and the attack went on, the fighters strafing the entire area.

"Finally, the planes flew away and the guards shouted, 'Up! March! Into position!' But I stayed where I was, hidden in the corn, holding my breath. And believe it or not, they marched off leaving me alone in the cornfield.

"I waited awhile, then crawled the opposite way in the corn. Finally, I felt safe and stood up and walked out of the field. I started to walk, and very soon came to a small country village. I began to get very nervous, as I was still wearing my prison uniform.

"At the edge of the village was a bicycle place. I thought, Better take a chance, and went inside. There was a Dutchman in the shop. I told him that I had just escaped from a prison camp. 'Can I have a bicycle?' I asked. 'I want to go home.'

"The man looked me over, then went to the back of the shop and pushed out an old but sturdy black bicycle. 'Here,' he said, pushing it toward me, 'go home. After the war you can return the bicycle.'

"I pedaled home, and my wife hid me through the Hunger Winter until now."

WITHIN A FEW weeks, goods began to appear in shopwindows—a winter coat, a pretty dress; but only in the windows. Nothing was for sale in the shops. A sign in the window of the shop would say FOR DISPLAY ONLY. Other shops showed cardboard imitations of milk bottles, cheese, and packets of good Dutch butter.

I heard that groups of Dutch children were being organized by the Allies for health holidays in Britain. These children were in such states of distress that something extraordinary was needed to build them up quickly.

Just as I had been sent from Vienna to Holland in 1920 as a hungry child with a tag around my neck, these Dutch children were put on ships in 1945 and sent across the North Sea to England for nourishment.

Day after day, Henk went to the Centraal Station and gave vouchers to returning Dutchmen, most of whom had lost everything and had either lost or been separated from their families.

Day after day, he would ask, "Do you know Otto Frank? Have you seen the Frank family—Otto, Frank, Margot, and Anne?" And day after day, head after head would shake, "No." Or, "No, I have not seen or heard of these people."

Undaunted by this, Henk would ask the next person, and the next, "Do you know the Franks?" Always expecting one more ravaged head to shake, he finally heard a voice reply to his question, "Mister, I have seen Otto Frank, and he is coming back!"

Henk flew home that day to tell me. It was June 3, 1945. He ran into the living room and grabbed me. "Miep, Otto Frank is coming back!"

My heart took flight. Deep down I'd always known that he would, that the others would, too.

Just then, my eye caught sight of a figure passing outside our window. My throat closed. I ran outside.

There was Mr. Frank himself, walking toward our door.

We looked at each other. There were no words. He was thin, but he'd always been thin. He carried a little bundle. My eyes swam. My heart melted. Suddenly, I was afraid to know more. I didn't want to know what had happened. I knew I would not ask.

We stood facing each other, speechless. Finally, Frank spoke.

"Miep," he said quietly. "Miep, Edith is not coming back."

My throat was pierced. I tried to hide my reaction to his thunderbolt. "Come inside," I insisted.

He went on. "But I have great hope for Margot and Anne."

"Yes. Great hope," I echoed encouragingly. "Come inside."

He still stood there. "Miep, I came here because you and Henk are the ones closest to me who are still here."

I grabbed his bundle from his hand. "Come, you stay right here with us. Now, some food. You have a room here with us for as long as you want."

He came inside. I made up a bedroom for him, and put every-thing we had into a fine meal for him. We ate. Mr. Frank told us he had ended up in Auschwitz. That was the last time he'd seen Edith, Margot, and Anne. The men had been separated from the women immediately. When the Russians liberated the camp in January, he had been taken on a very long trip to Odessa. Then from there to Marseille by ship, and at last, by train and truck to Holland.

He told us these few things in his soft voice. He spoke very little, but between us there was no need for words.

MR. FRANK settled in with Henk and me. Right away, he came back to the office and took his place again as the head of the busi-ness. I know he was relieved to have something to do each day. Meanwhile, he began exploring the network of information on Jews in the camps—the refugee agencies, the daily lists, the most crucial word-of-mouth information—trying everything to get news about Margot and Anne.

When Auschwitz was liberated, Otto Frank had gone right away to the women's camp to find out about his wife and children. In the chaos and desolation of the camps, he had learned that Edith had died shortly before the liberation.

He had also learned that in all likelihood, Margot and Anne had been transferred to another camp, along with Mrs. van Daan. The camp was called Bergen-Belsen, and was quite a distance from Auschwitz. That was as far as his trail had gone so far, though. Now he was trying to pick up the search.

As to the other men, Mr. Frank had lost track of Albert Dus-sel. He had no idea what had happened to him after he was trans-ferred from Auschwitz. He had seen with his own eyes Mr. van Daan on his way to be gassed. And Peter van Daan had come to visit Frank in the Auschwitz infirmary. Mr. Frank knew that right before the liberation of the camp, the Germans had taken groups of prisoners with them in their retreat. Peter had been in one of these groups.

Otto Frank had begged Peter to try to get into the infirmary himself, but Peter couldn't or wouldn't. He had last been seen going off with the retreating Germans into the snow-covered countryside. There was no further news about him.

Mr. Frank held high hopes for the girls, because Bergen-Belsen was not a death camp. There were no gassings there. It was a work camp—filled with hunger and disease, but with no apparatus for liquidation. Because Margot and Anne had been sent to the camp later than most other inmates they were relatively healthy. I too lived on hope for Margot and Anne. In some deep part of me, like a rock, I counted on their survival and their safe return to Amsterdam.

Mr. Frank had written for news to several Dutch people who he had learned had been in Bergen-Belsen. Through word of mouth people were being reunited every day. Daily, he waited for answers to his letters and for the new lists of survivors to be released and posted. Every time there was a knock at the door or footfalls on the steps, all our hearts would stand still. Perhaps Margot and Anne had found their way back home, and we could see them with our own eyes at last. Anne's sixteenth birthday was coming on June 12. Perhaps, we hoped, . . . but then the birthday came and went, and still no news.

Mrs. Samson returned to Hunzestraat. She moved back into her room. Her granddaughter had died of diphtheria in hiding in Utrecht, but her little grandson was alive. So far, Mrs. Samson had had no news of her daughter and son-in-law, who had disappeared that day at the Centraal Station. Nothing had yet been heard from her husband, reputed to be in England. She too was in a limbo of waiting for news.

Our vegetable man came back from the camp with frozen feet. I saw him back in his shop, and we greeted each other like long-lost friends.

Still, the shops were almost empty; we lived on rations. But reconstruction and renewal were in the works. Our spice company sold mostly *ersatz* goods, but business trickled in, keeping the company going.

One morning, Mr. Frank and I were alone in the office, opening mail. He was standing beside me, and I was sitting at my desk. I was vaguely aware of the sound of a letter being slit open. Then, a moment of silence. Something made me look away from my mail. Then, Otto Frank's voice, toneless, totally crushed: "Miep."

My eyes looked up at him, seeking out his eyes.

"Miep." He gripped a sheet of paper in both his hands. "I've gotten a letter from the nurse in Rotterdam. Miep, Margot and Anne are not coming back."

We stayed there like that, both struck by lightning, burnt thoroughly through our hearts, our eyes fixed on each other's. Then Mr. Frank walked toward his office and said in that defeated voice, "I'll be in my office."

I heard him walk across the room and down the hall, and the door closed.

I sat at my desk utterly crushed. Everything that had happened before, I could somehow accept. Like it or not, I had to accept it. But this, I could not accept. It was the one thing I'd been sure would not happen.

I heard the others coming into the office. I heard a door opening and a voice chattering. Then, good-morning greetings and coffee cups. I reached into the drawer on the side of my desk and took out the papers that had been waiting there for Anne for nearly a year now. No one, including me, had touched them. Now Anne was not coming back for her diary.

I took out all the papers, placing the little red-orange checkered diary on top, and carried everything into Mr. Frank's office.

Frank was sitting at his desk, his eyes murky with shock. I held out the diary and the papers to him. I said, "Here is your daughter Anne's legacy to you."

I could tell that he recognized the diary. He had given it to her just over three years before, on her thirteenth birthday, right before going into hiding. He touched it with the tips of his fingers. I pressed everything into his hands; then I left his office, closing the door quietly.

Shortly afterward, the phone on my desk rang. It was Mr. Frank's voice. "Miep, please see to it that I'm not disturbed," he said.

"I've already done that," I replied.

# CHAPTER EIGHTEEN

ONCE MR. FRANK had really settled in with us, he said to me, "Miep, now you must call me Otto. Now we are family."

I agreed to call him Otto, but not wanting to set a bad example for the others at work, I told him, "At home I'll call you Otto, but at the office I insist on calling you Mr. Frank."

"It's not necessary," he said.

"I insist."

Soon afterward, because small differences had developed between Mrs. Samson and us, the situation was no longer comfortable for us living there. We felt it was best to move. Henk's sister, Fenna, lived farther up our street. She offered rooms to us, and to Mr. Frank as well, so together we moved.

Mr. Frank was given a small room in the back with a washstand, and Henk and I had Fenna's bedroom. Fenna slept in the living room. We were lucky to make this arrangement, as housing in Amsterdam was very, very scarce. Of course, Berry came too.

The shops were still empty; anything but the barest essentials was impossible to come by. After so many years of nothing, we had almost gotten used to this. The whole last year of the war, Henk had not smoked very much. Now sometimes there were Canadian Sweet Caporals on the black market, and sometimes not. When there were cigarettes, Henk smoked.

I made our home as cozy as I could, and cooked meals for all of us from whatever I could scrape up. It was impossible to make interesting meals, as all the ingredients we had were basics, with no variety. But I had acquired a knack for making the best of little, and I kept everyone reasonably well fed and our home nice and cozy.

All of us were weak, depleted, slow-blooded. I had no reserve of energy anymore, but fortunately, I no longer needed great strength and energy. None of us was much for conversation, but our common memories kept us bonded together.

Slowly, our railways and bridges and dikes were being rebuilt. Otto told me that before they had gone into hiding, he had managed to place some of Edith's furniture from the Merwedeplein with friends. He had found that his possessions had been safe throughout the war, and now he would move them in with us.

The day arrived, and I saw the big grandfather clock that had come all the way from Frankfurt in 1933, the clock that needed to be wound every few weeks and ticked with the softest of heartbeats. I saw the small, delicate antique secretary, veneered with mahogany, carried through the room. Otto Frank said to me, "Edith would have been happy to know that you are using these things."

Then, Frank showed me the charcoal drawing of the sweet, big cat nursing its little kittens that had so touched me years earlier. He presented everything to me.

This charcoal particularly brought back so clearly the days of the Saturday get-togethers on the Merwedeplein. The days of passionate political talk, rich cakes, and good coffee; of sweet, shy

Anne, so small then, coming out with pretty Margot to greet the adults and have a piece of cake. Anne would hold her cat, Moortje, in her arms, and she would dangle down nearly to the floor, almost too heavy for a small girl to hold.

Quickly, I put these thoughts aside. I wanted not to think about what had been before.

One day, two bicycles arrived for Mr. Frank from friends of his in England. "Miep," Frank told me, pushing a sleek, shiny new English bicycle toward me. "One for you and one for me." I took it. I had never before in my life had a brand-new bicycle. No one in the neighborhood had anything new. I imagine that they eyed our new bicycles jealously.

Another package arrived for Mr. Frank. This one bore elaborate labels from America, from friends who had safely spent the war there. Otto opened the package carefully. We both looked at the contents spread across the table.

There were tins, and American cigarettes, and several small packets. Frank suggested I open them and take a look at what there was. The first I opened sent an aroma of cocoa up into my face. It was overwhelming. I felt the texture, so soft and powdery, the color so dark brown.

Seeing it and smelling the cocoa, I began to cry.

Otto said, "Take it, make it."

I couldn't stop crying. It was unbelievable to me that I was seeing real cocoa again.

THE FINAL LISTS of Jewish survivors were posted by the Red Cross. Of those who had been deported by the Germans, very few had returned to the Netherlands—not even one in twenty. Of those who had gone into hiding, at least one-third had survived. All those who had survived had lost just about everything.

Mr. Frank's lodger, the man Henk and I had played our charade with, had been deported to the camps. But he had survived and come back. The older man who had asked us to keep his beautiful Shakespeare had not come back. So the book remained on our shelves, just in case he ever returned. Neither had my upstairs neighbor come back, the lady who had asked us to care for her cat, Berry. So Berry lived on with us.

Slowly, bit by bit, we learned that Albert Dussel had died in the Neuengamme camp. That Petronella van Daan had died either in Buchenwald or in Theresienstadt on the day it was liberated. That Peter van Daan hadn't died on the death march away from Auschwitz, but had somehow survived it and been placed in Mauthausen, only to die there on the very day that the camp was liberated by the Americans.

Through information gathered from eyewitness survivors, we learned that Margot and Anne had been separated at Auschwitz from their mother, Edith Frank, who had spent the last weeks of her life there alone. Margot and Anne had been transferred to Bergen-Belsen, where they had been relatively healthy at first, but then, in the early months of 1945, had both fallen ill with typhus. In February or March, Margot had succumbed, and then Anne, totally alone, had succumbed to typhus as well, just a few short weeks before the liberation of the camp.

Even though the final lists of survivors had been posted, there were many displaced persons, and borders were not what they had been, so there was no way to know for sure the fate of many others who did not return. For some, it was possible to not give up hope.

Never once did we hear from Karel van der Hart after the war, but we heard somewhere that he'd gone to America.

In the evenings, after Henk, Otto, and I had returned from our offices and I'd fixed our evening meal, Otto began to translate bits of Anne's diary into German for his mother, who lived in Basel. Mr. Frank would include these translations with his letters to her.

Sometimes he'd come walking out of his room holding Anne's little diary and shaking his head. He'd say to me, "Miep, you should
hear this description that Anne wrote here! Who'd have imagined
how vivid her imagination was all the while?"

But when he would ask me to listen to what she'd written, I'd
have to say no. I could not bring myself to listen. It was much too
upsetting to me.

Because of Frits van Matto's unsympathetic personality, Jo
Koophuis and Otto Frank gently nudged him out of the business.
They didn't fire him, but they persuaded him that he might have
more of a future elsewhere. New warehousemen were hired.

Nineteen forty-six came and still we stayed poor; still there
was nothing.

On the fifteenth of May, 1946, Elli Vossen got married and
left the Prinsengracht. A young man was hired to take Elli's place.
Coming as she did from a big family, six sisters and one brother,
Elli had always dreamed of having a big family of her own. Right
away, she was pregnant, and very happy that her lifelong dream was
so quickly starting to come true.

I was now past my middle thirties. My childbearing years were
quickly passing. My own dream of motherhood had greatly changed
because of what had happened in Holland. I was glad no child of
ours had had to endure the terrible war years. After the war we did
not bring up the subject of having children.

I also had a great deal of trouble believing anymore in the
existence of God. When I'd been a little girl in Vienna, my parents
had been practicing Catholics. They took me to church a few times,
but I didn't like it. I was such a little girl—maybe three, four, or
five—I didn't really understand what was going on in the service,
but I felt affected by the darkness of the huge church, and by its
enormous size and the cold I felt inside. My aversion to church
made me beg to be excused from attending. My parents didn't insist that I go. So I never went back.

When I came to Leiden, my adoptive family never made me go to church either, so as I grew up, I didn't conform to any religion. Always, though, I never doubted the existence of God. That is, until the war. Then, by the time the war was finished, my sense of God had been poisoned and only an empty hole was left.

Henk had been a nonbeliever before and throughout the war, and he continued that way.

But I had a craving to read on the subject, and I began to read the Old Testament. Then I read the New Testament. Then, with deep interest, I read studies of many different religions: books on Judaism, books on Catholicism, Protestantism, anything I could lay my hands on.

I never spoke about my reading to anyone. I just read and read. Everything I read was rich and interesting, yet I was always hungry for more. The dark years had pulled down my inner supports, and I was looking for something to replace them.

ALTHOUGH A SLOW reconstruction and renewal was taking place, we Dutch continued to harbor a deep and strong feeling of hatred for the suffering we'd been made to endure at the hands of our savage German oppressors. For five solid years we'd been without contact with the outside world. We'd been utterly humiliated, brought to our knees; the lives of good, innocent people had been interrupted and destroyed. We felt no stirrings of forgiveness.

In 1946, Queen Wilhelmina called our first national elections. Anton Mussert, the head of the Dutch NSB, was executed by a firing squad in The Hague, and Arthur Seyss-Inquart, the Nazi Reichskommissar of the Netherlands, was hanged after a trial at Nürnberg. People argued back and forth about what was "right" in wartime and what was "wrong." Many traitors were punished. But somehow, revenge and justice brought little satisfaction.

In December of 1946, we decided to move into another apartment in our quarter. We'd stayed much too long with Henk's sister on Hunzestraat. Henk and I had a friend whose wife had recently died, a Mr. van Caspel. He had a large apartment to himself and a small daughter, a girl of nine, away in boarding school. He invited us to share his rooms.

Henk and I discussed the situation with Otto. Otto said that if it was all right, he'd like to move along with us to this apartment. Naturally, we said he'd be very welcome to stay with us, but we knew that he had so many friends and contacts that he could probably find better lodgings than what we had found.

"I prefer staying with you, Miep," he explained. "That way I can talk to you about my family if I want."

In fact, Mr. Frank rarely talked about them, but I understood what he meant. He could talk about his family if he wanted to. And if he didn't want to, in silence we all shared the same sorrow and memories.

So OTTO, HENK, AND I moved to Jekerstraat 65 together as 1947 began. Henk had begun to have a headache every day, a blinding headache. Not one to complain about himself, he said little about these headaches and did his best to go on about his daily business.

Every Saturday night, Henk and I, Mrs. Dussel, and several other friends would gather and play canasta together. Mr. Frank never played with us. But he had begun to have small gatherings of friends for coffee on Sundays. These were all Jews who had survived untold suffering. They'd come together on Sunday afternoons, asking one another, "Who's left in your family?" or "Did your wife come back?" or "What about your children? Your parents?" They'd exchange information about where they'd been—Auschwitz, Sobibor—facts about transports, dates; but never about what had happened to them personally. I could see that it was too difficult to talk about many things, and when they were together, it was not necessary.

At one of these Sunday get-togethers Frank mentioned that he had a diary written by his daughter Anne. One of the men at the gathering asked Frank if he might read it. Mr. Frank was reluctant, but gave the man some of the bits that he had translated for his mother in Basel, the sections that he'd been unsuccessfully trying for more than a year to get me to read.

After he'd read the excerpts, this man asked Frank if he might read the whole diary, that he was very much impressed with the excerpts and had a great curiosity to read more. Again with great reluctance, Mr. Frank gave him more to read.

Then the man asked Frank for permission to show the diary to a friend of his, a well-known historian. Frank was against it, but his friend cajoled and cajoled, and finally Frank said yes.

After he had read Anne's diary, the historian wrote an article about it for the Dutch newspaper *Het Parool*, which was now thriving, but had started as an underground paper during the war. The historian began a campaign to get Mr. Frank to allow Anne's diary to be published. Frank was very much against such a thing, and was adamant in his refusal. The historian and his friend eventually persuaded Otto Frank. They said that it was Frank's duty to share Anne's story with others, that her diary was a war document and very important because it expressed a unique voice of a young person in hiding.

So much persuasion began to make Frank feel that it was his duty to forgo his own sense of invaded privacy. Finally, although very reluctant, Frank agreed to allow a small, edited edition to be printed by Contact Publishers in Amsterdam. It was printed with the title *Het Achterhuis* ("*The Annex*"). Again and again, after it was published, Otto would ask me to read Anne's writing, but I continued to refuse. I simply could not bring myself to do it.

The printing of *Het Achterhuis*, which was Anne's name for the hiding place, was praised in some quarters, but there was indif-

ference on the part of many people who had lived through such unpleasant situations themselves. The last thing they wanted was to
read about such experiences. No one in Holland had had an easy
time during the war. Most people had suffered immeasurably. Most
people wanted to forget the war, to put it behind them and move on.

Nonetheless, Anne's diary was reprinted and gathered a wider
audience. Always Otto would tell me, "Miep, you must read it."
But always I couldn't. I couldn't relive the miseries, and I wouldn't
rekindle the terrible losses.

Henk too declined to read Anne's words.

AT LAST, food supplies, though still sparse, were being restored.
Again healthy, fat Dutch cows grazed in the countryside. The trains
began to run again, and the Amsterdam streetcars as well. Rubble
had been cleared away.

During the occupation, there had been just two kinds of
Dutch people: those who collaborated and those who resisted. Political and religious and class differences had been forgotten. It was
simply we Dutch against our German oppressor.

After the liberation, the unity quickly disappeared and people
again divided into groups and factions that were at odds with each
other. Everyone returned to his old ways, to his own class, to his
own political group. People had changed less than I would have
thought.

Many who had moved into the Jewish apartments in South
Amsterdam had stayed on. The neighborhood no longer had a
Jewish flavor. In fact, there was not much in common among people in the neighborhood anymore. It had lost its distinctive progressive atmosphere. It would never be the same as before. Amsterdam was changed too, a modern city rather than the friendly town
it had been.

With three grown men now at home—Henk, Otto, and Mr.

van Caspel—there was much I needed to do to care for them properly. Sometimes Van Caspel's daughter would come to spend a weekend with us. It was important to me that our home be clean and tidy and meals always be served on time. Mending needed to be done, and washing. And everyone needed a ready ear for listening.

At the office, real products were again for sale. The business had never ceased to function at any time. Since his return, Otto Frank had become once more the slightly nervous, soft-spoken man he'd been before the hiding time. The change that had taken place when he'd gone into hiding, the calm, authoritative personality he'd assumed, had vanished.

But Frank's interest in the business seemed to be waning. Since the publication of Anne's diary, letters had begun to come to him from children and adults. Conscientiously, Mr. Frank answered each letter. His office on the Prinsengracht became the place where he conducted matters pertaining to Anne's diary.

Then on a beautiful, warm day in 1947, I rode my bicycle to the Prinsengracht for the last time. Quietly, I said goodbye to everyone. I had given notice that I would no longer be employed by the firm. I was now fully responsible for the care of three men. I had decided that the care of these men and our home was now my full-time job. I was no longer the young girl longing for the freedom and independence that a job would give. Nothing in Amsterdam was as it had been before, and neither was I.

The second printing of the diary sold out and another printing was planned. Mr. Frank was approached with the idea of permitting the diary to be translated and published abroad. He was against it at first, but then he succumbed to the pressure on him to allow the diary a more widespread audience.

Again and again, he'd say to me, "Miep, you must read Anne's writing. Who would have imagined what went on in her quick little mind?" Otto was never discouraged by my continuing refusal. He would always wait awhile and then ask me again.

Finally, I gave in to his insistence. I said, "All right, I will read the diary, but only when I'm totally alone."

The next time I was totally alone, on a warm day, I took the second printing of the diary, went to my room, and shut the door.

With awful fear in my heart, I opened the book and turned to the first page.

And so I began to read.

I read the whole diary without stopping. From the first word, I heard Anne's voice come back to speak to me from where she had gone. I lost track of time. Anne's voice tumbled out of the book, so full of life, moods, curiosity, feelings. She was no longer gone and destroyed. She was alive again in my mind.

I read to the very end. I was surprised by how much had happened in hiding that I'd known nothing about. Immediately, I was thankful that I hadn't read the diary after the arrest, during the final nine months of the occupation, while it had stayed in my desk drawer right beside me every day. Had I read it, I would have had to burn the diary because it would have been too dangerous for people about whom Anne had written.

When I had read the last word, I didn't feel the pain I'd anticipated. I was glad I'd read it at last. The emptiness in my heart was eased. So much had been lost, but now Anne's voice would never be lost. My young friend had left a remarkable legacy to the world.

But always, every day of my life, I've wished that things had been different. That even had Anne's diary been lost to the world, Anne and the others might somehow have been saved.

Not a day goes by that I do not grieve for them.

# EPILOGUE

In 1948, Queen Wilhelmina abdicated in favor of her daughter, Juliana. Her half-century reign ended. Henk won a Dutch lottery that year, and we were able to get away from Holland for a short vacation in Grindelwald, Switzerland. Otto Frank came with us. For the first time since the war he saw his old mother in Basel. During the first half of 1948, Henk's terrible headaches, which had lasted an entire year, began to lessen in intensity. During our holiday in Switzerland the headaches ceased entirely, and they never returned.

After Anne's diary was translated into English and published in America and elsewhere, it quickly became a great success. Other translations were made, and everywhere around the world people read Anne's story. A play was based on the diary, which fictionalized and dramatized the story and the characters. The play was a spectacular success. In Amsterdam the first performance was on November 27, 1956. Elli and her husband, Jo Koophuis and his wife, and Henk and I were all invited. Victor Kraler had emigrated to Canada the previous year. For me, it was a very strange experi-

ence to see the play. I kept looking for my real friends to come on-
stage and not actors and actresses.

Then a movie was made. The premiere of the movie at the
City Theater in Amsterdam was on April 16, 1959. All of us were
again invited. Queen Juliana and her daughter Crown Princess
Beatrix were present. Mrs. Koophuis, Elli, and I were presented to
them. As far as I know, Otto Frank never saw the play or the
movie. He did not want to.

Everywhere, great attention was paid to the diary. Mr. Frank
had not become the director of the company again after the war.
More and more of his time was spent dealing with matters pertaining to the diary. Finally, the company moved to a new address and
Mr. Frank had no more association with the business. Mr. Koophuis
remained as director until he died in 1959. Mr. Kraler lived in Canada until his death in 1981. Once Elli was married and having children, she put her early life at the office behind her. Her memories
of those youthful years grew vague, and she was totally wrapped up
in her life as a mother and wife until her death in 1983.

Once Otto Frank was no longer associated with the business,
he gave his full attention to the diary. Anne Frank had become famous everywhere. As Mr. Frank and anything or anyone related to
Anne gained more and more publicity, Henk and I withdrew. Neither of us liked receiving special attention. We preferred anonymity
and privacy.

Then in 1949 a great event occurred. At the age of forty, I became pregnant. On July 13, 1950, our son Paul was born. Now our
little household included Otto, Mr. van Caspel, Henk, me, and our
little Paul.

While I was in the hospital having Paul, Mrs. Samson, our
former landlady, came to visit me. Her husband had returned from
England.

By 1950, things began to return to normal in Amsterdam.

Food was not a problem anymore, but never could I throw out left-over food. Even if a potato was bad, or a crust of bread had turned black, I'd find some use for it, like tossing it out for the birds. Sometimes along the canals in Amsterdam, a German tourist would now be seen showing his wife or sweetheart around. He'd tell her, "This is where I was stationed during the war."

In the fall of 1952, after living with us for seven years, Mr. Frank emigrated to Switzerland to be near his mother. He remarried in November of 1953 in Amsterdam and took his new wife with him to Basel. His wife had experienced a similar fate. She had been in Auschwitz too, and had lost all her family except one daughter. Mr. Frank had found an extraordinary woman. He and she had much in common and lived in harmony together until his death in 1980. Never once in all the years did Mr. Frank forget to call us on our wedding anniversary, July 16.

Although never a day goes by that I do not think about what happened, there are two days that are always particularly hard for us. On the 4th of May, the official Dutch day of mourning, we never go out. Many people go to church, the Queen included. Some lay flowers on the places where Dutch Resistance Fighters were executed or burned. There is a commemoration ceremony at Dam Square where the Queen and her husband lay a wreath at the foot of the National Monument. At 8 P.M. sharp, all the streetlights are lit. Trains and streetcars stop; cars stop, bicycles stop. People stand still. Most people go outside when the lights go on. Funeral music is played, then the Dutch national anthem. All the flags are at half-mast all day. Everyone stays quite silent.

The other terrible day is August 4, the day of the arrest. On that day too, Henk and I stay at home all day. We act as though the day were not happening. Neither of us will look at a clock all day. I stand at the window all through the day, and Henk, on purpose, sits with his back to the window. When we sense that it's about five o'clock, that the day has passed, we experience a sense of relief that the day is finished.

In 1948, the Dutch police made an investigation into the betrayal of our friends in hiding. According to police records, someone *had* betrayed our friends. No name was recorded on the written report, just that a person had received 7½ guilders per Jew—that is, a total of 60 guilders. We knew that our friends had to have been betrayed. Some had suspicions as to who the betrayer was. But Henk and I did not know. Mr. Frank was the only one who could have done something. He chose not to.

Another investigation took place in 1963 because the diary had reached such a level of international renown. There came a public outcry to punish the betrayer of our innocent friends.

I received a telephone call from the police that they would like to come and interview me concerning the arrest on that day long ago, August 4, 1944. It was a terrible moment for me when the policeman on the phone told me, "You are one of the suspected people, Mrs. Gies, because you were born in Vienna."

I said, "Come and speak to me whenever you want."

He came to our apartment. Henk and I spoke with the policeman together. It was chilly that day, and we had a coal fire burning. The fire was burning low, and Henk went out to fetch some more coal.

As soon as he was gone, the policeman leaned close to me and said, "We don't want to disturb your marriage, Mrs. Gies. Please come tomorrow at nine o'clock to see us. Alone."

I must have looked oddly at him, because he continued, "Mr. van Matto told us in our interview with him that you had a . . . how shall I say? . . . an 'intimate' . . . uh, 'friendly' relationship with a man high in the Gestapo. And that you also had a 'friendly' relationship with Mr. Koophuis."

The blood must have drained from my face. I could feel my blood pressure shoot up. I told him, "I won't reply to these charges. When my husband comes back, please say to him exactly what you've just said to me."

I could see that he wasn't pleased about this. We sat there across the room from each other. Henk came back with more coal. He fed the fire and sat down. Then the policeman said to Henk, "Mr. van Matto told us in our interview with him that your wife had a 'friendly relationship' with a man high in the Gestapo, and also that she had a 'friendly relationship' with Mr. Koophuis. What do you say to this?"

Henk turned to me and said, "I take my hat off to you, Miep. I don't know when you could have conducted all these 'friendly relationships.' In the morning, you and I left together to go to our offices. Every day we had lunch together at your office. During the evening you were always with me—"

The policeman cut him off. "All right, stop."

He then asked whether I thought Frits van Matto was the betrayer.

I told him, "I'm convinced he's not."

He asked whether I knew that others suspected Van Matto and that Anne herself in the diary writes about the distrust toward him of the people in hiding.

I again told him that I didn't think it was Van Matto.

A few weeks later, the same policeman told me, "I'm going to Vienna to see Silberbauer, the Green Police officer, to ask him if he remembers who the betrayer was. At the same time, I'm going to ask him why he let you go when the others were sent to camps."

"Good," I said. "When you come back, I'd appreciate it if you'd tell me what he says."

When the policeman returned from Vienna, he came again to see me. He told me that when he'd asked Silberbauer why he'd let me go, Silberbauer had replied, "She was such a nice girl." As for the betrayer, he'd said, "I don't remember. There were so many betrayals during those years."

Silberbauer had become a policeman in Vienna. Because of his Nazi activities, he had been suspended from his job for one year. The year had passed and he was again working on the police force.

The policeman also told me that when he'd spoken again to Frits van Matto, who remained the strongest suspect, although there was no proof, he had told Van Matto that notwithstanding the bad things he'd told the police about Miep, Miep had insisted that he was not the betrayer.

The policeman asked me why I insisted on this. I told him that the reason that I was convinced of it was that during the war one of the agents for our company had confided to me that Van Matto had his own son in hiding at home. I had kept the secret through the war and afterward. Because of this, Henk, Mr. Frank, and I had concluded that despite his unpleasant personality, Van Matto was not the betrayer.

Mr. Frank didn't wish to have a trial on the subject of the betrayer. He simply said, "I don't want to know who did it." Although Van Matto remained the leading suspect by some, others suspected some NSBers who had been living across the garden and might have observed some movement behind the dirty white curtains. Perhaps, as Anne had worried, one of the thieves who had broken into the factory had been the betrayer. Regardless of all the theories through the years, including several totally ridiculous ones, there was never any proof. I'm sure that if the police had had proof, they would have made an arrest.

That same Dutch policeman later told me that when he had gone to Switzerland to interview Mr. Frank on the subject and had mentioned that I was being investigated, Mr. Frank had told him, "If you suspect Miep, you suspect me too."

## Afterword: My 100th Birthday

When those last words in the original epilogue to *Anne Frank Remembered* were written, my husband, Jan (whom Anne called "Henk" in the diary), and I were considered old—my husband in his eighties, me in my late seventies. I could not have known that I would be lucky enough to live to my one-hundredth year. Nor could I have imagined the strangeness I would feel at having outlived almost everyone who shared the terrible times with me, including Jan.

His hat still hangs alongside mine on our hat rack near the front door. His watch is still stretched out on top of the television set. There is an oil painting of him on one wall of my apartment and a painting of Anne on another. There is a framed photo of Otto Frank near the end of his life, along with other photos of family and friends. There are awards I've received and mementos on various surfaces around the apartment.

The pieces of antique furniture given me by Otto Frank that had belonged to Edith remain. They include the large grandfather clock made in Frankfurt long ago that fills an entire wall. Near to the time Jan died, this clock stopped working. So far, no one has been able to repair it.

I am surrounded by memories but live entirely on my own, although my son, Paul, and his wife, Lucie, see to my well-being.

Had Anne Frank lived, she would be celebrating her eightieth birthday a few months after I hope to celebrate my hundredth. No doubt she would be encircled by children and grandchildren, as well as copies of published books and prizes won for writing them. I believe she would have realized her wish to become a celebrated writer.

Although the story I told in this book remains unchanged, I

am surprised by how many new and remarkable facts have been revealed in the twenty years since its publication.

When Otto Frank was preparing the original publication of the *Diary*, he edited it for simplicity and sense, as well as length. He decided to leave out what he thought was too personal or possibly hurtful to anyone still living, or even to some people no longer alive. He believed it would be polite to continue shielding many true identities. Anne had devised pseudonyms when revising the diary with the thought that she might publish parts of it after the war. As I have already explained, I used these pseudonyms too.

This is no longer necessary because that veil of secrecy was lifted when two new and different renditions of Anne's diary were published—*The Critical Edition* and *The Definitive Edition*.

Over the years, attacks against the diary's authenticity have been made by Holocaust deniers and neo-Nazis, people who, for reasons of their own, wish to denigrate it. Sometimes confusion was created by Anne's rewritings, too. The Dutch Institute of War Documentation decided to address these problems and attacks once and for all. This is why all of Anne's collected writings underwent a forensic investigation in order to authenticate them scientifically as her own.

After this was done, *The Diary of Anne Frank: The Critical Edition* was published. *The Critical Edition* includes background information about the Franks, about their arrest and deportation, as well as the details of the forensic investigation that proves when the diary was written and by whom—in other words, that it is genuine. It contains all of Anne's writings that were scattered on the floor of the hiding place during the arrest. I am eternally grateful I was able to preserve them. It explains the rewrites and various changes she made during the latter part of hiding in the hope of publication when the war ended; at the time, it seemed like the war would soon be over and she would be free. This edition is intended for scholars rather than for ordinary readers.

A few years later, the foundation to which Otto Frank willed the diary's copyright decided the time had come to make the diary more complete. What came to be called *The Diary of a Young Girl: The Definitive Edition* was published. This new, expanded edition restores many of Anne's diary writings that were left out of the original publication – 30 percent more. The added material illustrates in greater detail Anne's development as a writer and thinker. It immediately became a bestseller.

Because of the personal nature of some of Anne's remarks, some people greeted the new publications in a sensational way. This was unfortunate because such sensationalizing can easily detract from Anne's ability as a writer, which sparkles just as brightly in these expanded editions as it did in the original version.

Both the definitive and the critical editions use real names, so there is no reason for me to maintain secrecy about identities any longer.

As I mentioned, my husband, whom Anne nicknamed Henk, was actually named Jan. Elli Vossen's real name is Elisabeth Voskuijl. We called her "Bep." Jo Koophuis's real name is Johannes Kleiman. Victor Kraler is Victor Kugler. The van Daans are the van Pelses – Peter, Auguste (or "Gusti"), and Hermann. Dr. Albert Dussel is really Dr. Fritz Pfeffer. Our landlady Mrs. Samson's real name is Stoppelman.

Anne's friend Lies Goosen is really Hannah Goslar. Jopie de Waal is Jacqueline van Maarsen. Mrs. Blik is Sientje Blitz. Mrs. Coenen, daughter of Mrs. Stoppelman, is Mrs. Cohen. The Nieuwenhuis family is the van Nieuwenburg family. Van Caspel is Ab Cauvern. Van Matto is van Marren. The company name Koolen & Co. was actually Gies & Co. Travies N.V. was Opekta Company.

A German journalist named Ernst Schnabel, and then a Dutch filmmaker named, Willy Lindwer, among others, decided to find and interview people whose paths had crossed the Franks' after their arrest. These survivors gave testimony about what happened to the people in hiding between the arrest in August 1944 and the war's end in the spring of 1945. Detailed information, including eyewitness accounts of my friends' suffering and deaths, became known to the world.

I would have preferred not to know many of these details, but I have learned them nonetheless.

After *Anne Frank Remembered* was published in English and Dutch, it was published in eighteen other languages. Jan and I, and our coauthor, Alison Leslie Gold, who has since become a close friend, were amazed. The book sold well and was honored with awards. Letters began to arrive from all over the world. I answered every one of them, so I became very busy.

A film titled *The Attic* was made from our book. It too won awards. Much of the film was made right on the streets of Amsterdam where the real events once happened. When Jan and I were invited to visit the set, we had the eerie experience of watching actors say the same words we had once said on those streets. In fact, the first time I saw the young English actress who was to play Anne I almost fainted because she could have been Anne's twin. Eerie indeed.

We were proud that, though it was only for a movie, even fifty years later building owners in Amsterdam did not want to allow the Nazi swastika flag to be displayed on their walls.

Despite our age, Jan and I did what was asked of us after the book was published. We traveled to many countries and met many Holocaust survivors. When we met with school children in Germany and Austria, some of whom were descendents of Nazis, some said to us, "Our parents won't talk about what happened in the war. Our grandparents won't either. Please tell us what happened."

Because I could speak to them in German, and because I was originally from Vienna—in other words, because I was one of them and not an outsider—I was able to tell them the true story of what happened. I could and did tell details that their parents and grandparents had chosen not to discuss with them.

It was at this moment that Jan and I were truly glad that we had let Alison persuade us to tell our story. We realized that telling the truth of what happened from our perspective was necessary, and that speaking with these schoolchildren was the last important task of our lives.

Soon afterward, what seemed like a tidal wave of interest in Anne Frank, and in us, came flooding in.

The documentary film *Anne Frank Remembered*, whose title seemed to pay homage to our book, won an Academy Award for best documentary feature. I was invited to attend the ceremony in Hollywood. When the winner was announced, the director and I went onto the stage before an audience that had risen to their feet in an ovation.

It was a great honor, but Anne should have been standing there.

More documentaries were made, more interviews requested. But when Jan became sick, we stopped traveling and declined invitations. On January 26, 1993, he died at home in our bed while I was there with him.

When I was able, I went on alone.

It was a surprise to me when letters written in English by Anne and Margot were put up for auction in America. The owners of the letters were sisters.

In the spring of 1940, wanting to teach her students about a wider world, a teacher in Danville, Iowa, offered her class a chance to become pen pals with children in Europe. The teacher had a list of names and addresses she had collected while traveling. One of her students, Juanita Wagner, age ten, chose someone from the list who was also ten years old and who lived in Amsterdam, Holland.

Juanita later explained that in her letter she wrote about her older sister, her family's farm, and life in America. She mailed the letter and hoped she would receive a reply.

She did.

The postman brought not one but two letters with exotic Dutch stamps written on pale blue stationery. The one addressed to Juanita was signed "Your Dutch friend, Annelies Marie Frank." It was dated "29 April 1940, Monday." In it, Annelies—Anne—described her family, her school, her picture card collection, and her friends. She enclosed a postcard of Amsterdam and a small photo of herself.

The second letter was for Juanita's fourteen-year-old sister, Betty Ann. It was from Anne's older sister, Margot Betti—also fourteen. Margot had written about school, sports, Amsterdam, her family's apartment, and the Dutch weather. When Margot wrote that because of the times in which they lived, and because Holland was such a small country bordering on Germany, her family did not feel safe, the American girls did not realize why.

Juanita later described how she and her sister were overjoyed to have foreign friends and soon wrote back. They waited for replies, but none ever came.

They did not know that less than two weeks after Anne and Margot mailed their letters, Germany attacked Holland and everything changed. They did not understand the danger their pen pals were in because they did not know they were Jewish.

A museum in Los Angeles now has Anne's and Margot's letters to Juanita and Betty Ann on permanent display for all to see.

In recent years, the boyfriend whom Anne wrote about in her diary just before going into hiding was convinced to appear publicly at a few events. Among them was a tribute on what would have been Anne's seventy-fifth birthday. He was Helmuth Silberberg, nicknamed "Hello." Anne never knew that, soon after she went into hiding, Hello and his parents also went into hiding near Brussels. He managed to get a forged identity card and survived.

After the war he went to America, where his name became Ed Silverberg. He is a tall, white-haired, smiling man with a youthful face. I can't imagine that Anne would not still find him attractive. In her diary Anne said that Hello called her a "pep tonic," which I think describes her well.

In this book, I mention the letters and small packages I couriered between Fritz Pfeffer (called Dr. Dussel in the book) and his Frau, Charlotte, called Lotte. Charlotte always assumed that Fritz was in hiding somewhere out in the countryside, and that I was passing along the letters to another courier or someone from the underground. Of course she did not know I was passing them hand-to-hand directly. Because Charlotte was not Jewish she was able to survive the war, living in Amsterdam the whole time. For a time after the war, Charlotte, Otto, Jan, and I played cards together. Charlotte died in 1985.

A few years later, an astonishing discovery was made. A packet of letters and photos was found by someone strolling through the lively flea market on Waterlooplein in Amsterdam. Among them were the love letters between Fritz and Charlotte that I had couriered. The photographs documented the tenderness of their relationship. The photos of Dr. Pfeffer reveal the handsome, cultured man I knew, rather than the buffoon that Anne so unkindly described in her diary.

It is not well known that this unflattering portrayal of Fritz in the diary, and the dramatic license taken by the writers who adapted the diary in order to craft the various plays and films derived from it, caused great unhappiness to our friend Charlotte, as well as sadness for Otto, Jan, and myself over the years. This portrayal, once done, could not be made right, and that broke Charlotte's heart.

Because of the discovery of the love letters in the market and other revelations, it is no longer a secret that before Charlotte and Dr. Pfeffer got together, they had both been married. Both had sons from their first marriages. After we found out that Fritz had died in the Neuengamme concentration camp, we discovered that Lotte's first husband and her son had died in Auschwitz, and that Fritz's former wife had died in the concentration camp Theresienstadt.

We later found out that Dr. Pfeffer's son had survived in England and went to America after the war. He called himself Peter Pepper. For his own reasons, he chose not to ever meet anyone connected to his father—Charlotte, Otto, or me—until 1995, when he decided to meet me. Our charged reunion was filmed for the documentary *Anne Frank Remembered*. It was a remarkable moment when I set eyes on Fritz's son, who, in many ways, resembled his father. We shook hands. Our eyes met. There was no need for him to thank me for trying to help his father, but he did. At that moment, neither of us could have known that he would die only two months later. How strange life can be.

Since the publication of *Anne Frank Remembered* I have received thousands of letters from around the world, mostly from school children who have questions to ask me. I have done my best to answer all of them. When my age began to make this difficult, a Dutchman named Cor Suijk began to visit every few weeks to assist me. Even if he had to drive from Aachen, Germany, or fly from meetings in Omaha, Nebraska, Cor has never failed to show up with a joke and a little news.

In a folder on the table beside me are letters to me written by children and adults in La Barre, France; Palmerston, New Zealand; Omaha, Nebraska; Hobe Sound, Florida; Hannover, Germany; Staffordshire, England; Svenljunga, Sweden; Istanbul, Turkey; Amsterdam, Holland; Jerusalem, Israel; Teresbpolis, Brazil. And more. I cannot rest until they are answered.

Cor Suijk was a close friend of Otto Frank. He had worked with the Dutch Resistance during the war. Although he was only a teenager at the time, he was sent to a concentration camp. He has sometimes told how he witnessed a large raid in Amsterdam and will never forget what he saw and heard. Men were being put on a streetcar by soldiers. Women were calling out the names of their husbands or brothers or sons. Children were calling for their fathers and uncles.

For many years Cor has worked to promote Holocaust education all over the world. He speaks many languages. This has been very useful for his work, and for helping me answer letters I have received from so many different countries.

As it happened, Cor was the source of one of the most unexpected surprises in recent memory. For many years he remained silent about the fact that Otto Frank had given him five original pages from Anne's diary for safekeeping. Cor explained that Mr. Frank had asked him to keep these pages to himself until after the death of Mr. Frank's second wife. When Cor released the news of these previously unimagined pages, the announcement created controversy.

In these pages, Anne muses on very private matters. Her comments have been understood as critical of her parents' marriage. Anne wonders if her father loves her mother as much as her mother loves him. She judges whether or not this love is romantic or unromantic.

We must remember that these are only Anne's opinions. Although her diary shows her maturity and development over the twenty-five months in hiding, she was still essentially a child. It must also be remembered that Mr. and Mrs. Frank and everyone else were living under great tension without any privacy while in hiding. Such circumstances do not seem to me the best in which to judge a marriage.

I knew Mr. and Mrs. Frank as a married couple for ten years. In my opinion, he was always a good husband and father, and she was always a good wife and mother.

In 2007 another discovery was made, this one of a sorrowful nature. A cache of letters in a manila envelope—over eighty letters and documents—was discovered among tens of thousands of scraps and documents in an archive at the Yivo Institute for

Jewish Research in New York. These were urgent letters written by Mr. Frank to his American business connections. There were also letters to friends and relatives, including Edith Frank's two brothers, Julius and Walter Hollander, who had gone to America in 1939. In these letters, Mr. Frank sought help to get visas to a neutral country or to America or Cuba. With every passing day, the letters show increasing desperation.

I knew at the time that Mr. Frank was making such inquiries. I urged him to try to get out of Europe. I knew that his hiding plan was the last resort. These letters evoke for me that terrible time long ago that most people cannot imagine anymore.

I was not surprised that the letters repeatedly mentioned Anne and Margot, and how much more important their fate was than his or his wife's. Nor was I surprised when Mr. Frank said in one of the letters that, if the family could not get out together, Edith urged him to go by himself or, if possible, to take the children with him. This is the kind of person Edith Frank was.

Another recent development concerns the great chestnut tree in the back yard adjacent to the hiding place. It is immense in size, even older than me, and unfortunately has not avoided sickness as it has aged. Because of fungus, rot, moth infestation, and dying roots, there is a danger that it will come crashing down either onto the museum that the hiding place has become or onto the neighbor's house. Experts agree that the tree should be cut down, but protests and outcries by both tree advocates and readers of the diary have developed into a worldwide cause. People consider it to be Anne Frank's tree. Anne mentions it many times in her diary. During the first spring in hiding—1943—Anne hardly noticed it. But soon she become infatuated by it. She would go up to the attic of the hiding place—sometimes with Peter—and, because the attic contained the only window that wasn't covered, she could look out at the branches of this same tree. In winter she admired drops of rain on the bare branches, in summer she admired it in full bloom.

She could see the sky and also an occasional seagull through the branches. She wrote that all these things she saw kept her from being unhappy.

I understand why the tree means something to people today,

just as it did to Anne. Though there have been reprieves, at the moment, the tree's fate is uncertain.

I knew almost nothing about my husband's underground work other than the small bits and pieces that unfolded during the war. I knew he was able to get illegal ration cards for the people in hiding, which meant we were able to obtain food for them. When Paul or I tried to speak to him about his life in the war, Jan always said "I'll tell you later, not now."

But later never came. Jan died without revealing the full story of his underground life.

Because of research done by my son, his friend Gerlof Langerijs, and others since Jan's death, I know now that he was a very active member of one of the underground groups made up of civil servants. These helpers sliced up the map of Amsterdam, and each of them would visit people in their slice as part of their work. They delivered goods, medical supplies, ration coupons, and whatever else they could. This was very dangerous work, and Jan was almost caught several times when he visited addresses that were betrayed to the Germans.

There was a violent part of this organization, but if Jan ever carried weapons, I don't know about it. Jan arranged hiding addresses all over town and also outside of Amsterdam. He must have saved scores of people, mainly Jews, but also men who did not want to have to work in Germany—*Arbeitseinsatz*—and other people who were sought by the Nazis.

He kept silent about this work, as did his fellow underground workers. On the day of his funeral, several men from his group were present. They shook my hand, but kept to themselves and remained silent about their wartime activities.

My son regrets that we didn't keep the pressure on Jan to tell. I am of the same opinion.

Much of the new material gathered about our saga has been interesting or surprising. Unfortunately, some of it has not always been flattering or totally substantiated. Various incorrect pieces of information have seeped into the growing mountain of Anne Frank–related materials as well.

I compliment the authors and filmmakers, and I value their work. But I believe it is important that the correct historical facts should always be observed. A few unresolved clues should not be made into history.

Some interpretations of certain events use negative or sensational words to describe things, and some people have, I believe unjustly, done harm to Otto Frank's memory. He was a man who had to deal with death coming toward him and his family. He always did the best he could under terrible circumstances, and does not deserve to be maligned.

New and controversial theories about the identity of the betrayer and the events leading to the betrayal have been stitched together in some publications. Because of new research, we now know that there were several more people with either motives or opportunities to betray my friends in hiding. While some of these theories are plausible, so far none has been proven by hard facts.

My final words on the betrayal are these: We shall never know.

As the lone survivor of this story, I am often asked for comments about these events. Sometimes I've given them; sometimes I've chosen to remain silent when I thought that was best. But I would like to take this opportunity to correct a few inaccuracies:

Jan and I did not go out to dinner in a restaurant on the night after the Germans attacked Holland on May 10, 1940, as one film shows us doing.

The man who came to arrest the people in hiding, SS Oberscharführer Karl Silberbauer, arrived at the hiding place on a bicycle, not in a shiny Mercedes car with a swastika flag on its hood as the same film showed.

Although Silberbauer had a pistol when he arrived that terrible August 4th, the pistol was never put to my head, as was incorrectly claimed in another version of the events of that day.

Nor was there ever a shotgun during the interrogation. And Anne did not scream during the arrest. Only Margot cried, but, according to Mr. Frank, she did so silently. These inaccuracies were also included in a film.

After the war, when I saw Mr. Frank from the front window of our apartment, I ran outside to greet him. It was recently written that I saw him arrive by car. This is incorrect. I saw Mr. Frank arrive on foot. I can still see him passing our window.

During the hiding time I lived for the day that the war would end, when I would be able to go into the hiding place, throw open the doors, and say to my friends, "Now go home!"

This was not to be.

Perhaps when the time comes for me to join Jan and our friends in the hereafter, I'll push aside the bookcase, walk behind it, climb the steep wooden stairway, careful not to hit my head on the low ceiling where Peter nailed the old towel to it. Upstairs Jan will be leaning against the edge of the dresser, his long legs stretched out, the cat Mouschi in his arms. All the others will be sitting around the table and will greet me when I enter.

And Anne, with her usual curiosity, will get up and rush toward me saying, "Hello, Miep. What is the news?"

I doubt I have very long to wait.

People ask me what it is like to have outlived almost everyone whose history I have shared. It is a strange feeling. Why me? Why was I spared the concentration camp after being caught helping to hide Jews? This I will never know.

I have tried to speak for Anne, but on several occasions I thought that she should have been the speaker. And let us not forget Margot, who kept her own diary, which was never found.

Apparently these things just had to be.

People also ask if there is anything I would like to say as I approach my hundredth birthday. The answer is, I have been very lucky. I came from far and I survived the war. I've been granted a long life. Perhaps the most valuable assets are that I can still think properly and my health—considering my age—is good.

For some reason I was given a great opportunity to find and shelter the diary, to be able to bring the message from Anne to the world.

I will never know why.